The Best of Sunshine City

An impertinent insiders' guide

By Don W. Martin & Betty Woo Martin

Pine Cone Press, Inc. ● Henderson, Nevada

BOOKS BY DON AND BETTY MARTIN

Adventure Cruising ● 1996
Arizona Discovery Guide ● 1990, 1993, 1994, 1996
Arizona in Your Future ● 1991, 1993, 1998
The Best of the Gold Country ● 1987, 1990, 1992
The Best of San Francisco ● 1986, 1990, 1994, 1997
The Best of the Wine Country ● 1991, 1994, 1995
California–Nevada Roads Less Traveled ● 1999
Inside San Francisco ● 1991
Las Vegas: The Best of Glitter City ● 1998
Nevada Discovery Guide ● 1992, 1997
New Mexico Discovery Guide ● 1998
Northern California Discovery Guide ● 1993
Oregon Discovery Guide ● 1993, 1995, 1996, 1999
San Diego: The Best of Sunshine City ● 1999
San Francisco's Ultimate Dining Guide ● 1988
The Toll-free Traveler ● 1997
The Ultimate Wine Book ● 1993, 1999
Utah Discovery Guide ● 1995
Washington Discovery Guide ● 1994, 1997

Copyright © 1999 by Don W. Martin and Betty Woo Martin
Printed in the United States of America. All rights reserved. No written material, maps or illustrations from this book may be reproduced in any form, including electronic media, other than brief passages in book reviews, without written permission from the publisher.

Library of Congress Cataloging-in-Publication Data
Martin, Don and Betty —
San Diego: The Best of Sunshine City
Includes index.
1. San Diego—description and travel
2. San Diego—history

ISBN: 0-942053-27-3
Library of Congress catalog card number: 98-91238

COVER DESIGN ● **Vicky Biernacki**, Columbine Type and Design, Sonora, Calif.

This book is dedicated to the memory of Father Junípero Serra, a guy with a gimpy leg who more or less started the whole thing.

JUST THE BEST; NOT ALL THE REST

This is a different kind of a guidebook. Instead of saturating readers with details on everything there is to see and do in the seventh largest city in America, the authors have sifted through San Diego's hundreds of lures and selected only the ten best in various categories. It is more than a mere book of lists, however. Each listing is a detailed description, with specifics on location, hours and price ranges.

Further, there is plenty from which to choose. *San Diego: The Best of Sunshine City* offers Ten Best lists in nearly fifty different categories. It is thus a great resource for visitors with limited time, visitors with lots of time and residents who'd like to make new discoveries about their community.

A guidebook focusing only on the best must, by its very nature, be rather opinionated. Some would even suggest that it's impertinent. Further, many readers may not agree with the authors' selections, which is part of the fun of reading it. In fact, readers are invited to make their own Ten Best selections. Details are in the back of this book.

This is the third in a series of "Ten Best" city guides by veteren travel writers Don and Betty Martin. Check your local book store for *The Best of San Francisco* and *Las Vegas: The Best of Glitter City*.

Keeping up with the changes

One of the fastest growing communities in America, San Diego is a city of constant change. Every time we go for a good seafood dinner or a beach fix, we find something new, and we visit often.

If you discover something afresh on your next visit, or if you catch an error in this book, let us know. Drop us a note if you find that a seafood restaurant has become a laundromat or the other way around. All who provide significant information that we've not yet uncovered will earn a free copy of one of our other publications. See the list in the back of this book.

We'd also like to invite you to submit your own nominations for future editions of *The Best of Sunshine City*. All who submit at least fifteen nominations will receive a free copy of the next edition. Use the form in the back of this book or—if you're reluctant to dismember it—a photocopy thereof.

Address your comments to:

Pine Cone Press, Inc.
631 Stephanie St., #138
Henderson, NV 89014

CONTENTS

A few words of thanks

The authors could not have written such a detailed and opinionated guide to San Diego without the assistance—and the opinions—of many other people. We are particularly grateful to these folks:

Joe Timko, national public relations manager for the San Diego Convention & Visitors Bureau, for providing us with an abundance of material on this fine city; and noted romance novelist and El Cajon resident **Sharon Ihle** and her husband **Larry,** who took the time to compile for us a lengthy list of their very favorite things in the area.

WELCOME TO SAN DIEGO!

I was first welcomed to San Diego several decades ago by a young lady in a short, tight skirt. Just out of boot camp at the Marine Corps Recruit Depot, I was walking up lower Broadway when she emerged from the shadow of a building and offered to show me a good time—for a fee. A kid fresh off an Idaho farm, I was too bashful and too poor to accept her hospitality. I recall that my monthly pay at the time was $82.50.

In the years since, I've been welcomed to San Diego many times—and not by ladies in mini-skirts. After finishing my hitch in the Marine Corps, I went to work for a daily newspaper in northern San Diego County, and had many occasions to spend quality time in this great city. Although I left the paper after a few years, I've never strayed far from San Diego, spending all of my subsequent years either in California or southern Nevada. My wife and I have watched San Diego grow from a midsize town to the seventh largest city in America. We've seen her blossom from a liberty port for sailors and Marines into a sophisticated, vibrant and exciting metropolis.

San Diego is one of America's top tourist destinations, attracting more than fourteen million visitors a year. In fact, tourism is the city's third largest industry. Visitors are lured by its miles of beaches, island resorts, a splendid city park sheltering several museums and outstanding zoo, a fine Mexican community in its Old Town section, major league sports, good shopping, hundreds of restaurants and many cultural offerings.

One might say that the city offers too much for visitors. It would be impossible to sample all of its lures during a one or two week vacation, or during a brief convention visit. Who can take time to sort through this abundance and choose the very best of San Diego?

Fortunately, we can. We spent months canvassing this exciting city, seeking out the best attractions, the sandiest beaches, the best tamale ever to emerge from a corn husk, the trendiest shops and cutest cafés, the best places to hike and bike, even the best vista points and picture spots. Having accomplished this, we toured the rest of San Diego County to find its best attractions, its most scenic drives and tucked-away beaches.

After sifting through every corner of San Diego—city and county—we saved the very best, just for you.

Don W. Martin
Hanging out with a burrito in Old Town

I would not give you five dollars for the whole of it. I would not take it as a gift! It doesn't lie right! Never in the world can you have a city here.
— Alonzo Horton, upon arriving in San Diego in 1867

Chapter one

SAN DIEGO!
YOU ARE MY SUNSHINE

When we call San Diego "Sunshine City," we aren't referring just to its reputation as one of the sunniest major municipalities in America. It does indeed enjoy a sun-blessed climate the year around and in fact it's warmer in winter than that other famous sunspot, Las Vegas. Also, while thoroughly sunny in summer, it doesn't suffer the sizzling temperatures of its desert neighbor. Average July high is 73 degrees in San Diego; it's 105 in Glitter City.

This is a room temperature city; year around average daily temperature is 70 degrees.

San Diego is sunny in disposition, as well. Mellowed by a rich Latin heritage, the city wears an easy-going grin. It's more casual than San Francisco, less intense than Las Vegas and not as restive as Los Angeles. There is more of a resort feel to this sunny, beach-rimmed city. While L.A. frets over gridlock, smog and sprawl, San Diego seems more positive about its growth. It has eased traffic congestion with a light rail system and has almost eliminated urban decay by virtually rebuilding its downtown core. Although the area is growing rapidly, central San Diego has remained reasonably compact.

7

This is not to suggest that it's a small town. With a population topping a million, San Diego is the seventh largest city in the country. It's also one of America's most visited cities, drawing more than fourteen million tourists a year. Since it brims with restaurants, hotels, attractions, parks, beaches and even a couple of resort islands, those visitors may be hard pressed to make the best choices. That, of course, is the purpose of this book, as we pointed out in the introduction.

First, however, a look at San Diego—how it came to be, and how to get there and get around. And when we speak of San Diego in this book, we refer to both the city and the county. Although most chapters concern the City of San Diego and its contiguous communities of Ocean Beach, Mission Beach, Pacific Beach, La Jolla and Coronado, we've set aside Chapter Fourteen to explore the rest of the county. If San Diego the city is compact, San Diego the county is not. It's the sixth largest county in America and it offers its own special lures—everything from a famous observatory to mountain woodlands to desert parks to an old gold mining town. And of course, a grand string of beaches!

Finally, because thousands of other visitors do so, we cross the border into Baja California to point out the Ten Best lures of Tijuana and beyond.

AN UNAUTHORIZED HISTORY

In a sense, San Diego is where California began, for it's the site of the first in a chain of missions established by Spanish friars. Padre Junípero Serra, limping from an infected leg, alternately walking and riding a mule, arriving above San Diego Bay in July of 1769. The president of New Spain's Baja California missions, he had traveled in the company of soldiers led by Captain Gaspar de Portolá, who had been dispatched to colonize Alta (Upper) California. Serra held mass on a brushy hilltop on July 16, then he set about to establish a mission. A few soldiers were left behind to build a garrison or presidio to protect the new enterprise and the main body continued northward.

Currently a candidate for sainthood, Serra is described by local author Michael McKeever as "a fifty-five-year-old Franciscan priest, known for his sharp tongue and a fondness for chocolate." (From *A Short History of San Diego,* © 1985, published by Lexicos, San Francisco, Calif.) Although statues and sketches of Friar Serra are common, no one really knows what he looked like because no life portrait exists.

The aim of those early padres was to bring The Word to the native people while also requiring them to do most of the work of building and maintaining the missions. And if the natives were tools of the missionaries, the friars were tools of the king of Spain. That great colonial empire wanted to establish a foothold in Alta California before it was claimed by Russian fur trappers from the north or Yankee settlers from the east.

ATTAINING SAINTHOOD:
REALLY STRANGE BEDFELLOWS

The patron of San Diego achieved sainthood in a very odd—some would say macabre—way. Saint Didacus was born in the Canary Islands, became a priest and spent most of his adult life caring for students and patients in the infirmary at Spain's University of Alcalà near Madrid. He died there in 1463.

In 1562, Carlos, the son of Philip II of Spain, was seriously injured in a fall from a horse and lay near death. The century old body of Didacus was exhumed and placed in bed with the injured son, and the kid awoke the next morning feeling just fine. Well, maybe he was a bit grossed out, but he was cured. The king appealed to the Pope to canonize this long dead padre for the miraclous cure of his son, and his wish was granted.

However, Spain had been weakened by recent wars; it lacked the powerful armies and the funds needed for a major occupation. Officials chose a low-key and low-budget approach—dispatching smaller military units, accompanied by priests who hoped to convert the local folks to Christianity. Soldiers were used mostly to protect the padres from reprisals by unwilling converts. While this was a thinly-veiled land grab, it was at least more humane than Spain's brutal conquests of the native peoples of South America and Mexico. Of course, the indigenous people of Alta California had no gold to steal.

Unfortunately, the soldiers often were brutal to the native people, cuffing the men about and—well—abusing the women. Indians of the San Diego mission, who were called *Kumeya'ay* (pronounced *KOO-me-eye*), revolted in 1775 and killed one of its priests, Father Luis Jayme. He became the first Catholic martyr on the California frontier.

Spanish officials had known about coastal California for more than a century. Legendary explorer Juan Rodríguez Cabrillo, cruising up the coast of Baja California, dropped anchor in a long, narrow bay on September 28, 1542, scaring the loincloths off the local *Kumeya'ay*. He named it San Miguel Bay, after Saint Michael. Cabrillo stayed only a few days and then continued north along the coast. Unfortunately, he died four months later from gangrene after a shipboard accident. The next visitor didn't appear until November of 1602, when Sebastián Viscaíno cruised into Cabrillo's bay. Wanting to leave his own mark, he renamed it for Saint Didacus of Alcalá, whose feast day was November 12. Like Cabrillo, Viscaíno didn't stay long. He continued north to discover another large bay, which—in the spirit of political discretion—he named for his mentor, the Count of Monterey, who was viceroy of New Spain.

More than a century and a half later, when Spain decided to settle Alta California with the cross and the sword, Monterey—not San Diego—was their primary destination. It became the mission headquarters and ultimately the capital of Spanish California. Sorry about that, local historians. San Diego wasn't even California's first town. That honor went to—good grief!—San José.

Knowing the way to San José

The Spanish made a distinction between missions, which were church-run agricultural colonies, and *pueblos* or towns, which were settled by civilians. Pueblo San José de Guadalupe was founded in 1777 by a group of settlers from Sonora, Mexico, led by Captain Juan Bautista de Anza. Part of the group continued northward to establish California's second city, Yerba Buena, better known these days as San Francisco. And these were hardly the first settlements founded by the Spanish in present-day America. New Mexico's Santa Fe traces its roots back to 1607, thirteen years before the Pilgrims set foot on Plymouth Rock.

San Diego more or less *evolved* as a secular town. In 1774, Father Serra moved his mission from its hilltop site six miles inland to present-day Mission Valley. This put his operation closer to the native villages and their fields, and it kept them away from pesky soldiers. The military garrison remained atop what is now Presidio Hill and eventually a few folks—mostly discharged soldiers—began settling around its base. Some sent for their wives in Mexico; a few married natives. They traded at the mission, for there was still no town. In fact, none was yet needed. Most missions had become vast agricultural enterprises and cottage industries. They produced leather, woven fabric, candles, wine and other frontier staples, and they made money by selling these goods to settlers and travelers. (One study, which used old records to calculate how much wine the missions produced and how much they didn't sell, suggested that many of the padres must have been sloshed much of the time. The Indian converts weren't permitted to imbibe.)

In 1821, Mexico won its independence from Spain and the new government granted huge tracts of land to men who had fought for her liberty. A golden era of great *ranchos* began, and these spreads—some over a hundred thousand acres—competed with the missions for commerce.

Two issues concerned the new government of Mexico—the growing numbers of Americans settling in Alta California and the power of the Catholic church, as represented in its mission holdings. To clip the church's wings and open more land to its own people, it enacted the Secularization Act of 1833. This stripped the missions of their vast landholdings and converted the mission chapels into parish churches. However, many frontier towns were too small to support them. Some were abandoned; others were taken over by local governments and used for everything from storage facilities to cattle barns.

The poor Indians were simply turned loose into a world that was no longer theirs. Some wandered into the hills, although many became *vaqueros*—cowboys on the great ranchos. Others wound up as servants and virtual slaves of Mexican settlers. A few, frustrated and angered, raided the settlements, but they were quickly crushed by the military. A popular punishment was to drape a rebellious native over a cannon barrel and beat him to death.

Finally, a real town

The small settlement near the mission grew slowly. It was designated as San Diego *pueblo* on January 1, 1835, boasting a population of about 400. With a large natural harbor not far away, the new town became a trading center, particularly for cowhides and tallow, which were produced on the surrounding ranches and shipped to eastern America and beyond. Leather was in such demand and cattle were so plentiful that their hides were more valuable than their meat. These skins became known as "California banknotes." Richard Henry Dana, a seaman aboard an American ship that sailed into San Diego Bay in 1835, wrote about the hide trade in *Two Years Before the Mast.*

If San Diego the *pueblo* enjoyed moderate prosperity, San Diego the mission did not. It was secularized in 1834 and its lands were given to a retired soldier. Padres struggled for more than a decade to keep the church going, then it finally was boarded up in 1846.

In that same year, the United States declared war on Mexico. When it ended, our southern neighbor was forced to surrender California, along with most of Arizona, New Mexico and Texas, under terms of the 1848 Treaty of Guadalupe Hidalgo. Weakly-defended California fell into American hands even before the war ended. Many *pueblos* submitted without a fight. However, a particularly bloody battle occurred in December of 1846 in the San Pasqual Valley northeast of San Diego. Andrés Pico's Mexican troops soundly defeated the Army of the West, led by General Stephen Watts Kearny. Although Pico won, he realized that his forces were outnumbered by the growing ranks of Americans and ultimately would be defeated. He withdrew to San Diego and surrendered the city to Colonel John Charles Frémont on January 17, 1847. In a final insult, American troops used the old mission has a barracks and its outbuildings as stables.

Abraham Lincoln returned California's missions to the Catholic church in 1862, although the abandoned San Diego de Alcalá continued to crumble. Serious restoration finally began in the 1930s, helped by contributions from local citizens and a foundation established by newspaper mogul William Randolph Hearst. Now fully restored, it's an active parish church.

San Diego the *pueblo* enjoyed moderate growth until 1849 when the California gold rush drew peoples' attention northward. Gold, not cowhides, became the key to prosperity and the little adobe village dozed in the sunlight. By the middle 1850s, California's three largest cities were San Francisco, Sacramento and Stockton. Los Angeles was eighteenth in size and San Diego was too small to count. Dozens of rowdy northern California mining camps were larger. In fact, many San Diegans headed for those mining camps, further depleting the town's population.

"It doesn't lie right!"

One of San Diego's problems was that it was poorly situated. It rimmed a weedy plaza at the foot of Presidio Hill, separated from the waterfront by more than a mile of muddy, rutted road. Then in 1867, entrepreneur Alonzo Erastus Horton stepped from the deck of a steamship onto the rickety dock, rode a bumpy wagon up to the dusty village and exclaimed: "I would not give you five dollars for the whole of it. I would not take it as a gift! It doesn't lie right! Never in the world can you have a city here."

Horton decided to build a new town, down by the bayfront, where it belonged. He bought nearly a thousand acres of "sagebrush and mudflats" at about twenty-seven cents an acre and began platting a city. He even gave away land to people who would agree to develop them. "Horton's Addition" is now downtown San Diego.

The city was off and running and it has never looked back. Three years after Horton's arrival, gold was discovered in central San Diego County. The new mining camp of Julian began pouring its wealth into the growing city. Although the gold ran out within four years, whaling in and about San Diego Bay kept the economy rolling for a bit longer. Then wealthy tourists began arriving, drawn by the mild climate and sandy beaches.

Although hard times have hit San Diego—an Old Town fire in 1872, the end of Julian mining, the depletion of whales, the 1930s Depression—the city has climbed steadily upward. With its clear skies, it became an early aviation center, particularly after one Charles Lindbergh sent a telegram to local airplane builder T. Claude Ryan in 1927. It asked Ryan if he could construct a "whirlwind engine plane capable of flying nonstop between New York and Paris." Later, the growing city became a major military center, for a sudden and unfortunate reason. After the Japanese attacked Pearl Harbor in 1941, the headquarters of the U.S. Pacific Fleet was relocated to San Diego. Its Marine Corps Recruit Depot, established back in 1911, was expanded to handle a rapid influx of new boots and several aircraft and other war industries were based there.

After the war ended, many sailors, Marines and defense plant workers decided they liked what they'd seen of San Diego, and growth continued. It does so to this day.

GETTING THERE

Although San Diego is tucked far down into America's southwest corner, it's a relatively easy reach, served by three freeways, a busy airport and Amtrak. Sunshine City's areas of visitor interest are rather widespread so a car is necessary unless you intend to spend most of your time lounging around a resort pool. If you're flying in, plan on renting some wheels.

San Diego International Airport, which locals prefer to call Lindbergh Field, is practically downtown, built on a mudflat along San Diego Bay. For airport and general flight information, call (619) 231-2100. The city is served by Aeromexico, (800) 237-6639; Alaska Airlines, (800) 426-0333; America West, (800) 235-9292; American and American Eagle, (800) 433-7300; British Airways, (800) 247-9297; Continental, (800) 231-0856; Delta, 241-4141; Midwest Express, (800) 452-2022; Northwest, (800) 225-2525; Reno Air, (800) 736-6247; Southwest, (800) 435-9792; TWA, (800) 892-4141; United (800) 241-6522; and US Airways, (800) 428-4322.

Airport transportation: Since the airport is near downtown, a cab ride is brief and costs only about $10 to $15. Shuttle companies offer service for a bit less; two of the more active ones are Cloud 9 Shuttle at (800) 9-SHUTTLE or (619) 278-8877 and Public Shuttle at (619) 990-8770. San Diego Transit runs bus service to the airport; it's cheaper but slower; (619) 233-3004.

Rental cars: All major rental car companies have airport service. If you're looking for bargains, several local firms claim extra low rates. (These are *their* claims; not ours.) Many don't have airport offices although most provide pickup and return. Among those we found in the Yellow Pages are Accent Car Rental, (800) 295-5331 or (619) 224-9924; Admiral Car Rental, (619) 696-9900; Bargain Auto Rentals, (619) 299-0009; California Rent-A-Car, (619) 238-9999; City Rent-A-Car, (800) 736-8693 or (619) 223-6444; Courtesy Auto Rentals, (619) 497-4800; Ladki Car Rental, (800) 245-2354 or (619) 525-2222; Rent-a-Wreck, (619) 223-3300; Rent For Less, (619) 273-4758; and West Coast Rent A Car, (619) 544-0606.

Taxis: Cab service around San Diego is provided by Airport Cab, 280-5555; All Cities Cab, (619) 291-2997; American Cab Company, (619) 234-1111 or 292-1111; Co-Op Silver Cabs, (619) 280-5555; Crown City Cab, (619) 437-8885; Dial A Cab, (619) 274-8294; Diamond Cab, (619) 474-1544; Orange Cab, (619) 291-4444 or 291-8888; Radio Cab, (619) 232-6566; Red Top Cab, (619) 531-1111; San Diego Cab, (619) 226-8294; Shield Cab, (619) 235-8736; Silver Cabs, (619) 280-5555; USA Cab, (619) 231-1144; and Yellow Cab, (619) 234-6161.

Amtrak has frequent runs between the city and Los Angeles, with other San Diego County stops in Solana Beach and Oceanside. Trains operate out of the city's handsome old Santa Fe depot at 1050 Kettner Boulevard at the foot of Broadway; (800) USA-RAIL or locally (619) 239-9021.

Greyhound gallops from a terminal at 120 W. Broadway, with service north on Interstate 5 through California to Oregon and Washington, northeast to Las Vegas and Salt Lake City on I-15 and east on I-

8 through Yuma to Phoenix, with connections beyond; (800) 231-2222 or locally (619) 239-8082.

Public transit: The Metropolitan Transit System operates the city's buses and the San Diego Trolley, one of America's first modern light rail systems. The bus network covers greater San Diego, while the trolley offers main line service to Old Town, Mission Valley, downtown, Seaport Village and south through coastal communities to the border at Tijuana, Mexico (see below). Unlimited ride passes for both buses and trolleys are available for one day to a month. Individual fares vary, based on distance. The system has very generous senior fares that don't change with the zones; it was less than a dollar the last time we rode. For fare and schedule information, call (619) 233-3004 or (619) 685-4900 for automated touch-tone info. Or check with the Transit Store downtown at 102 Broadway; (619) 234-1060. It's open weekdays 8:30 to 5:30 and weekends noon to 4. Ask for a "Welcome kit," containing everything you need to know about San Diego's public transit system.

GETTING ABOUT

Interstate 5 is the area's main north-south freeway corridor, cutting inland through San Diego and ending just short of the border above Tijuana. It provides quick access to downtown; take the Front Street/Civic Center exit to get to the heart of things. Incidentally, if you're staying downtown, a quick way to catch I-5 is to follow one-way First or Fifth streets north; you'll soon encounter northbound and south bound on-ramps.

Interstate 805 runs farther inland along the city's eastern flanks, roughly paralleling I-5's course; it passes mostly through suburban neighborhoods. Another suburban route, the Martin Luther King Jr. Freeway (Highway 94), travels northeast from downtown.

From the east, I-8 follows the course of the creek-sized San Diego River through Mission Valley, passing above Old Town and ending just short of the beach below Mission Bay Park. The I-15 freeway drops down from Riverside and San Bernardino, travels inland through San Diego County and joins the tangle of other freeways near the downtown area. If you plan to explore the beaches of San Diego County, old U.S. 101 stays closer to the ocean than I-5. North Torrey Pines Road above La Jolla blends into this coastal route.

Where to play tourist

While downtown is relatively compact, greater San Diego is spread over many miles, as are its attractions. Visitor lures and most of its more interesting restaurants and shops are focused in these areas:

Mission Bay Park is a 4,600-acre aquatic playground created in the 1960s when a swampland north of San Diego Bay was dredged. It was shaped into a network of lagoons, beaches, parklands, picnic areas

and playgrounds—about half land and half water. It has several resorts and many miles of jogging, walking and biking paths and it's
home to Sea World Adventure Park.

Mission Beach and **Pacific Beach** are north of Mission Bay.
Both are typical shoreside communities with bikini shops, small cafés,
smaller houses and a few beach resorts. Mission Beach is home to Belmont Park, a classic restored amusement center with a roller coaster,
fun zone and a large indoor pool where Johnny Weismuller and Esther
Williams once splashed for the cameras. The area's other coastal community is **Ocean Beach,** a small enclave just below the channel entrance to Mission Bay. Immediately above Pacific Beach is **La Jolla**,
expensive, trendy and situated above a beautiful wind-sculpted crescent called La Jolla Cove.

Old Town at the base of Presidio Hill is where the pueblo of San
Diego began. Much of the area is now Old Town San Diego State Historic Park, with shops, cafés and small museums installed in ancient
adobe buildings. Old Town deteriorated quickly after Alonzo Horton
shifted the city center to the bayfront. It survived as a shantytown and
eventually as a tourist attraction, with Mexican pottery and trinket
shops and small cafés. I recall from my early days in San Diego that
one of these places was called "Ramona's Marriage Place," which was a
good trick, since Helen Hunt Jackson's book *Ramona* was pure fiction.
In fact, she wrote it not in San Diego (although she had visited there)
but in a New York hotel room.

Balboa Park is San Diego's crown jewel—an emerald, actually.
Draped over mesas and ravines above the city, the 1,400-acre park is
home to most of San Diego's museums, the world renowned San Diego
Zoo, an outdoor organ pavilion, a sports complex, space and science
center, landscaped gardens and a splendid collection of Moorish-Spanish buildings. Most were created for the 1915 Panama-California International Exposition, which heralded the completion of the "Big Ditch"
across Central America.

Downtown is the commercial heart of San Diego and the legacy
of Mister Horton. Until the 1970s, much of his new town had deteriorated into an urban slum of flophouses, saloons and whorehouses
called Stingaree. Sailors and Marines on liberty would grab their pay
envelopes and head for lower Broadway and Stingaree for a weekend
of partying. Most of this region has been redeveloped into a trendy
shopping and dining area. Horton Plaza is a modern mall spread over
six blocks—the result of urban renewal by bulldozer. Just to the east, a
sixteen block section of old Stingaree has been gentrified into Gaslamp
Quarter. Here, venerable brick and masonry buildings were preserved
instead of demolished. Designated as a national historic site, Gaslamp
is pleasing collection of cafés, boutiques and specialty shops.

Several neighborhoods are tucked into the hills above downtown
and the most interesting of these is **Hillcrest**. It's home to many eth-

nic restaurants, specialty shops and galleries, and it's the city's primary gay community.

The waterfront adjacent to downtown is a popular tourist venue. Its focal point is the Embarcadero with a bayfront promenade, several seafood restaurants, a floating maritime museum and cruise ship terminal. Just to the south is Seaport Village, a nautical theme shopping complex on the site of the old Coronado Ferry terminal. A gracefully curving 2.3-mile long bridge now connects Coronado to downtown San Diego. **Coronado** is an attraction in its own right with its miles of beaches, petite downtown shops and the legendary Hotel del Coronado. Often referred to as an island, Coronado is linked to the mainland several miles to the south by a skinny six-mile-long landspit called Silver Strand.

The Golden Triangle ten miles north of the city is an upscale and architecturally dramatic enclave with hotels, condos, shopping complexes, the prestigious Salk Institute and other medical centers, and the San Diego campus of the University of California. A few decades ago, these brushy hill were undeveloped except for a Marine Corps rifle range called Camp Matthews. In 1964, the federal government turned the base over to the University of California, and the area has been growing by quantum leaps ever since. It has two visitor lures—Scripps Institution of Oceanography's Birch Aquarium and Torrey Pines State Reserve. Also, visitors can tour the campus of the glistening white Mormon Temple, whose spires rise just east of I-5 like a ghost castle.

Where to relax and sleep

San Diego County has more than 45,000 hotel and motel rooms. The city's highrise hotels are mostly downtown, while its resorts are in several outlying areas. Its two most imposing new hotels, the Marriott and Hyatt Regency, are on the waterfront just beyond downtown.

Two resort areas are just minutes from San Diego International Airport. Harbor Island is a nicely landscaped manmade appendage thrusting into San Diego Bay opposite the airport, and Shelter Island is a similar artificial landfall just to the west off Point Loma. Several resorts are spaced about Mission Bay and a large collection of hotels is inland along I-8 in Mission Valley. Most of these stand along a frontage road called Hotel Circle. Incidentally, San Diego currently suffers an excess of hotel rooms. Since most visitors prefer downtown or the coastal resort areas, you can find some good prices in Mission Valley.

The area's finest resort is the venerable Hotel del Coronado, a national historic landmark dating from 1888 and the showplace of Coronado. With its gleaming white walls and orange-roofed towers, it's one of the world's most photographed hotels.

Can't afford the Del? San Diego's main motel row is along El Cajon Boulevard, a continuation of Washington Street heading east from the Hillcrest District. Rosecrans Street (State Route 209), which leads to the tip of Point Loma, is another motel area, although prices generally are higher than on El Cajon Boulevard. You'll also find several motels mixed in among the resorts along Hotel Circle in Mission Valley.

Getting camped?

San Diego isn't exactly RV and tent camp country. We found only two RV parks here, both adjacent to Mission Bay—Campland on the Bay, (800) 422-9386 or (619) 581-4260; and De Anza Harbor Resort, (800) 924-7529 or (619) 273-3211. These are not inexpensive; prices approach those of motels. Campland permits tents; De Anza does not.

RV parks are plentiful in surrounding communities. You'll find coastal camping at state beaches, city parks and/or private campgrounds in Cardiff by the Sea, Encinitas, Carlsbad and Oceanside. These fill up quickly in summer, so get a campground directory and make reservations early. Inland, camping is available at Cuyamaca Rancho, Anza-Borrego Desert and Palomar Mountain state parks.

Making a run for the border

Visiting Mexico is a simple matter, particularly if you're going only to Tijuana and you don't plan to stay more than seventy-two hours. More extensive trips require a bit of advance preparation. To visit Tijuana, you merely walk or drive through the international border crossing at San Ysidro. Mexican regulations require an original birth certificate plus a photo I.D. or a passport for entry into Mexico, although officials usually will wave you through. You'll need a picture I.D. such as a driver's license to get back into California.

We recommend that you walk across the border or use buses or Tijuana taxis. This is the world's busiest border crossing and vehicles often face long delays getting back into California. Also, you must obtain Mexican auto insurance if you drive across the border, since Mexico doesn't recognize American or Canadian policies. As a pedestrian, you'll find plenty of shopping just inside the border and along Avenida Revolución. It's about a mile from the border, via a marked pedestrian route. For more on visiting Mexico, see Chapter Fifteen.

Our favorite San Diego moments

When you get to know a town as well as we know San Diego, you tend to make lists—mental or written—of your preferred places and favorite moments. We wrote ours down:

1 *ADMIRING THE VIEW FROM MOUNT SOLEDAD* • *At the end of Mount Soledad Road in eastern La Jolla. Gates open from 8 a.m. to midnight; free. GETTING THERE: Two roads reach Mount Soledad. From La Jolla, turn inland onto Nautilus Street from La Jolla Boulevard, just over a mile south of downtown and drive uphill, follow-*

ing directional signs. Or follow I-5 north from San Diego and take the Grand/Garnet Avenue exit, which puts you on Mission Bay Drive. Continue north about half a mile on Mission Bay, go west (left) about a quarter of a mile on Garnet and turn right up Mount Soledad Road.

A couple of miles inland from the coast of La Jolla, 822-foot Mount Soledad provides a fine view of the greater San Diego area. The panorama sweeps west over La Jolla's red rooftops to the Pacific Ocean; south to Mission Bay, Point Loma, San Diego Bay, Coronado and the downtown highrises; east to wooded and thickly populated inland hills; then north to the Golden Triangle and finally back around to the Torrey Pines area and La Jolla peninsula. We like to get up there just before sunset, settle onto a bench or lie back on the grass at the base of the Mount Soledad cross. As the sun sizzles into the Pacific, surrounding hills fade to dark velvet and lights begin to twinkle.

If you're visiting here for the first time, drive up to Mount Soledad in the daylight. It's a great place to get your bearings while enjoying an absolutely splendid view.

2 EATING FISH & CHIPS AT POINT LOMA SEAFOODS •

2805 Emerson St.; (619) 223-1109. GETTING THERE: Drive southeast on Rosecrans Street, turn left onto Emerson and follow it a few blocks to its terminus at the Municipal Sportfishing Pier.

For decades, Point Loma Seafoods has been serving some of the cheapest fish fare in San Diego. It's not a fancy restaurant; it's a bustling, sometimes chaotic fish market with the busiest takeout counter in the city. Residents and tipped-off tourists happily swarm this place from mid-morning through early evening. There are several reasons for its popularity. Its sourdough seafood sandwiches, fish and chips, shrimp Louis, seafood plates and shrimp and crab cocktails are tasty and remarkably inexpensive. And it's in a pleasant setting—adjacent to the Municipal Sportfishing Pier just off Shelter Island. Folks can take their booty into a spartan yet comfortable dining area or—as we prefer—sit outside on a patio or alongside the dock, admiring the boats.

Never mind that you're eating off paper plates with plastic forks, and that sulking pigeons and aggressive seagulls eye your food with undisguised jealousy. Sitting at pier side, inhaling the fresh air and eating affordable seafood is one of San Diego's definitive moments.

3 RIDING THE FERRY TO CORONADO • *San Diego Harbor*

Excursions, 1050 N. Harbor Dr.; (619) 234-4111. San Diego departures are on the hour from 9 to 9 Sunday-Thursday and 9 to 10 Friday-Saturday. Coronado departures are on the half hour 9:30 to 9:30 Sunday-Thursday and 9:30 to 10:30 Friday-Saturday. GETTING THERE: San Diego Harbor Excursions is at the waterfront, near the foot of Broadway. To reach Ferry Landing Marketplace, cross the Coronado Bridge and go right on Orange, then right again onto First Street.

One of my earliest San Diego memories, when I was a Marine fresh out of boot camp, was riding the old auto ferries between San Diego and Coronado, and then strolling around that cute little community. Of course, Marine privates can't afford cars so I'd go as a foot passenger, sitting on one of the benches along the rail, admiring the San Diego skyline and watching the water slip past. For a kid fresh off an Idaho farm, that was quite an experience. It still is.

Ferries have been crossing the bay to Coronado since 1886, then they stopped running when the San Diego-Coronado Bay Bridge was opened in 1969. Service was reinstated by San Diego Harbor Excursions in 1987, although it has been hit by inflation. The original fare was ten cents and now it's two dollars. The new service carries passengers only, but that's all right. I still prefer to sit along the railing and stare at the water.

4 *ENJOYING AN ORGAN RECITAL AT SPRECKELS PA-VILION* • *In Balboa Park at 2211 Pan American Rd.; (619) 702-8138. Free public concerts every Sunday from 2 to 3, plus Monday evening concerts at 8 in July and August. GETTING THERE: Spreckels Organ Pavilion is just south of El Prado, off Plaza de Panama.*

There's no better way to spend a sunny afternoon or balmy evening than to sit in this pavilion while the 4,445 pipes of the world's largest organ fill the air with the sound of music. The organ was given to the city in 1914 by sugar magnates Adolph and John Spreckels just prior to opening of the Panama-California International Exposition.

5 *EATING A SHAVED ICE AT MISSION BEACH* • *Available at Big Olaf's at 736 Ventura Place and Ice Heaven Hawaii at Ventura Place and Strand Way. GETTING THERE: Ventura Place borders the parking lot of Belmont Park. Take I-8 west to Mission Bay Park and follow West Mission Bay Drive through the park to Mission Beach; the drive blends into Ventura Place.*

We first found shaved ice—not to be confused with crushed ice—in Hawaii. Not pulverized, it's shaved from a large rotating ice block and served in a paper cone with flavoring poured over. We lean toward piña collada, although the rainbow ice is fun, particularly if the preparer is skilled at making pretty colored patterns. We like to take our chilly treats to the nearby beach promenade, sit on a bench or planter and watch the passing parade of rollerbladers, cyclists and runners.

6 *WATCHING NIGHTFALL FROM BALI HAI* • *2230 Shelter Island Dr.; (619) 222-1181. GETTING THERE: To reach Shelter Island, head southwest toward Point Loma on Rosecrans Street (State Route 209) and turn left onto Shelter Island Drive. After a few blocks, spin around a traffic circle and go briefly northeast.*

This restaurant, currently known as Sam Choy's Hawaii at the Bali Hai, occupies the tip of Shelter Island, with a splendid view of San Diego Bay, the city skyline and Coronado. Either the bar or the window-walled dining room are great places to watch the light of day fade to dusk. The last rays of the sun glint off downtown highrises then, as darkness gathers, city lights come alive, as if in reflection of the stars above. On the night of the full moon, when the lunar disk rises above the city as the sun disappears behind Point Loma, the effect is absolutely awesome. The proper drink for this event? Obviously, a tropical libation called the Coronado Sunset—a blend of rum, fruit juice and piña collada mix.

7 ATTENDING A PERFORMANCE AT THE STARLIGHT BOWL • *Balboa Park; (619) 544-7800. Performances June through early September. GETTING THERE: The Starlight Bowl is just south of Pan American Plaza, adjacent to the Aerospace Museum.*

One of our earliest San Diego memories is sitting in the Starlight Bowl, watching and listening to a performance of *The Merry Widow*. It was called the Starlight Opera then, although it wasn't and still isn't opera. The original company did light opera and musicals and the present group, Starlight Musical Theater, produces classic Broadway shows. Terraced into a hillside, the amphitheater was built for the 1935-36 California Pacific International Exposition as a Depression era WPA project. It has entertained millions of lovers of musicals through the decades. The tenors and sopranos often have to freeze in mid-note while a jet bound for Lindbergh field rumbles overhead. Still, an evening at the Starlight Bowl remains one of San Diego's finest moments.

8 EXPLORING GASLAMP QUARTER • *Downtown San Diego, bounded by Broadway, Fourth and Sixth avenues and Market Street. GETTING THERE: Take the Front Street/Civic Center exit from I-5. Follow Front Street south, cross Broadway, pass the edge of Horton Plaza and turn right on G Street. You're in the heart of the Gaslamp.*

Streetwalkers were common in the old Stingaree when I was a young Marine. Since the area has become trendy Gaslamp Quarter, streetwalking has taken on a new meaning. We enjoy strolling past the boutiques and cafés, pausing to peer at menus posted in windows and perhaps having lunch or a glass of wine at an outdoor table. That's a nice feature of the Gaslamp—virtually every restaurant offers *al fresco* dining and sipping.

9 WALKING ABOUT SAN DIEGO BAY'S "ISLANDS" • *Harbor Island is opposite San Diego International Airport and Shelter Island is off Point Loma. GETTING THERE: To reach Harbor Island, take any airport exit from I-5, then go west on Harbor Drive to the island*

turnoff. For Shelter Island, continue on Harbor Drive about two miles to Point Loma, turn left (south) onto Rosecrans Street, then left again onto Shelter Island Drive.

Both of the "islands" in San Diego Bay are manmade peninsulas, dredged up from the mud and enhanced with grassy lawns, palm trees, swimming areas, promenades, marinas, resorts and restaurants. Shelter Island was created in the 1950s when the main ship channel was deepened and excess mud was dumped onto offshore shoals. Harbor Island followed a decade later, as berths at the San Diego Naval station were deepened to accommodate large aircraft carriers.

The peninsulas, shaped like putting irons, are more than a mile long and each has a concrete promenade running its length. They provide fine views of the bay, Point Loma, Coronado and downtown San Diego's highrises. For serious boat watching and people watching, relax at one of the many benches along the way, or simply sprawl on the adjacent lawns.

10 DINING IN THE CASA DE BANDINI GARDEN • *In Old Town at 2660 Calhoun St.; (619) 297-8211. Mexican fare; lunch through dinner daily. GETTING THERE: Take the Old Town exit from I-5 or I-8 northwest of the city. The restaurant is just northeast of the plaza.*

Housed in a nicely restored 1829 adobe, Casa de Bandini is one of Old Town's more popular restaurants. Although the interior is handsomely decorated, we prefer dining in the courtyard garden. It's lushly landscaped and busy with trellises, arbors and fountains, made even brighter and cheerier by colored lights and strolling mariachis. Even chilly evenings can be comfortable, since heat lamps keep things cozily warm. The food is a cut above typical tourist fare. The kitchen has been improved in recent years, and several seafood and California-Mexican entrées have been added to the traditional Hispanic menu.

The buildings are beautiful, the setting is lovely; the note of San Diego's fair is simply charming. —The *Saturday Evening Post*, commenting on Balboa Park's 1915 Panama-Pacific Exposition

Chapter two

PLAYING TOURIST
Doing what the others do—only differently

San Diego ranks with San Francisco and Los Angeles as one of California's most visited cities. Although balmy weather is one of Sunshine City's greatest drawing cards, people come for its many attractions as well. Balboa Park, the San Diego Zoo, Sea World and Mission Bay Park are its major lures. However, there are dozens of other reasons to set your compass for San Diego, and this chapter focuses on both the obvious an the hidden lures of this sunbathed city.

As we mentioned in the introductory chapter, when we discuss attractions in San Diego, we include the contiguous communities of Ocean Beach, Mission Beach, Pacific Beach and La Jolla, which are just up the coast and—in fact—part of metropolitan San Diego. We also include Coronado, which is a separate community.

That other San Diego list

In addition to the book you hold in your hands, another good source for the city's better offerings is the annual "San Diego's Best Readers Poll," published as an insert to the *Union-Tribune* in late August. It has more than 130 different lists, with the best three in each category. It's geared more toward local readers, and includes such strange subjects as "Best Car Wash" and "Best Padre" (a baseball player, not a priest). We questioned some of the dining selections in a recent edition, such as Denny's for best breakfast and Pizza Hut for best pizza. These franchise places are okay, although we'd hardly consider them to be the very best the town has to offer. Also, the survey includes a category for "Best Fast Food" which, of course, is a self-canceling phrase.

However, we found the list useful and we'll admit to checking out some of its selections. It gave us several good leads and we sometimes agreed with the *Union-Trib's* readers. Pick up a copy if you're in town during August. For back issues, you can call the *Union-Tribune* at (619) 299-3131.

A NOTE ABOUT OUR LISTINGS: Before we begin, we should point out that each Ten Best list starts with our personal favorite, followed by the next nine in alphabetical order. Thus, there are no losers in this book; only winners and runners up. (When items aren't directly related, our ten selections are listed in no particular order.)

PRICING: Since prices frequently change, we use dollar-sign price codes to indicate the approximate cost of adult admission to various attractions: *$* = under $5; *$$* = $5 to $9; *$$$* = $10 to $14 ; *$$$* = $15 to $19 = *$$$$$* = $20 or more. And you already know that prices are almost always less for seniors and kids.

WHEN TO VISIT THE TEN BEST ATTRACTIONS

Every visitor to San Diego wants to see its main attractions. It's hardly necessary to compile a list suggesting that you go to Balboa Park and the San Diego Zoo, that you pay your respects to Mission San Diego de Alcalá, play in Mission Bay Park and say "Hi!" to Shamu at Sea World.

However, these places aren't much fun if you have to burrow through thick crowds, stand in long ticket queues and inhale diesel fumes from tour buses. We therefore take sightseeing a step further, not only selecting our Ten Best San Diego attractions, but suggesting the best times to go see them.

For starters, autumn is the best time to do just about anything here because the weather is wonderfully balmy and Sunshine City is almost unfailingly sunny. Tourists crowds are thinner since visiting kids have had to leave for school, taking their parents with them. Spring is fine as well, since the summer crowds haven't yet arrived and rainfall is relatively light here. Of course, all of you may not have a spring or autumn option, so we'll try to find other ways around the crowds by suggesting the best days to visit.

1 BALBOA PARK IN THE MIDDLE OF A WEEKDAY • The

park Visitor Center is in the northwest corner of the House of Hospitality, off Plaza de Panama, across from the San Diego Museum of Art; (619) 239-0512. A seven-day "Passport" costing just over $20 provides admission to about ten of the park's museums and other attraction. With a value of more than $60, it's well worth the investment. Passports are available at the various museums and attractions that honor them. GETTING THERE: Take the Laurel Street exit from I-5 and go uphill, or go north on Fifth Avenue from downtown and turn right onto Laurel, which becomes El Prado (The Promenade) as it enters the park.

If we had time to visit only one attraction in San Diego, it would be Balboa Park, a 1,200-acre mecca of recreation, culture and critters occupying several lumpy mesas creased by wooded canyons. It is a park like no other in America, containing one of the world's largest zoos, most of San Diego's important museums and a fine collection of Spanish-Moorish buildings left over from two international exhibitions.

And the best time to visit this vast complex is midday on a weekday, to avoid both weekend crowds and the commuter traffic that swirls around this area in the early morning and late afternoon. (It doesn't go through the park itself, although getting here and away might be a chore during commute hours.) Of course, with so many attractions and appeals, a thorough visit to the park will require more than one weekday midday. Incidentally, Since Balboa Park is so large, a free tram hauls visitors from one area to the next, daily from 9 to 5:15. Pick up a park map marked with tram stops at the Visitor Center.

City founders set aside this wooded area northeast of downtown for a city park way back in 1868, although development was slow in coming. When San Diego hosted the Panama-California International Exposition in 1915 to celebrate completion of the Panama Canal, a large chunk of this city-owned land was selected for the site. Planners decided to save several of the elaborately detailed Spanish-Moorish exhibit buildings as a focal point for the park. More structures from the 1935-36 California-Pacific International Exposition, built with Depression era WPA labor, contributed to this architectural bounty. Most of these buildings remain today, restored to their intricate finery.

Balboa Park's many attractions appear elsewhere in this book under their own listings. Even without its specific lures, this is a grand place to spend the greater part of a day. Hike its many trails into pine and eucalyptus groves, stroll through one of the park's theme gardens, spread a picnic lunch in Pepper Grove or on a cool lawn, or simply find a place to relax and listen to the 100-bell carillon chime the time from the 200-foot California Tower.

If we could change one thing in Balboa Park, we'd close the entire length of El Prado to vehicle traffic. The section from Plaza de Panama east to Plaza de Balboa is a true promenade. However the segment from the west gate to Plaza de Panama is open to vehicles. And despite its pretty name, Plaza de Panama is—good grief!—a parking lot. C'mon city planners; you can do better than that!

2 **BELMONT PARK IN MIDSUMMER** • *3146 Mission Blvd.; Mission Beach; (619) 491-2988; roller coaster information (619) 488-1549; Plunge information (619) 488-3110. Most rides operate Sunday-Thursday 11 to 10 and Friday-Saturday 11 to 11 in summer, then Sunday-Thursday 11 to 5 and Friday-Saturday 11 to 9 the rest of the year. Grounds admission free; various prices for rides. GETTING THERE: Take I-8 west to Mission Bay Park and follow West Mission Bay Drive through the park to Mission Beach. Mission Bay Drive blends into Ventura Place beside the amusement center's parking lot.*

We normally steer clear of popular attractions in summer. However, this is a summer kind of place. The only remaining beachside amusement park in southern California, Belmont Park is meant to be enjoyed on a warm sunny day, when you can play on the rides, then splash in the nearby surf. (Avoid it on summer weekends, however.)

Ready for a trip into the past? Climb aboard the all-wooden Giant Dipper roller coaster, and take a plunge in The Plunge, a 175-foot indoor pool where Esther Williams and Johnny Weismuller once plunged for the movie cameras. Or catch a ride on the old fashioned Tilt-a-Whirl or the antique carousel. If you'd like to return to the present, there's a large video game parlor called Prime Time and—good grief!—even a MacDonald's.

Ventura Place, the short street opposite Belmont Park's car lot, also resembles a beachside retreat from yesterday, with its shaved ice and hot dog parlors, swimsuit shops and even a tattoo parlor.

Belmont Park was built by San Diego benefactor and sugar magnate John D. Spreckels in 1925 as the New Mission Beach Amusement Center. Later closed and falling into ruin, it was given to the City of San Diego and renovated in the late 1980s. Its Giant Dipper is listed on the National Register of Historic Places.

3 **BIRCH AQUARIUM ON A SUMMER WEEKDAY** • *Scripps Institution of Oceanography, 2300 Exhibition Way, La Jolla; (858) 534-3474. Daily 9 to 5. MC/VISA, AMEX; $$ plus $ parking fee. GETTING THERE: Go north about nine miles on I-5 from the I-8 interchange and turn west onto La Jolla Village Drive, which becomes North Torrey Pines Road. About a mile from the freeway, turn left onto Expedition Way.*

This fine aquarium and ocean science center is a popular draw for class field trips, so we usually avoid it on school days. So many students will have their little noses pressed to the display tanks that it may be hard to see the octopi and moray eels. On weekends, kids and parents crowd the place, so summer weekdays may be best.

Through the generosity of the Scripps newspaper publishing family, the San Diego Marine Biological Association established an institution in 1903 "to carry out a biological and hydrographic survey of the waters of the Pacific Ocean adjacent to the coast of southern California; (and) to build and maintain a public aquarium and museum."

Thus began one of the world's foremost marine biology labs, the Scripps Institution of Oceanography, now operated by the University of California. Its Birch Aquarium is one of the oldest and most respected on the West Coast. Although it lacks some of the monumental exhibits of newer places such as the Monterey Bay Aquarium and the Oregon Coast Aquarium in Newport, it is a fine facility, with a strong focus on the sea life of southern California and Baja California. Folks can admire multicolored fish and coral reefs in thirty aquarium exhibits, including a 70,000-gallon tank with an undulating kelp forest.

The excellent "Blue Planet" display focuses on the importance of water to life on earth—without which there would be none. Interactive exhibits chart wave movements and allow visitors to generate thunderstorms. Particularly fun is a simulated grocery shelf display sponsored by Von's Markets, where visitors can use scanners to read barcodes and learn the role that sea life plays in the production of our foods and other essentials.

4 CABRILLO NATIONAL MONUMENT ON A CLEAR DAY

● *1800 Cabrillo Memorial Drive; (619) 557-5450. Daily 9 to 5:30; longer hours in summer; $$. GETTING THERE: The easiest approach is to follow Rosecrans Street (State Route 209) southwest to Point Loma; you can pick it up near the junctions of I-5 and I-8.*

Remember that tired cliché about clear days and seeing forever? Cabrillo National Monument occupies the very tip of Point Loma, providing stellar vistas of San Diego Bay, the city skyline beyond and the green hillsides above. You can watch ship traffic enter the harbor, watch planes take off and land from North Island Naval Air Station and San Diego International Airport, and admire the detail of the San Diego skyline.

This also is one of California's most important historic sites. A graphic at the entrance to the interpretive center says it best:

Here we commemorate the bravery and determination of a handful of men of many nationalities who served the flag of Spain and the cross of Christianity in exploring the new word...

On September 28, 1542, Portuguese navigator Juan Rodríguez Cabrillo, sailing under the Spanish flag, entered nearly landlocked San Diego Bay. He spent six days waiting out a storm and checking out the local Indians, then he continued northward. The museum chronicles the exploits of Cabrillo and other early navigators in the employ of Spain, who were the first outsiders to discover and explore the west coast of America.

This small national monument's other featured attraction is the old Point Loma Lighthouse, occupying a bluff above the museum and visitor center. It served only thirty-six years because it had a fatal flaw; sitting 433 feet above the sea, it often was shrouded in fog. A new lighthouse was built lower down on the point in 1891 and is still in use. Old Point Loma Light is now a museum, furnished as it would have been when Robert Israel and his wife Maria kept the light burning for ships seeking passage into San Diego Bay.

5 *MISSION BAY PARK ON A SUNNY WEEKDAY* • *Northwest of downtown above the I-5 and I-8 junctions. Park headquarters is at 2581 Quivira Court; (619) 221-8900. GETTING THERE: Take the Mission Bay exit from I-5 and go toward the ocean or follow I-8 west and take West Mission Bay Drive northwest. To reach park headquarters, turn onto Quivira Way near the Hyatt Islandia, drive south away from the Hyatt and follow the road to its end.*

Once a mosquito-ridden swampland so inhospitable that Juan Cabrillo called it False Bay, Mission Bay rivals Balboa Park as San Diego's most popular playground. It's so large that it is rarely congested, even on warm sunny days. It can get crowded on summer weekends, however. Mission Bay is home to Sea World and six major resort hotels; many are listed elsewhere in the book. However, its best attraction is its great aquatic outdoors—more than twenty-five miles of beaches, acres of lawns, several marinas and water sports areas and miles of walking and biking trails.

Mission Bay is so large and complex that it's easy to get lost. To help find your way about, pick up a map at park headquarters; copies are in a rack outside the entrance if the office is closed.

Reclamation of this swampland was started in the 1950s and when it was completed, old False Bay had been fashioned into a 4,600-acre recreation area, about half water and half land. Even with several resorts, marinas and Sea World, about seventy-five percent of the park is open space.

6 *MISSION SAN DIEGO DE ALCALÀ DURING MASS* • *10818 San Diego Mission Rd.; (619) 281-8449. Mission open daily 9 to 5; $. Sunday mass at 7, 8, 10, 11 and noon, and at 5:30; Saturday at 5:30 p.m. and daily at 7 a.m. and 5:30 p.m. GETTING THERE: Follow I-8 about seven miles east from San Diego and take the Mission Gorge Road exit (near the I-15 interchange). Pursue Mission Gorge north for about half a mile through a thick commercial area, then go left on Twain Avenue for another half mile; the mission is on your right.*

Whether or not you're a Catholic, you'll get a better sense of the history and charm of this ancient church if you're here during mass, when the voice of the priest and the sounds of music mingle with echoes of the past. Sit beneath those great beam ceilings and imagine yourself in San Diego during its formative years, when this was a haven not for Catholic parishioners and curious tourists, but for frontier priests and *Kumeya'ay* Indians. However, there were no pews then; the native converts sat on reed mats on the floor.

Before or after mass, you can follow a self guiding tour—with a brochure—from the gift shop, past a typically spartan padre's cell, then through the church and into the gardens. A nicely done museum traces the mission's history from its founding through its glory days as an agricultural empire to the Mexican period when its lands were removed, and finally to American occupation and restoration.

Initially established atop Presidio Hill in 1769, the mission was moved to this site in 1774 to be closer to the Indians' agricultural fields—and to get them away from the sometimes pesky soldiers of the presidio. After the American conquest of California, it suffered the indignity of being used as a cavalry barracks from 1846 until 1862, then it was restored to the Catholic Church by order of President Lincoln. Some of the present structures date from 1813, although they've undergone considerable reconstruction and restoration. Mission San Diego has been a parish church since 1941.

7 OLD TOWN DURING CINCO DE MAYO ● *Old Town San Diego State Historic Park; (619) 220-5422. For Fiesta Cinco de Mayo information, call (619) 299-6055. Park visitor center and historic buildings open daily 10 to 5. Free walking tours daily from 10:30 to 2. Various hours for other Old Town facilities. GETTING THERE: Take the Old Town exit from I-5 or I-8 northwest of the city.*

Cinco de Mayo is celebrated in Old Town with food and crafts booths, brightly costumed dancers and other Hispanic capers. Most festivities occur during the week that includes May 5, which is what *Cinco de Mayo* means. (The date commemorates the Battle of Puebla, when an outnumbered Mexican force defeated the invading armies of Napoleon III in 1862.)

Of course, the first week of May is a pretty narrow window for planning a San Diego trip. Actually, just about any time is fine for visiting here, except on weekends. It rivals Balboa Park and Sea World in popularity, and we found it rather crowded even on a cloudy January Sunday.

Old town is a multi-faceted place. The historic park, a traffic-free six square block area, has several exhibits in restored or reconstructed buildings. You'll find everything from adobe homes to the first office of the *San Diego Union,* dating from 1868. Filling one end of Old Town is Bazaar del Mundo, a wonderfully gaudy shopping complex. Interspersed among Old Town's historic structures are many specialty shops and Mexican restaurants, and others are on nearby streets.

Many of Old Town's features—notably its restaurants and shops—are covered elsewhere in this book. One of our favorite places is the

Seeley Stables, a large barn that houses a fine collection of coaches and surreys from the town's earlier days. A second story display area tells the story of the American cowboy, whose roots are traced to the *vaqueros* of the Mexican Southwest. The stable also contains the state park information center, open daily 10 to 5.

The park's largest and most authentic exhibit is the courtyard style Casa de Estudillo with several rooms and workshops furnished to the early 1800s. If you're a longtime San Diego resident or a past visitor, you'll recall a time when it wasn't authentic at all. San Diego benefactor Adolph Spreckels bought the crumbling ruin in 1909 and had it converted into an inn, and it later became a curio shop and tourist trap. Until 1966, it was known as "Ramona's Marriage Place," based on Helen Hunt Jackson's novel *Ramona,* about a señorita who falls in love with an Indian. Many tourists didn't realize that Señorita Ramona was a fictitious character and Ms. Jackson wrote her book in a New York hotel room. (To be fair, she did visit this area in the 1800s and her novel may have been based on some actual events.)

8 SAN DIEGO MARITIME MUSEUM ON A WEEKEND •

1306 N. Harbor Dr.; (619) 234-9153. Daily 8 to 8; $$. GETTING THERE: The three ships that comprise the maritime museum are at the San Diego waterfront alongside Harbor Drive, opposite downtown.

Why a weekend for the maritime museum? For one thing, this facility doesn't draw the heavy crowds of places like the San Diego Zoo, so weekends are usually fine. However, it can get chaotic on some weekdays when local schools conduct field trips. We don't begrudge the little darlings' desires to learn more about ships and sailing. However, it can get a bit hectic when they swarm—jabbering happily—up and down the gangways.

Three historic ships comprise this floating museum—the 1863 sailing bark *Star of India,* the 1898 ferryboat *Berkeley* that once plied San Francisco Bay and the unusual steam Yacht *Medea,* built in 1904. The *Star of India* is the star of the show, at least in longevity. This fine old sailing ship was acquired by a local group 1927, and it has been on display at the waterfront since 1948. The two other ships were added later. The main deck of the *Berkeley* is a museum devoted to sailing, with a special exhibit on yachting, since the World Cup race has been staged off San Diego. Her upper deck is relatively original, complete with rows of passenger seats and ornate woodwork. Also intact is the boiler room, with its huge steam engines, coal bins and a sooty mannequin "stoker." From the *Berkeley,* you can take a gangway down to the *Medea* and peer into a restored turn-of-the-century dining salon, smoking lounge and other elegant oak-paneled accommodations.

The next door *Star of India* is one of the oldest completely restored sailing ships in America. Her small passenger and officers cabins have authentic turn-of-the-century furnishings and the cramped crew quarters—rough tiered bunks—look ready for occupancy. The grand old *Star* cruised all over the world and circled the globe twenty-two times. She hauled everything from lumber along the American coast to English immigrants bound for New Zealand.

9 SAN DIEGO ZOO DURING FEEDING TIME • *2920 Zoo Drive in Balboa Park; (619) 234-3153. Daily 9 to 9 in summer and 9 to 4 the rest of the year. MC/VISA, AMEX; general admission $$$$; combination ticket including admission plus tram tour, kids' zoo and sky tram $$$$$. Combo tickets also available for the San Diego Wild Animal Park. GETTING THERE: Take Park Boulevard into Balboa Park and follow signs.*

When we suggest visiting the zoo during feeding time, we're referring to the animals', not yours. When you visit the zoo, check on meal times at the various animal enclosures. All of earth's creatures—including two-legged ones—are more active and more usually interesting at the dinner table. Signs out front also indicate when the rare pandas are on display; they usually come out during cool weather.

Covering more than a hundred acres, with 4,000 animals representing 800 different species, this is one of the world's most honored zoological parks. The San Diego Zoo is a pioneer in the development of realistic animal habitats without bars or cages. It's easy to lose yourself in the wonder of this place and pretend you're in a real rainforest, a tropical gorilla habitat or strolling alongside a hippo wallow. The Polar Bear Plunge is so realistic that you'll forget you're in semi-tropical San Diego. You can see eighty percent of the zoo's exhibits by hopping aboard a tram, although interaction among some of the animals and the tram drivers distracts from the reality of the settings. We like to stroll leisurely along the zoo's many paths and view the critters quietly, and preferably on a slow day, which means an off-season weekday. (The animals usually are more active on cooler days, so winter visits are just fine.)

In addition to housing one of the world's largest animal collections, the San Diego Zoo is famous for its research and conservation work. It has bred many rare and endangered species, including the California condor and the only copulating koalas outside of Australia. The zoo's current effort is to get two giant pandas on loan from China to mate, although *Shi Shi* and *Bai Yun* don't seem to like one another much.

10 SEA WORLD ADVENTURE PARK IN THE OFF-SEASON • *In Mission Bay at 1720 South Shores Rd.; (619) 226-3815 or (619) 226-3901 for recorded information. Daily 10 to dusk; later evening hours in summer. MC/VISA, DISC; $$$$$. Admission includes all shows; parking and some rides are extra. GETTING THERE: Follow I-8 west from the I-5 interchange and take the Mission Bay exit north; Sea World comes up shortly on your right.*

San Diego's most popular attraction gets very crowded in summer, so plan an off-season visit if possible. The critters there don't mind the cooler weather and they'll put on a fine show for you. If you must go in summer, plan on a weekday and get there early. You can beat the crowds by arriving when the gates open.

Sea World gained international note a couple of decades ago when its Shamu became the globe's first performing killer whale. Shamu is still there, leaping high out of the water and splashing the first seven rows of the seating section, although he's not the original. Like Betty Crocker, Shamu has become a trade name. He and other captive killer whales have done much to gain sympathy for these noble beasts by performing in aquatic parks and appearing in films such as *Free Willie*. (Noted marine mammal illustrator Pieter Folkens, who we met on a wildlife cruise, once mused that—since killer whales eat dolphins—perhaps someone should do a movie version of *Flipper* and call it *Free Willie's Lunch*.)

Although Shamu is Sea World's star, you can catch several other shows and view a good assortment of aquatic critters, including dolphins (safely out of Shamu's range), penguins, otters, walruses and hundreds of fish varieties in aquarium tanks. Recent additions to this aquatic park are manatees, those highly endangered sea cow type critters from the American South. Wild Arctic is another new exhibit, with polar bears, walruses, seals and other critters from the frozen far north. Sea World is highly respected as an aquatic research center, although the park has gotten a bit hokey. Among its exhibits are a motion simulator ride, "Mission: Bermuda Triangle," and a playland area called "Shamu's Happy Harbor."

THE TEN BEST MUSEUMS

Museum-hopping is easy in San Diego, since most of the city's cultural archives are in Balboa Park. Many are housed in those splendid Spanish-Moorish buildings left over from the international expositions of 1915 and 1936. Several museums have been improved and expanded in recent years, so if you haven't visited them for a while, expect to find some things new.

If you plan to see several museums in Balboa Park, buy a seven-day "Passport," which provides more than $60 worth of admissions for just over $20. It's available at any of the park's participating museums.

NOTE: Many of the city's museums are closed on Monday, particularly those in Balboa Park.

1 *REUBEN H. FLEET SCIENCE CENTER* ● *In Balboa Park;* (619) 238-1233. *Various hours for space theater showings; Science Center open daily at 9:30; closing times vary with the seasons. MC/VISA,*

DISC; $$; combination Science Center and Omnimax movie admission $$$. GETTING THERE: The Science Center is at the far eastern end of El Prado, on Plaza de Balboa.

Completely redone in 1999 and nearly doubled in size, the Fleet Science Center is easily San Diego's finest museum. Further, it's more than a science museum. In addition to many state-of-the-art interactive exhibits, it offers a planetarium and wide screen theater where Omnimax and Imax films are shown. Often, two are scheduled at a time, shown alternately shown during the day.

A really cute exhibit in the Science Center is called "About Faces," in which you capture your image on freeze-frame video and learn that it isn't really symmetrical. You can manipulate that old mug with some very comic results. And do you want to know how computers talk to you and to one another? Traveling light bars demonstrate how binary signals, which translate the alphabet into ASCII language, send messages back and forth. You can become an instant computer programmer and transmit "I love you" or "Pick up a loaf of bread on the way home" to your significant other. At another computer exhibit, you can access the internet, punch in "www.weather.com" and see how miserable things are back home while you frolic in sunny San Diego. One of the science center's most appealing attractions—particularly for kids— is SciTours, which takes visitors on a wild motion-simulator ride through space.

At the museum's gift shop, you can buy science-oriented stuff such as glow-in-the-dark night sky charts and real space food used by the astronauts; would you believe freeze-dried ice cream?

2 MINGEI INTERNATIONAL MUSEUM • *In Balboa Park at 1439 El Prado; (619) 239-0003. Tuesday-Sunday 10 to 4; closed Monday; $$. GETTING THERE: Mingei is in the House of Charm on the southwest corner of Plaza de Panama.*

Although located in one of El Prado's old Spanish colonial buildings, the Mingei is an airy, modern museum with several permanent exhibit halls around a second-floor mezzanine. The main floor, called the Rotunda Gallery, is used for changing shows. The focus of this fine museum is on international folk art and decorative items used in the daily lives of various ethnic groups. One of the larger exhibits depicts the art and culture of Indonesia and New Guinea, with multicolored masks, dolls, fertility symbols and shadow puppets. A Japanese collection features contemporary decorative bottles, bowls and jars.

Another major exhibit—unless it has been disassembled before you get there—displays the multicolored folk art and furniture of central Europe. Items include cheerful wedding bonnets and costumes, and— tee-hee—a marriage bed with elaborately painted headboards. (It looked too small for two people, but then...)

3 **MUSEUM OF CONTEMPORARY ART** • *700 Prospect St., La Jolla; (858) 454-3541. Tuesday-Saturday 10 to 5 (until 8 p.m. Wednesday), Sunday noon to 5; closed Monday. Also at 1001 Kettner Blvd., downtown San Diego; (619) 234-1001. Tuesday-Saturday 10 to 5 (until 8 p.m. Friday), Sunday noon to 5; closed Monday. $. GETTING THERE: The La Jolla museum is just up from La Jolla Cove in the downtown area, at Prospect and Draper. The San Diego branch is at Kettner near Broadway, across from the Santa Fe depot.*

We have a theory that most modern artists are actually humorists who enjoy pulling the collective public leg, and that people attend their exhibits to prove they're enlightened about current cultural trends. And so, in this quite beautiful museum overlooking La Jolla Cove, art patrons nod solemnly at exhibits of a disassembled plastic Jesus, little squares in varying shades of beige, and a pair of boxing gloves hanging by duct tape from a draped rubber tarp. (This one, according to the artist, is making a racial statement about Blacks in the ring.) As we stared quizzically at an important exhibit by the late British artist Francis Bacon of "The Papal Tortures of 1953," a guide explained: "Notice how the yellows draw your eyes right to the soul of the painting." We stared at this blurry portrait of a screaming Pope, nodded in agreement, then moved on to a large metal sculpture of a two-headed half-man, half-woman sprouting from a TV set. That's what happens when you watch *The Simpsons* too often.

The museum's downtown extension is smaller, with equally curious art. Both have very nice selections of books on art and artists.

4 **SAN DIEGO AUTOMOTIVE MUSEUM** • *2080 Pan American Plaza in Balboa Park; (619) 231-2886. Daily 10 to 5:30 in summer and 10 to 4:30 the rest of the year. MC/VISA; $$. GETTING THERE: Go southwest from Plaza de Panama, past the Spreckels Organ Pavilion and you'll see the museum on your right.*

Not large as auto museums go, the San Diego version nonetheless offers a very select display of yesterday vehicles. The first item you see may be the most impressive—a showroom quality 1954 Kaiser Darrin. Vehicles range from horseless carriages such as a topless 1909 International Harvester "Farm Wagon" to more contemporary rigs such as early Ford Mustangs and one of the first Datsun 240-Zs. Car buffs will drool over a really cool 1974 Lamborghini Countach 500-S. And dearie, you certainly can remember the 1957 Chevy Bel Air with a wrap-around windshield, and that really hot Chrysler 300.

The museum also has a nice collection of "woodies," popular during the Fifties and Sixties as surfer wagons, plus a large gathering of vintage motorcycles. And of course it has a *Back to the Future* type DeLorean. The museum's 1981 model is identical to the one used as an automotive time machine in the movie.

5 SAN DIEGO AEROSPACE MUSEUM • *2001 Pan American Plaza in Balboa Park; (619) 234-8291. Daily 10 to 4:30. MC/VISA; $$. GETTING THERE: It's next door to the Automotive Museum.*

This rivals the Fleet Science center as the best museum in San Diego. Extensive and comprehensive, it traces the history of flight from early balloon ascents to the Wright Brothers' flight through the development of commercial and combat aviation and into the space race.

In front of this sleekly modern museum, you'll see what is perhaps the sexiest airplane ever built—the Lockheed A-12 Blackbird. Inside, you'll encounter a full-scale flyable replica of Charles A. Lindbergh's *Spirit of St. Louis* and an extensive exhibit concerning his epic flight from New York to Paris. Why is San Diego so excited about Lucky Lindy? Because his aircraft was built about a mile from here, by the Ryan Aviation Company.

You'll next pass through the International Aerospace Hall of Fame honoring more than a hundred flight pioneers, from those who built them to those who flew them. And then your walk through aviation history begins. There's Wilbur and Orville, fiddling with their Kittyhawk Flyer; beyond are more planes of the early twentieth century, including rare items such as a flyable Japanese Zero and Russian MiG-15. Women fliers are honored, from Amelia Earhart to daredevil lady barnstormers. A special exhibit focuses on the Flying Tigers, volunteer American pilots who flew P-40 Tomahawks for China in the opening days of World War II. Coming full circle, literally and figuratively in this well laid out museum, you'll see space capsules, satellites and astronaut regalia.

This is a busy, delightfully cluttered place. Planes sit on the floor and hang from ceilings; exhibits cover the walls and spill into side rooms. With so many things to see, and so many videos to watch, you could spend most of a day here. It's one of the most comprehensive air museums in America, perhaps exceeded only by the Smithsonian and the Museum of Flight in Seattle.

6 SAN DIEGO MUSEUM OF ART • *In Balboa Park at 1450 El Prado; (619) 232-7931. Tuesday-Sunday 10 to 4:30; $$. GETTING THERE: The museum is on the north side of Plaza de Panama.*

Housed in one of the park's wonderfully filigreed Spanish-Moorish buildings, this is *the* art museum of San Diego. It hosts major traveling exhibits and contains the city's largest and most eclectic art assortment. Serious collections include works by early Spanish and Italian artists; French pre-impressionist and impressionist art, with Renoir, Monet, Degas, Matisse and the like; the works of early and contemporary American artists; and an extensive Asian art collection of figurines, vases, Chinese prints, screens, calligraphy and Buddha images. Particularly interesting is an exhibit of Japanese woodblock paintings that had been collected by Claude Monet, who was a great admirer of this art form.

In startling contrast to all of the above, step into a gallery of California art and stare quizzically at objects such as six two-by-fours thrust through an iron ring, two black bars on a white canvas, and multi-colored candles melting over a beat-up suitcase. If Van Gogh had found such an easy route to public acceptance of his art, perhaps he wouldn't have been so tortured and he'd have left this earth with both ears attached.

7 *SAN DIEGO MUSEUM OF HISTORY* ● *In Balboa Park at 1649 El Prado; (619) 232-6203. Tuesday-Sunday 10 to 4:30; $$. GETTING THERE: The museum is in Casa del Balboa about midway down El Prado.*

Although it sits by the sea, San Diego has a desert climate. Thus, the city's story is the story of water, and it's effectively told in this museum. You're first greeted by a handsome 1866 Concord stagecoach that once operated in these parts, then you step into an exhibit entitled "Eden in the Desert," concerning the city's efforts to obtain water. A particularly ironic episode occurred when one Charles Hatfield was hired by the city for $10,000 to bring rain during a 1915 drought. He did whatever it is that rainmakers do, and the skies opened up, causing the worst flood in San Diego's history. City officials said they would pay him only if he accepted full responsibility for the flood damage; Mr. Hatfield left town penniless.

The museum focuses particularly on the city's development since California was admitted to the Union in 1850. It also mounts major traveling exhibits, including some that aren't related to local history. (When we last visited, we saw a display concerning one of America's great urban parks—not Balboa, but Central Park in New York City.) The museum is operated by the San Diego Historical Society.

8 *SAN DIEGO MUSEUM OF MAN* ● *1350 El Prado; (619) 239-2001. Daily 10 to 4:30; $$. GETTING THERE: The museum is just inside Balboa Park's west gate in the California Building.*

The most interesting exhibit at this fine anthropological museum consists of hairy and anatomically complete replicas of our ancestors. Oddly, this display is chronologically reversed, so walk to the far end and start back. You'll find replica bones of the famous three-million-year-old missing link Lucy, discovered in 1974 in Ethiopia. (Incidentally, her name came from *Lucy In the Sky with Diamonds*, a song by the Beatles that the anthropologists played in camp the night after her discovery.) From here, following the exhibit toward its entrance, you'll encounter increasingly taller and more erect critters, ending with Cro-Magnon man of 20,000 years ago. Other than needing a shave and a haircut, he looks quite like us.

Another exhibit traces human conception, with actual videotapes of a female egg cell being fertilized by a rambunctious male sperm and then growing into a fetus. Other displays focus on native people of the Southwest and Mexico—how they lived before we outsiders came, and how we have disrupted their lives. In the "Life and Death on the Nile" exhibit concerning gods and mummies of ancient Egypt, you can feed a dollar bill into a machine and produce your own personal *cartouche*, spelling out your name phonetically in Egyptian hieroglyphics.

9 *SAN DIEGO NATURAL HISTORY MUSEUM* • *In Balboa Park at 1788 El Prado; (619) 232-3821. Daily 9:30 to 5:30 in summer and 9:30 to 4:30 the rest of the year; open until 6:30 on Thursdays; $$. GETTING THERE: The museum is at the far eastern end of El Prado, opposite the Fleet Science Center.*

While not elaborate, this is an interesting and nicely done museum, featuring the flora, fauna and geology of San Diego County and neighboring Baja California. An exhibit on area gems and minerals is styled as a mining tunnel, with the usual glow-in-the-dark flourescent stuff. In the paleontology display, you'll likely be surprised to learn that walruses once hung out in San Diego County. The museum's best display is a life-sized diorama of Anza-Borrego Desert State Park with a stuffed bighorn sheep among the pretend rocks, and the nighttime lairs of an owl and a fox. If you have kids along, they'll like the creepy-crawly displays of both live and mounted bugs. The museum also mounts changing exhibits with specific natural history themes.

10 *TIMKEN MUSEUM OF ART* • *1500 El Prado in Balboa Park; (619) 239-5548. Tuesday-Saturday 10 to 4:30 and Sunday 1 to 4:30; closed Mondays and all of September; free. GETTING THERE: The Timken is immediately east of the San Diego Museum of Art.*

One of the most attractive of the city's museums, this modern facility is a showplace of Italian marble with bronze accents and fabric walls. It was opened in 1965 as a gift to the city from two art-collecting spinster sisters, Anne and Amy Putnam, and Henry H. Timken of Timken roller bearing fame. Most of the art came from the Putnams and Timken financed the building. It displays selected works of several European masters and American artists, plus a really fine collection of Russian religious icons. Among the more recognized artists represented here are Peter Paul Reubens, François Boucher and Rembrandt. The museum's finest works are the icons—brilliantly painted altar screens and figurines of the Russian Orthodox Church.

THE TEN BEST THINGS TO DO IN SAN DIEGO

Blessed with a benign climate, San Diego is a city where people *do* things. This isn't couch potato country, folks!

1 *GO WHALE WATCHING* • *H&M Landing, 2803 Emerson St.; (619) 222-1144. WEB SITE: www.hmlanding.com. Whale-watching season generally is from mid-December through March, with the best sightings from December through early February. GETTING THERE: Take the Rosecrans Street (Highway 209) exit from I-5 or I-8, follow it southwest through Point Loma and turn left on Emerson. H&M is at the sportfishing pier at Emerson and Scott.*

Each winter, about 25,000 California gray whales make a dramatic 14,000-mile round trip cruise between the Bering Sea off Alaska and Baja California. They pass close to the coast in several places, particularly on their southward journey. One of these is Point Loma, and several local firms conduct two to three-hour whale watching trips from San Diego Bay. The senior member of this leviathan-spotting fleet is H&M Landing, which has been doing these trips for nearly half a century. It has been suggested that H&M invented whale watching. During peak season, whales are almost always spotted, since the boat captains are experienced in finding and tracking them. The whales don't seem to mind the attention.

The tracking experience is rather dramatic. The captain spots a glossy, barnacle-encrusted back in the distance and eases closer. The great whale often swims just off the bow, visible beneath the surface. Then it comes up for a breath of air, spouts water vapor with a great sigh, arches its back, flips its mighty fluke and gracefully slips beneath the sea. On a recent trip, our boat cruised within a few dozen yards of a forty-footer, which—with no sign of duress or distress—moved serenely along, diving and then reappearing every few minutes. The whale and the boat cruised together for nearly half an hour.

For the ultimate whale watching trip, book an eight to eleven-day voyage down the Baja Peninsula aboard the *Spirit of Adventure.* This small expedition boat is operated by Mike Keating in cooperation with H&M. It enters Baja lagoons where the whales spend the winter, and guests scoot about in small skiffs, often getting close to reach out and touch these magnificent beasts. Whales are only part of the show. The groups walk among sea elephant colonies, swim with dolphins and porpoises and see tens of thousands of seabirds. Some trips cruise around the tip of Baja California and enter the Sea of Cortez. For information, contact H&M or *Spirit of Adventure* Charters, 1646 Willow St., San Diego, CA 92106; (619) 226-1729.

2 *TAKE A SAN DIEGO BAY CRUISE* • *San Diego Harbor Excursions, 1050 N. Harbor Dr., (800) 442-7847 or (619) 234-4111; and Hornblower Cruises, 1066 N. Harbor Dr., (619) 686-8715. GETTING THERE: The two firms are side-by-side on the Embarcadero, below downtown, near the base of Broadway.*

These two firms market essentially the same voyages on San Diego Bay—one and two-hour sightseeing trips and dinner cruises. Both also have whale-watching trips from mid-December through March. Prices are similar for the two firms—around $50 for a dinner cruise that includes dancing; about $12 for a one-hour sightseeing cruise and less than $20 for two hours, and about $20 for whale watching. San Diego Harbor Excursion also operates the Coronado ferry service, at $2 each way. The harbor cruises are quite pleasant and almost always flat calm. Since San Diego Bay is nearly landlocked, it takes a nasty storm to roil the waters. On the one-hour cruises, you'll loop the bayfront, passing assorted ships and cruising under Coronado Bridge and along the Coronado shoreline. On the two-hour cruise, add the U.S. Naval Submarine Base, the tip of Point Loma, North Island Naval Air Station, and Shelter and Harbor islands. The longer cruise is definitely worth the added cost. On both, the onboard narrator will tell you more about San Diego Bay than you probably ever wanted to know.

3 *TOUR THE TOWN BY TROLLEY • Old Town Trolley Tours; (800) 868-7482 or (619) 298-TOUR. WEBSITE: www.historictours.com. Periodic departures from Old Town and eight other points in San Diego and Coronado;* **$$$$$**.

Why a trolley tour instead of a comfortable air conditioned bus? What in heck is *transportainment* and what did Wyatt Earp have to do with San Diego? Curiosity drove us to take a ride around San Diego and Coronado on one of the propane-driven rubber-tired rigs of Old Town Trolley Tours. It's an interesting concept: These narrated historical trips cover about thirty miles and stop at nine different places. Passengers can hop on and off at will, taking a break between segments to do a bit of prowling on their own.

As the trolley clang-clangs along, the driver-guide points out places of interest and offers tidbits of history—such as the fact that Wyatt Earp spent some time in San Diego, and that Lindbergh Field was built in 1928, the year after Charles Lindbergh completed his epic New York to Paris solo flight. They play "history quiz" with the passengers (we won a souvenir coin for knowing who discovered the Pacific Ocean) and sometimes sing along with the trolley's recorded musical soundtrack. And that, folks, is *transportainment*.

Incidentally, sit on the right side of the trolley, since you'll be closer to the bay when it ding-a-lings along the Embarcadero, and you'll get a better view of the San Diego skyline as it crosses the San Diego-Coronado Bay Bridge.

4 *TAKE THE PLUNGE AT THE PLUNGE • Belmont Park, 3115 Ocean Front Walk (at Ventura Place); (619) 488-3110. Opens at 5 a.m., with various closing hours; $ per swim; other fees for special activities. GETTING THERE: Take I-8 west to Mission Bay Park and follow*

West Mission Bay Drive to Mission Beach; it becomes Ventura Place and ends at the Belmont Park car lot.

You can dive into history when you take a dip in The Plunge, the huge indoor swimming pool at Belmont Park that dates from 1925. One of the oldest and largest public indoor pools in America, it measures 175 by sixty feet, with several lap lanes and plenty of space for just splashing about. The Plunge has an extensive program of swimming lessons and aquatic workouts.

Never mind that there's a pervading smell of chlorine in the air; you're swimming in an historic landmark. When it was opened as part of John D. Spreckels Mission Beach Amusement Center, it was billed as the world's largest indoor saltwater pool. It has been the scene of Hollywood water spectaculars starring Esther Williams and Johnny Weismuller, and big bands once played for dancing on the mezzanines. Beginning to show its age in the 1930s and 1940s, it was given to the state and then the City of San Diego. It was converted to fresh water, then completely renovated in the late 1980s as part of the Belmont Amusement Park's restoration.

5 **TAKE THE PALOMAR PLUNGE** • *Gravity Activated Sports, Inc., 16220 Highway 76, Pauma Valley; (800) 985-4GAS or (760) 742-2294. Reservations required; MC/VISA, AMEX. GETTING THERE: Pauma Valley is in northern San Diego County. Call about directions and/or hotel pickup.*

Gravity Activated Sports, as the name implies, specializes in downhill bicycle trips in San Diego County. Participants are driven by van to a launch point, then they enjoy a gravitational ride downhill. Packages include bike rental and gear, lunch and a souvenir T-shirt. The firm's most popular outing starts with a tour of Palomar Observatory, followed by a 5,000-foot downhill glide to the base of Palomar Mountain. Among other trips are the Desert Descent through Montezuma Valley to Anza-Borrego Desert, a ten-mile Temecula Valley winery tour (mostly level; no gravity boost) and a nineteen-mile off-road ride for intermediate to advanced mountain bikers.

6 **PLAY ON MISSION BAY** • *Mission Bay Park is northwest of downtown above the I-5/I-8 junctions. GETTING THERE: Take the Mission Bay exit from I-5 and go toward the ocean or follow I-8 west and take West Mission Bay Drive northwest.*

There's no better place to play under San Diego's sun than at Mission Bay Park, that 4,600-acre aquatic playland with marinas, miles of beaches and lots of calm, warm water. In case you didn't bring the proper gear for a day of water play on Mission Bay, you can rent it. Here are some outlets: **Seaforth Boat Rental** near the Hyatt Islandia Hotel at 1641 Quivira Road (223-1681) rents paddleboats, jet skis, kayaks, motorboats and sailboats. **Mission Bay Sportcenter** at 1010 Santa Clara Place (488-1004) rents water sports equipment and offers instruction in kayaking, sailing, surfing, waterskiing and windsurfing. **San Diego Sailing Center** at 1010 Santa Clara Place (488-0651) has windsurfing and kayaking lessons and rentals. **Windsport Kayak & Windsurfing Center** at 844 W. Mission Bay Drive (488-4642) has rentals, sales and lessons for windsurfing, sea kayaks, body boards and paddle skis.

7 BIKE OR SKATE ALONG THE BEACH • *Ocean Front Walk between Mission Beach and Pacific Beach. GETTING THERE: Drive through Mission Bay Park on West Mission Bay Drive; the route ends in Mission Bay at the corner of Mission Boulevard and Ventura Place.*

An old-fashioned seaside boardwalk once connected Mission Beach to Pacific Beach, about three miles north. It's all paved now and formally called Ocean Front Walk, although some locals refer to it as the boardwalk or promenade. There are long stretches of sandy beach, volleyball courts and other play areas on one side, and beachfront homes, rentals and beach businesses on the other. It's a busy recreational thoroughfare, open to walkers, runners, cyclists, rollerbladers and rollerskaters. Joining this parade is a great way to get a workout.

Didn't bring your gear? **Hamel's** at Ocean Front Walk and Ventura Place in Mission Beach (488-5050) rents rollerblades and skates, bikes and beach accessories.

8 TAKE THE COASTER UP THE COAST • *Coaster commuter train service; (619) 233-3004 in San Diego or (760) 722-6283 from coastal north county. WEB SITE: www.sdcommute.com. GETTING THERE: The Coaster leaves from the Amtrak station at the foot of Broadway in downtown San Diego.*

The Coaster is a commuter train that calls on shoreside communities between San Diego and Oceanside. Although it's designed for commuters, this is a great scenic excursion as well, since the trains travel through attractive communities and—in many areas—right along the beach. The trains use double-deck commuter cars with comfortable, roomy seating.

You can reach the Coaster depot from just about anywhere in the city via the San Diego Trolley or Metropolitan Transit buses. The trolley links with the Coaster at its Santa Fe and Old Town stations. Old Town is handy, since there's ample free parking on an adjacent lot—although this tends to fill up later in the day.

Starting from the Amtrak station, the Coaster stops at Old Town and Sorrento Valley, and then the coastal communities of Solana Beach, Encinitas, Carlsbad (two stops) and Oceanside. It runs nine times daily in each direction on weekdays and four times on Saturdays. There is no service on Sunday.

9 *CATCH THE "TIJUANA TROLLEY"* • *The San Diego Trolley's San Ysidro/Tijuana Blue Line. Trains run every fifteen minutes from 5 a.m. to 9 p.m., then every thirty minutes until 1 a.m. For schedule information call (619) 233-3004 or (619) 685-4900 for automated touch-tone phone information.*

If you plan to visit Tijuana during your San Diego stay, a relatively painless approach is aboard the San Diego Trolley. The train stops within a few feet of the international border and you can either walk across through a covered pedestrian facility, catch a bus for a dollar or a cab for about $5. For more on visiting Tijuana, see Chapter One, page 17, and Chapter Fifteen, page 214.

The "Tijuana Trolley" trip to from San Diego to San Ysidro isn't scenic, since the route travels mostly on back streets, passing clothes lines, junkyards and trailer courts. It parallels the I-5 corridor, taking you through the ordinary blue collar industrial towns of National City, Chula Vista and San Ysidro. However, the trolleys are comfortable since the trains move along well-maintained railbeds. And the trip is cheap; two dollars each way the last time we went. (If you drive down, you'll have to pay several dollars for parking on the California side, unless you plan to drive into Tijuana, which we don't recommend for brief visits.) This isn't rapid transit; the trolley makes several stops and takes about forty minutes. But what's the rush; aren't you on vacation?

10 *CATCH A PADRES GAME* • *At Qualcomm Stadium; (619) 641-3131 for the stadium, (619) 283-4494 for the Padres and (619) 297-2373 for tickets by phone from Ticketmaster. The season runs from mid-April to early October. Day games start at 1:05; night games at 7:05. GETTING THERE: Qualcomm Stadium is at the junction of I-8 and I-805 north of downtown. A painless way to get there is aboard the San Diego Trolley; the Blue Line stops within walking distance of the ballpark.*

Every sports fan knows that San Diego has two major league ball clubs—the baseball Padres and football Chargers. While Charger tickets are tough to get, game-day tickets usually are available for the Padres. And you can get better seats by calling in advance. Sales have been up in recent years after the Padres' brushes with the World Series, so advance tickets are a good idea.

The Padres became a major league team in 1969 after decades in the minors, and they won their first National League championship in 1984. They share Qualcomm Stadium with the Chargers. Built in 1967, the park originally was called Jack Murphy Stadium in honor of the highly respected *San Diego Union* sports editor who helped bring major league baseball to the city. Recently, a local firm called Qualcomm bought stadium sponsorship and poor old Jack's monument was given an ugly new name.

Incidentally, if you want to try your luck at getting San Diego Charger tickets, the number is (619) 280-2121.

OTHER PROFESSIONAL AND UNIVERSITY TEAMS ● In addition to the Padres and Chargers, several minor league and university teams compete hereabouts. Among them are the **San Diego Gulls** of the West Coast Hockey League, (619) 224-4625; **San Diego Sockers** of the Continental Indoor Soccer League, (619) 224-4171; **San Diego State University Aztecs**, competing in the Western Athletic Conference in football and basketball, (619) 283-7378 or (619) 594-6947; and the **University of San Diego Toreros** basketball team, playing in the West Coast Athletic Conference; (619) 260-4600. The WAC football champion goes to the Holiday Bowl in Qualcomm Stadium in late December.

GETTING TICKETED ● For sporting events in San Diego and elsewhere in southern California, two of the larger ticket agencies are Premier Tickets, (619) 295-7000 and Ticketmaster, (619) 220-TIXS. Several other agencies are listed in the San Diego Yellow Pages under "Ticket sales."

THE TEN BEST OVERLOOKED ATTRACTIONS

We define "overlooked attractions" as lures—small or large—that most visitors fail to visit, usually because they aren't publicized in many other guidebooks. Some of our selections are out of the way and hard to find, while others are rather obvious.

1 MISSION TRAILS REGIONAL PARK VISITOR & INTERPRETIVE CENTER ● *1 Father Junípero Serra Trail; (619) 668-3275. Daily 9 to 5; free. GETTING THERE: Take I-8 about seven miles east to the Mission Gorge Road turnoff, follow it just over four miles northeast and turn left into the interpretive center.*

Visitors rarely discover this fine interpretive center, although it's an easy reach from downtown. The imposing two-story stone structure is the focal point of Mission Trails Regional Park, which covers nearly 6,000 acres of rough-hewn hills and brushland along the creek-sized San Diego River. A network of trails winds through this arid landscape and along the river's riparian course. The interpretive center has nicely done exhibits and touch-screen videos on the flora, fauna, geology and native people of this area.

As you walk from the main floor to a mezzanine display area, you'll trigger a recording of night sounds made by coyotes, owls and other nocturnal critters of the region. You can use spotter scopes on the center's upper balcony to study geological features and look for critters in the bushes of this rough-hewn terrain area.

From the visitor center, you can drive or hike about two miles along Father Junípero Serra Trail through nearby Mission Gorge. At the far end, a short interpretive trail leads from a picnic area to the site of the West Coast's first engineered irrigation project. A fourteen-foot-high stone dam was built across the river by Indian labor between 1813 and 1816 to divert water to Mission San Diego's agricultural lands six miles away. A section of the dam has been rebuilt.

NAVIGATIONAL AND PARKING ADVISORY ● Although hikers and bikers can go both ways on the Father Junípero Serra Trail, it's a one-way trip for vehicles. To get back to San Diego, continue on this route until it merges with Mission Gorge Road. Follow this about four miles to the town of Santee, then go south on Freeway 67 to I-8. Gates on both ends of the trail are closed from 7 p.m. until 8 a.m. April through October and from 5 to 8 the rest of the year. If you park here after closing time, you'll get locked in.

2 **AFFORDABLE VIP CLASSICS** ● *861 Fifth Ave.; (619) 232-6864. GETTING THERE: It's downtown, on the edge of Gaslamp Quarter, at the corner of E Street.*

This auto dealership housed in one of Gaslamp Quarter's old buildings will appeal to classic car buffs. As the name implies, the firm sells used cars that—by design or reputation—have become classics. The showroom is set up like an auto museum, with each car labeled and described. Most have been impeccably restored. When we last strolled through, the merchandise on display included a Jaguar XKE, an early Ford Mustang fastback, a 1969 Camero Z-28, early model Corvettes and an Austin Healey. We noted—with a wince—that some of the cars selling for tens of thousands of dollars were the same models that we once owned and then sold for a song.

3 **BROADWAY FLYING HORSES CAROUSEL** ● *Seaport Village at 849 W. Harbor Dr.; (619) 234-6133. Daily 10 to 10 in summer and 10 to 9 the rest of the year; $. GETTING THERE: From downtown, follow Broadway toward the bay, turn left on the Pacific Highway and follow it to the end; it blends into Harbor Drive. From the waterfront, follow Harbor Drive or Pacific Highway south. The Carousel is in the southeast corner of Seaport Village.*

Are you and the kids jaded by the age of computer amusements? For a dollar each, you can take a spin into history on this great old carousel at the Seaport Village shopping center. It was built for New York's Coney Island in the 1880s by legendary carousel master Charles I.D. Looff. The glistening, hand-carved wooden horses, dogs, goats and other carousel critters have been meticulously restored. As you spin dizzily around on your favorite steed, listening to the baritone melodies of the Wurlitzer pipe organ and let your mind drift back to a more gentle era, before the days of video game violence and virtual reality.

4 CORONADO HISTORICAL MUSEUM • *1126 Loma Ave.; (619) 435-7242. Wednesday-Saturday 10 to 4 and Sunday noon to 4. Free; donations appreciated. GETTING THERE: Cross the Coronado Bridge from San Diego, turn left onto Orange Avenue and follow it about a mile to downtown Coronado. Turn right on Loma Street and the museum is three doors down, on your left.*

This little museum of Coronado's memories is housed in an 1898 Victorian. Exhibits are nicely displayed if rather limited; you can see them all in a few minutes. Displays include properly modest bathing turn-of-the-century attire, artifacts of Hotel del Coronado and historic photos of the community. One of the two small exhibit rooms focuses on Coronado's link to the mainland. Ferries had been crossing the bay to San Diego since 1886, then they stopped running the day the San Diego-Coronado Bay Bridge was opened in 1969. Service was reinstated in 1987, although it has been hit by inflation. Original fare was ten cents and now it's $2.

5 FIREHOUSE MUSEUM • *1572 Columbia St.; (619) 232-FIRE. Thursday-Friday 10 to 2 and weekends 10 to 4; $. GETTING THERE: The museum is at Columbia and Cedar streets. To get there, go north from downtown on one-way India Street, then go right up Cedar.*

This is a surprisingly extensive museum tracing the history of firefighting, with more than a dozen old rigs from hand-drawn hose carts and steam engines to early hook and ladder trucks. It's housed in Station Number 6, one of San Diego's earliest firehouses. Rarest member of the collection is an 1841 Rumsey hand pumper that had to be filled by a bucket brigade. Other rigs include a 1917 American LaFrance chemical engine and a 1942 Seagrave hook and ladder truck with a 100-foot aerial ladder. Many of the fire rigs were used in San Diego, while others have been imported from elsewhere.

Other exhibits include firemen's hats and uniforms, assorted equipment, and photos and news clippings about historic conflagrations in San Diego and elsewhere. A volunteer group called the Pioneer Hook and Ladder Company maintains and staffs the museum. If you're curious about the history of firefighting, the curator-on-duty likely will be a real fireman.

6 JUNÍPERO SERRA MUSEUM • *2727 Presidio Drive above Old Town; (619) 297-3258. Tuesday-Saturday 10 to 4 and Sunday noon to 4 in summer; Friday-Sunday 10 to 4:30 the rest of the year; $$. Combination tickets available with Villa Montezuma and the Marston House, listed below. GETTING THERE: The museum sits atop Presidio Hill; drive north through Old Town, turn right onto Taylor Street then right again onto Presidio Drive and follow signs.*

The mission style Junípero Serra Museum atop Presidio Hill is one of San Diego's most visible landmarks. Some observers mistakenly think that it *is* the mission. Despite its high visibility atop the hill, most tourists overlook this interesting archive. It was practically empty when we visited on a January Sunday, although Old Town just below was rather crowded. The museum, containing relics and exhibits concerning the founding of San Diego's mission and presidio, was a gift to the people of San Diego by department store owner George W. Marston. He bought the property to save it from development, had the museum built in 1929 and deeded it to the city. It's now operated by the San Diego Historical Society.

As we noted in the opening chapter, Mission San Diego de Alcalà was established on this hilltop in 1769, along with a presidio or fortress. Five years later, the mission was relocated six miles inland while the presidio remained. It was abandoned after America took over California, although a bastion called Fort Stockton was built by U.S. troops farther up the hill. A short drive past the museum will take you to that site. Nothing remains there except some monuments concerning the fort and the Mormon Battalion that occupied it briefly; see below. Tree-shaded Presidio Park just below the fort site is a nice place to picnic or just lie in the grass.

7 **MARSTON HOUSE** • *3525 Seventh Ave.; (619) 298-3142. Weekends only, noon to 4:30; $$; combination ticket available with Villa Montezuma and Serra Museum. GETTING THERE: Follow one-way Fifth Avenue about 2.5 miles north from downtown, turn right on Upas Street and drive two blocks toward Balboa Park.*

This large brick and stucco 1905 American craftsman mansion was the home of philanthropist George Marston. It's in an old money neighborhood on the shoulder of Balboa Park, which Marston also helped develop, along with Presidio Park and the Junípero Serra Museum. The interior of redwood, oak and pine has a rather clubby, functional look typical of a craftsman or "arts and crafts" home. This style became popular early in the twentieth century, when architects had grown tired of Victorian filigree. Marston's daughter Mary willed the home to the city after her death at the age of 106, and it's now operated by the San Diego Historical Society. Visitors are taken on tour by docents, who point out the straightforward style of the house and its furnishings. After the tour, one is free to wander about the elaborate park-like grounds.

8 **MORMON BATTALION VISITORS' CENTER** • *2510 Juan St.; (619) 298-3317. Daily 9 to 9; free. GETTING THERE: It's immediately northeast of Old Town at the corner of Juan and Harney streets.*

This facility is interesting if you're a fan of Western history and/or a member of the Church of Jesus Christ of Latter-Day Saints. The Mormon Battalion was comprised of nearly five hundred volunteers who, despite years of persecution, agreed in 1846 to march to San Diego and help American forces wrestle California from the Spanish. In what was to become the longest infantry march in American history, the battalion covered two thousand miles in six months. Ironically, the Mexican War had ended by the time they reached San Diego in January of 1847, so the military put them to work, improving and guarding Fort Stockton atop Presidio Hill. After being discharged later that year, several headed north to San Francisco and Sutter's Fort (Sacramento). Some were involved in the discovery of gold at Sutter's Mill. Most eventually worked their way back to Salt Lake City, even as other folks were headed for California, seeking the gold that the Mormons had helped discover.

Operated by the Mormon Church, the center has several historic exhibits and paintings relating to the epic crossing. A very well done film chronicles the adventures of the Mormon Battalion. It's all free and you can learn about the Mormon church if you wish, although the gentle folks at the visitor center won't press the issue.

9 SAN DIEGO MODEL RAILROAD MUSEUM ● Balboa Park; (619) 696-0199. Tuesday-Friday 11 to 4 and weekends 11 to 5; closed Monday; $. GETTING THERE: It's in the basement of Casa de Balboa Building off El Prado.

This is the kind of place where you might pause briefly out of curiosity, and then emerge a couple of hours later, grinning like a kid. This is not a model railroad layout; it is many. All have been carefully assembled by volunteers of various area model railroad clubs. You'll find all sizes of toy trains here, from the large 1/48th scale "O" gauge to the tiny "N" gauge with trains shrunk to 1/160th of actual size. The model layouts are elaborate and trains range from historic narrow gauge models to the sleek aluminum cars of the Santa Fe Chief.

You can press your nose to the Plexiglas with the other kids and watch tiny trains disappear into tunnels and try to guess where they'll emerge. They resemble sinuous mechanical snakes as they crawl through their extensive layouts. Follow their progress as they chuff over the San Diego desert to Arizona, or slowly spiral up Tehachapi Pass above Los Angeles, one of the most difficult rail grades in the country. And if you really want to act like a kid again, you can take over the controls and race a choo-choo against your traveling companion in the Toy Trains Gallery.

10 VILLA MONTEZUMA ● 1925 K St.; (619) 239-2211. Weekends only, noon to 4:30; $$; combination ticket available with the Marston House and Serra Museum. GETTING THERE: The museum is at K and 20th Avenue. To reach it from downtown, go east about a mile on Market Street, cross I-5, then go right three blocks on 20th to K Street.

This is one of San Diego's most startling sights—an elaborate Victorian mansion with filigree façades and leaded glass windows, sitting in a rather scruffy Hispanic neighborhood. Villa Montezuma and the Marston House are both operated by the San Diego Historical Society and they offer interesting contrasts. Marston's mansion is rather austere within, yet it occupies a beautiful park-like setting, while Villa Montezuma is incredibly ornate inside, and it sits on a barren street corner.

The "villa" was built in 1877 by bachelor concert pianist and novelist Jesse Shepard. It's one of San Diego's most elaborate historic structures, with an ornate Queen Anne tower topped by a Russian Orthodox onion dome. The equally intricate interior has been meticulously restored; it's a stunning study in carved and lacquered woods, linquesta borders and ceilings, marble fireplaces and leaded glass windows. Docents give continuous tours, pointing out finer details of the house's wonderfully overdone décor. It's a virtual museum of European and American antiques, although none of them are original to the house. After building his home at the staggering cost of $20,000, Shepard speculated in local real estate, lost his fortune and had to sell the property and its furnishings.

Let the stoics say what they please, we do not eat for the good of living, but because the meat is savory and the appetite is keen. —Ralph Waldo Emerson

Chapter three

SALSA CITY
A HIGHLY OPINIONATED DINING GUIDE

Although San Diego has never suffered a shortage of burritos, being the largest American city near the Mexican border, it was not considered a serious culinary haven until quite recently. Several decades ago, the zenith of local dining—both literally and figuratively—was to take visiting Auntie Maude up the outside elevator of the El Cortez Hotel and feed her overdone filet mignon in its skyroom restaurant. And if the visitor were your rich uncle, you'd take him to the Grant Grill downtown, with its great men's club ambiance and impeccably attentive service.

For decent seafood, you adjourned to Anthony's Star of the Sea at the waterfront, and for proper Mexican food, you sought out one of the mom and pop cafés in Old Town that hadn't yet been discovered by tourists.

Today, San Diego rivals—dare we say it?—San Francisco with its variety of both upscale and inexpensive restaurants. Virtually every ethnic dining persuasion is represented here, from Afghani through Peruvian to Vietnamese. Unlike San Francisco, Sunshine City has no major Chinatown or Japantown, although Asian restaurants are quite numerous. Oddly, the largest concentration is in a commercial area around Balboa Avenue and Convoy Street north of downtown, which is also the city's automobile row; see Chapter Thirteen, page 182.

Like other cities, San Diego embraces the faddish *nouveau* and "new American regional" cuisines, which seem to be preoccupied with raspberry purée, air dried beef and sun dried tomatoes. Or is it air dried tomatoes and sun dried beef?

The local dining scene is so bounteous that the highly regarded Zagat Survey added San Diego to its restaurant guides in 1997. And it's so volatile that the guide was updated a year later, with the addition of nearly fifty new cafés and the deletion of more than half that number.

We particularly like the abundance of outdoor restaurants, appropriate to the city's benign climate. Many of these *al fresco* cafés have heat lamps, enabling them to carry their fresh air service into the cool winter and the cool of the evening. You'll find a good number of restaurants with outdoor dining in Gaslamp Quarter, the Hillcrest District just above Balboa Park and along the India Street restaurant row. That's an area in the Middletown district northwest of downtown, which is rarely visited by tourists; see Chapter Thirteen, page 181.

Restaurant selections in this and other chapters represent our dining experiences and the recommendations of others. We were not influenced by freebies for we accepted not a single gratuitous meal, nary a taco nor sun dried tomato, from any café in town.

In our listings, we use simple strings of dollar signs to indicate the price of a typical dinner with entrée, soup or salad, not including drinks, appetizers or dessert: *$* = less than $10 per entrée; *$$* = $10 to $19; *$$$* = $20 to $29; *$$$$* = "Did you say you were buying?"

THE TEN VERY BEST RESTAURANTS

With hundreds of restaurants in San Diego, how can one possibly select the very best? Obviously, by being quite arbitrary. We dined anonymously at each of our "Ten Very Best" selections (and at many more to narrow the field down to ten), paid the check, left a reasonable gratuity and departed, like true phantom diners.

Our choices represent a broad culinary cross-section. You will note that we are not strong on trendy "American contemporary" restaurants whose offerings are more artistic than filling, and whose salads aren't ample enough to keep a rabbit regular.

1 GEORGE'S AT THE COVE ● 1250 Prospect St., La Jolla; (858) 454-4244. American, mostly seafood; full bar service. Lunch and dinner daily. Major credit cards; $$$. GETTING THERE: You'll find George in a shopping complex above La Jolla Cove in downtown La Jolla.

George Hauer's place is the finest restaurant in greater San Diego for several good reasons. The food is excellent, the view is grand and the prices are fair. *Bon Appétit* calls it "that rarity, a seaside showplace that also serves superb food." Actually, George's is two restaurants and both take splendid advantage of the views over La Jolla's sculpted beachfront. The upstairs Ocean Terrace is a rather casual deck, with umbrella tables and an open air vista of La Jolla Cove. There's nothing between diners and this great outdoors but a low glass partition. Downstairs is more stylish yet still casual, with drop lamps, spear-shaped wall sconces and impressionistic paintings on the walls. The most impressive wall, of course, is made of glass and provides an un-fettered view of La Jolla Cove. On our last visit, some of George's offer-ings included petit Angus filet, pan-seared salmon with Pommery mustard glaze, pan-seared whitefish in a pesto glaze with red wine and shallot sauce, and paprika-dusted sea bass with green chutney.

2 **AZZURA POINT** • *At Loews Coronado Bay Resort, 4000 Coronado Bay Rd.; (619) 424-4000. California-Pacific Rim fare; full bar service. Dinner nightly. Major credit cards; $$$$. GETTING THERE: Loews is about five miles south of downtown Coronado on Silver Strand, opposite Silver Strand State Beach. The restaurant is to the left of the lobby, on the mezzanine level.*

Creative cookery, pleasingly soft décor and fine views across San Diego bay are hallmarks of this upscale restaurant. The changing menu may offer savories such as grilled salmon with lentils, tomatoes and olives; Hawaiian snapper with caramelized kumquats; or roast saddle of rabbit. Dining excellence has its price, of course; figure on the high twenties into the thirties for dinner and you can go beyond $70 for the daily chef's menu, a multi-course dinner with appropriate wines. The look is both comfortable and dramatically simple, with bleached woods, chenille banquettes with leopard skin pattern throw pillows, wall sconces and potted fan palms. Tables are terraced to af-ford everyone that pleasing bay view.

3 **THE BELGIAN LION** • *2665 Bacon St., Ocean Beach; (619) 223-2700. French-Belgian; wine and beer. Dinner Thursday-Saturday. Major credit cards; $$$ to $$$$. GETTING THERE: The Lion is at the corner of Bacon and West Point Loma Boulevard. The easiest approach is to follow I-8 to its western terminus, go southwest on Sunset Cliffs Boule-vard, turn right onto West Point Loma and follow it west two blocks to Bacon.*

Hushed elegance bests describes this charming restaurant, housed in a pleasingly weathered bungalow. The interior suggests a French manor house with lace curtains, candelabra wall sconces and brocaded furniture fabric. Wine racks standing about the two dining areas suggest that this restaurant has a serious wine list. The menu, classic French with Belgian accents, changes periodically. It may feature savories such as sautéed sea scallops with sweet peppers, rabbit braised in red wine, sautéed chicken breasts with apples and apple brandy, and poached salmon with herb butter with Sauvignon Blanc and vegetable broth. The menu normally lists one of its most popular signature dishes—a cassoulet of duck, sausage, pork, lamb and white beans. In warm weather, guests can enjoy a pretty garden out front, sheltered from the passing traffic.

4 *DOBSON'S* • *956 Broadway Circle; (619) 231-6771. American; full bar service. Lunch weekdays, dinner nightly. Major credit cards; $$$. GETTING THERE: Not to be confused with Broadway, this is Broadway Circle, which is a U-shaped extension of Second and Third avenues downtown, in front of Horton Plaza. Dobson's is on the Second Avenue link.*

Having worked and lived in and about San Francisco for more than twenty years, we felt immediately at home in this place. Dobson's is the classic San Francisco—some would say New York or Chicago—business lunch venue, with warm wood paneling and bentwood chairs. It's also exceedingly popular for dinner. The first thing you encounter is a bar; there's an intimate dining area beyond and another upstairs. Dobson's occupies a narrow old brick building in the shadow of several downtown highrises. The up front bar is quite handsome, featuring a mirrored, arched back bar with leaded glass inlays. Although the place looks comfortable and clubby, the menu is rather contemporary, with fare such as ginger lime crusted salmon, marinated duck with raspberry sweet and tart sauce, and pepper crusted venison. However, you can still get an honest steak or veal chop. Dobson's is considered *the* downtown power lunch venue.

5 *GRANT GRILL* • *In the U.S. Grant Hotel at 326 Broadway; (619) 232-3121. American-continental; full bar service. Dinner nightly. Major credit cards; $$$ to $$$$. GETTING THERE: The Grant is in the heart of downtown, opposite Horton Plaza Park. The hotel is bounded by Third and Fourth avenues and the Grill is just off the lobby on the Fourth Avenue side.*

More years ago than I care to remember, I tried to impress a date by taking her to dinner at the Grant Grill. Oddly, I can't even remember her name, although I recall the service was so attentive that our waiter stood by and added ice cubes to our water glasses as they melted. The venerable Grill seems to have changed little since then. The service is still attentive and the décor is still warmly dark and clubby, with plush curved booths, dim lighting and thick carpeting. The menu has been upgraded somewhat, to include such contemporary fare as chicken linguine with prosciutto and radicchio, and grilled salmon with warm tomato relish. However, it still issues sturdy fare such as medallions of beef, mixed grill and rack of lamb with mint sauce. And the waiters still wear tuxedos and white gloves, although they seem more friendly than I recall from my first visit. But then, I was a timid youth. The food—both classic and *nouveau*—is excellent. The Grill continues to win dining awards.

6 LE FONTAINEBLEAU • *The Westgate Hotel, 1055 Second Ave.; (619) 238-1818. WEBSITE: www.westgateotel.com. French-California; full bar service. Lunch weekdays, dinner nightly. Major credit cards; $$$$. GETTING THERE: The Westgate Hotel is just off lower Broadway in the heart of downtown; Le Fontainebleau restaurant is on the mezzanine level.*

Le Fontainebleau is the most elegantly coiffed restaurant in San Diego, and possibly on the West Coast. This gracious dining room is a study in European finery, from its soft colors, Baccarat crystal chandeliers and plush floral carpeting to its brocaded burgundy chairs. The fare, under European-trained Chef René Herbeck, is French with California and Asian accents. Recent examples—although the menu changes periodically—were lobster spiced with ginger, Dover sole with julienne vegetables and smoked salmon sauce, tenderloin of beef with broccoli purée and black truffle sauce, and roasted duck breast with spices and *cous cous.*

7 MARINE ROOM • *2000 Spindrift Dr., La Jolla Shores; (858) 459-7222. American, mostly seafood; full bar service. Lunch Monday-Saturday, dinner nightly and Sunday brunch. Major credit cards; $$$$. GETTING THERE: From downtown La Jolla, head north on Prospect until it blends into Torrey Pines Road, go about a third of a mile, then fork left onto Spindrift. The restaurant is on your left, about a third of a mile down.*

The ocean view from this opulent and legendary restaurant is absolutely smashing, and occasionally the waves splash against the windows, much to the exhilaration of diners. They've splashed inside only twice in the more than sixty years that this restaurant has been in business, so keep your seat and enjoy your meal. The dining room is a careful study in simple elegance, with white nappery, floral carpet, brocaded chairs and scallop wall sconces. Of course, we spent most of our time looking at the wave-tossed beach, just beyond the restaurant's seaward wall of glass.

The menu follows current culinary trends of fresh fare, creatively spiced and elegantly presented. It changes with the seasons, so you may or may not encounter Alaskan halibut in a potato net with artichokes, lobster with morels and candied shallots, or salmon with mustard seeds, sweet spices and brioche.

8 *MR. A'S* • *2550 Fifth Ave.; (619) 239-1377. American-conti-nental; full bar service. Lunch weekdays and dinner nightly. GETTING THERE: The restaurant is located on the 12th floor of the Fifth Avenue Center near Laurel Street, just below Balboa Park. Take Laurel from I-5 or one-way Fifth from downtown.*

When we asked our friends Sharon and Larry Ihle of nearby El Ca-jon to select their favorite San Diego things, they picked Mr. A's for best restaurant, best view restaurant and best view bar. It certainly is one of the city's better dining venues, winner of several awards, in-cluding a rare four-diamond rating from AAA. Although it's perched atop a building filled with attorneys' offices, its quite elegant, with rich burgundy furnishings, plush carpeting and scalloped drapes. We rate it second only to Le Fontainebleau for opulence.

And the view? Awesome! Because it's situated atop a twelve-story building in the hills below Balboa Park, it has a splendid panorama far up and down the coast. The fare is continental with some American *nouveau* influences—roast prime rib of beef, rack of lamb with garlic herbs, veal chops with Cabernet Sauvignon sauce, breast of chicken with Marsala wine sauce, and grilled halibut with sun dried tomatoes and lemon butter.

9 *PRINCE OF WALES GRILL* • *Hotel del Coronado, 1500 Or-ange Ave., Coronado; (619) 435-6611. Contemporary American; full bar service. Dinner only. Major credit cards; $$$$. GETTING THERE: Cross the Coronado Bridge from San Diego, turn left onto Orange Avenue and follow it just over a mile.*

As part of the historic "Del's" ongoing renovation, the Prince of Wales has shed its staid clubby look and emerged with soft colors, golden accents and filmy scalloped drapes. One thing that remains is the fine ocean view through floor to ceiling windows. The menu is as contemporary as the décor. While it changes frequently, you may en-counter fare such as sea scallops with bulgur wheat, pilaf and *cous cous*; bass with bok choy, potato leek pancakes and black mussels; or grilled veal chop with air dried tomatoes, sorrel and feta cheese ri-sotto. Off the hotel's central courtyard and away from the hubbub of the lobby, it's regarded by locals as one of the area' most romantic res-taurants.

10 *RAINWATER'S ON KETTNER* • *1202 Kettner Blvd.; (619) 233-5757. American; full bar service. Lunch Monday-Saturday, dinner nightly. Major credit cards; $$$ to $$$$. GETTING THERE: The restaurant is on the mezzanine floor of a former warehouse at Kettner and B Street, two blocks above Broadway downtown.*

Rainwater's is a visual surprise. Although it occupies a fine old brick warehouse, the interior décor is both clubby and sleek, with dark furnishings in a light and airy space, deep curved booths and beaded lighting. The fare is hearty American with some interesting *nouveau* touches. The menu, subject to change, may offer ribeye steak, pork chops, veal chops, filet of ahi with fettuccine noodles, chicken breast with garlic-crusted mashed potatoes, or parchment salmon. Rainwater's is noted primarily as a serious steak and martini place—a magnet for power brokers from the nearby downtown office towers.

THE TEN BEST LOCAL FAVORITES

These are establishments that many locals say they favor—places that often are overlooked by visitors. They range from trendy restaurants where people go to be seen to diners where folks go just to eat. Our overall winner is a place that's been around since 1944.

1 **HOB NOB HILL** • *2271 First Ave.; (619) 239-8176. American; wine and beer. Breakfast through dinner daily. Major credit cards; $ to $$. GETTING THERE: Take one-way First Street west from downtown; it's on the corner of First and Juniper.*

Dearie, do you remember those waitresses with dark uniforms and little doily aprons? They're still here. Hob Nob Hill fits the bill as the city's best locals' restaurant. It has stood the test of time, having been in business for more than half a century; it serves breakfast through dinner; and it's remarkably inexpensive. Local folks can afford to eat here regularly. And they do, from pin-striped lawyers discussing the latest litigation over eggs Benedict to retired folks on a budget and ordinary working people in need of a cheap lunch. Although the building is rather austere, it's quite homey inside, with booths, wainscotting and hurricane lamp chandeliers. When we last checked, several dinners—chicken and dumplings, roast tom turkey, baby beef liver and grilled fish—were less than $10. Only the steaks and pork chops crept into the low teens. And these meals include soup or salad. Old Hob Nob was featured in *Gourmet* magazine recently as one of America's great hometown cafés.

2 **BANZAI CANTINA** • *3667 India St.; (619) 298-6388. Japanese-Mexican; wine and beer. Lunch and dinner daily. Major credit cards; $$. GETTING THERE: Banzai is at India near Chalmers, part of the restaurant row at the northwest end of India Street. Take an off-ramp from parallel I-5 or follow one-way India Street from downtown. NOTE: Because it's one way, to return downtown you must continue on India to Washington, go left under the freeway and left again onto Kettner. There are several I-5 on-ramps along the way.*

If you speak any Japanese, you'll know that "banzai"—despite its World War II reputation—just means "Hooray!" or maybe "Right on!" in current vernacular. That term is sometimes—but not always—appropriate for this curious blend of Asian, Mexican and Mediterranean cuisine. Among its interesting entrées are chicken breast with tamarind sauce and pineapple salsa, mahi mahi with pan-fried noodles and vegetables in a Chinese barbecue sauce, and a Japanese *bouillabaisse* with tofu, shrimp, calimari, clams, mussels and tuna. This trendily under-decorated café with a cheerful yellow interior and stark black furniture occupies a ground floor and mezzanine of an austere stucco building. More inviting is its wrought-iron patio with a few plants dangling from above.

3 **CREST CAFÉ** • *425 Robinson Ave.; (619) 925-2510. American; wine and beer. Lunch through late evening daily. Major credit cards; $$. GETTING THERE: It's between Fourth and Fifth avenues in the Hillcrest District.*

Straights and gays of Hillcrest keep this little café busy from sunup until well after dark. The fare includes herbal chicken, a quite lively jalapeño chicken salad, artichoke pastas and rather good luncheon hamburgers. The early morning crowd orders breakfast burritos, *machaca* (shredded beef, chipped onions and tomatoes with scrambled eggs) and Spanish scrambled eggs with jack cheese and salsa. The look of Crest is vaguely art deco, with glass bricks, chrome trim and drop lamps.

4 **CROCE'S and CROCE'S WEST** • *802 Fifth Ave.; (619) 233-4355. Southwestern; full bar service. Lunch and dinner daily. Major credit cards; $$$. GETTING THERE: This dual restaurant is in Gaslamp Quarter, between E and F streets.*

Created by the widow of singer Jim Croce, this is a popular hangout for downtowners—both for lunch and dinner. Tourists visiting Gaslamp Quarter are drawn here as well, not necessarily because they make a Croce connection, but because this restaurant is particularly inviting. Actually, it's two restaurants in adjoining old brick buildings—Croce's and Croce's West. The look is contemporary, contrasted by exposed brick, and several tables spill onto the sidewalk. Ms. Croce serves designer cuisine in this modernistic setting, with offerings such as salmon with coriander crust and papaya salsa, grilled swordfish with jalapeño Bèarnaise, and chicken molé with polenta and greens.

5 **DAKOTA GRILL AND SPIRITS** • *901 Fifth Ave.; (619) 234-5554. Contemporary American; full bar service. Lunch and dinner daily. Major credit cards; $$. GETTING THERE: The Grill is on the edge of Gaslamp Quarter at the corner of E Street near Broadway.*

Like Croce's, Dakota Grill is a see-and-be-seen place for downtowners. It's appealing mostly for its ambiance, although some local critics also give it high marks for food. Despite the Dakota name, the look is sorta' Southwest, with warm New Mexico colors, kokopelli figurines and Route 66 signs. (A cellar bar here is called "Route 66.") Dakota is easy to find because it occupies one of the few multi-story buildings in the Gaslamp; a hotel sits atop this ground-floor grill.

Although it's open only for lunch and dinner, an outside coffee bar called The Grind draws office-bound downtowners and those who aren't going anywhere, preferring to sit with the morning paper or play chess with a friend. The grill is mixed, ranging from Thai chicken salad and assorted barbecued ribs to gorgonzola ravioli and Southwest spiced chicken. Garlic mashed potatoes appears frequently with the entrées.

6 *HENNESSEY'S TAVERN • 4650 Mission Blvd., Pacific Beach; (619) 483-8847. American; wine and beer. Lunch and dinner daily. Major credit cards; $$. GETTING THERE: The Tavern is on the corner of Mission and Emerald.*

The problem with southern Californians is that they don't know how to create a proper Irish pub. They're always too bright and cheerful. They miss the point. The pub is supposed to be dark and moody, while the patrons are bright and cheerful. Thus it is with this Hennessey's chain, with outlets in several southern California cities. The Pacific Beach version, while not as Irish as it pretends, is a comfortable and inexpensive place where neighbor folks can get a good pint of stout and a shot of Bushmills. The menu is mostly American—sandwiches, steaks and chicken. It does list a token corned beef and cabbage dinner, but no bangers 'n' mash or shepherds pie. And what's this teriyaki chicken sandwich? Saints preserve us!

7 *HUMPHREY'S • In Humphrey's Half Moon Inn at 2241 Shelter Island Dr.; (619) 224-3577. American; full bar service. Breakfast through dinner daily. Major credit cards; $$$. GETTING THERE: To reach Shelter Island, head into Point Loma on Rosecrans Street (State Route 209) and turn left onto Shelter Island Drive. Humphrey's Half Moon Inn is just to the right of a traffic circle and the restaurant is a short distance beyond.*

Two things may surprise you about Humphrey's. Although it's on Shelter Island, it's not a tiki hut café and it's probably more popular with residents than with tourists. One of its local appeals is a lively entertainment menu, and we discuss that in Chapter Seven, Page 120. The dining menu is as trendy and upbeat as the entertainment. Among its "California Coastal Cuisine" selections are conch and crabcakes with shrimp, salmon with champagne and caviar, and sesame seed crusted mahi mahi. It also features several steaks and pastas, and specials such as Caribbean spiced lamb, and halibut with citrus teriyaki orange glaze. Both the restaurant and next-door lounge are sleekly modern and they have views of an adjacent marina.

8 **LAMONT STREET GRILL** • *4445 Lamont St., Pacific Beach; (619) 270-3060. American; full bar service. Dinner nightly. Major credit cards; $$$. GETTING THERE: The grill is between Balboa and Garnet in Pacific Beach, on the corner of Hornblend Street.*

In an area known for its funky cafés, Lamont Street Grill is rather a stylish establishment, with French windows, crisp white nappery and several cozy dining rooms divided by planters. Save the nearby beach shacks for lunch and Monday night football; this is where locals go when they feel in a romantic mood. The fare is well-thought-out American with continental accents, and might include chicken Dijon, properly done filets, and fresh catch of the day lightly cooked and properly seasoned. The Zagat guide calls it one of the city's "most charming restaurants." And to really turn on the charm, warm up your companion with a couple of drinks on the courtyard patio, beside its fireplace.

9 **MISSION CAFÉ** • *3795 Mission Blvd., Mission Beach; (619) 488-9060. American and Mexican; wine and beer. Breakfast through mi-dafternoon daily. MC/VISA; $. GETTING THERE: It's a block up from the beach at the corner of San Jose Street.*

Let's put it this way: Sitting at the next table was a teenager with dyed yellow hair and a pair of overalls seventeen sizes too big, and a well-dressed man, probably his father. We were guessing that they chose this funky, Berkeley-style place to seek common ground. They seemed to be getting along just fine. Mission Café, relatively clean and set with couches, plain tables and chairs, is where the beach folk come for leisurely breakfasts, Mexican accented lunches, assorted specialty coffees and power fruit drinks. A reading rack encourages patrons to linger. The décor is properly spartan and the service staff wears shorts, even in January. (My server kept calling me "Sir"; I wish they wouldn't do that.) The menu is vaguely health oriented although my big breakfast burrito contained enough yolks to send egg stocks soaring. However, you can get a stir fry of tofu, brown rice and zucchini. Most breakfast and lunch dishes are accompanied by black beans sprinkled with fresh cilantro and green onion spears; quite tasty. And portions here are *huge*.

10 **TIO LEO'S MEXICAN RESTAURANT** • *6333 Mission Gorge Rd. (between Rainier and Glacier), (619) 280-9944; and 5302 Napa St. (corner of Morena), (619) 542-1462. Mexican; full bar service. Lunch and dinner daily at both places; breakfast on weekends at the*

Napa Street location. Major credit cards; $$. GETTING THERE: For the first, take the Mission Gorge exit from I-8 (about a mile east of the I-8/I-15 junction) and drive north about three-quarters of a mile; it's on your right. For the Napa Street branch, take the Morena Boulevard exit from I-8 and go north across the San Diego River bed to Napa Street; it's located between Old Town and Mission Bay Park.

Neither tourist places nor mom and pop taco shops, Tio Leos are part of a small local chain of very attractive Mexican restaurants. They occupy Spanish style stucco buildings, with outdoor patios and cozy indoor dining areas accented by ceramic tile and fireplaces. Uncle Leo's menu is typical, with the usual range of things bound into tortillas, plus shrimp-chicken or shrimp-steak combos, crab quesadillas, and chilies colorado and verde. The restaurants also have "healthy choice" menus featuring items such as grilled eggplant tacos, chicken tacos and vegetarian burritos.

THE TEN BEST SEAFOOD RESTAURANTS

Water, water everywhere. A city sitting on one of America's largest natural harbors—a city with its own commercial fishing fleet had *better* have some good seafood restaurants. San Diego offers a broad choice, from old standbys to *nouveau* places where chefs do strange things to broiled salmon. Does raspberry purée really enhance the taste of seafood? This list ranges from pricey to budget, beginning with one of the city's oldest seafood gourmet rooms, which is still the best:

1 ANTHONY'S STAR OF THE SEA ROOM • 1360 N. Harbor Dr.; (619) 232-7408. Full bar service. Dinner nightly. Major credit cards; $$$ to $$$$. GETTING THERE: The Star of the Sea Room is on the waterfront below downtown; it's at the foot of Ash Street, beside the San Diego Maritime Museum.

The most enduring of the city's better seafood houses, this fine old restaurant has a pleasing turn of the century "nautical drawing room" décor with dark woods and beaded chandeliers. Diners are expected to look the part as well; this is one of the few restaurants in town that asks gents to wear jackets. If the look is classic, the menu is contemporary as the Star of the Sea Room attempts to keep pace with newer, trendier establishments.

The menu, which changes with the seasons, may contain such curiosities as wok-stirred frogs legs with ginger, garlic and chilies; sesame crusted mahi mahi with Thai basil pesto coconut cream; or sausage of Idaho sturgeon. Can one get a simple fresh fillet, lightly done? Certainly; you need only to ask what's just been caught. The menu does state: "The whims of nature control the availability of these creatures from the sea."

2 **BLUE POINT COASTAL CUISINE** • *565 Fifth Ave.; (619) 233-6623. Full bar service. Lunch and dinner daily. MC/VISA, DISC; $$$. GETTING THERE: This coastal cuisine is found inland, at the corner of Fifth and Market in Gaslamp Quarter.*

Blue Point one of those corporate-owned cafés that, while serving innovative seafood, is a bit too contrived. The dark furniture, plush banquettes and huge tub light fixtures are right out of a decorator's studio, and the menu uses "hook, line and sinker" to categorize its appetizers, entrées and desserts. Cute, huh?

It's evident that the chef likes to fiddle with the fish, offering griddled mustard catfish with jalapeño tartar sauce; pan seared walleye pike with soda cracker, bacon, tomato pancake; and Southwestern shrimp scampi with cilantro, pesto and corn cake. Yes, you can get fresh fish lightly done without all those trappings. Just ask your server. And you can eat indoors beneath those overpowering tubs or outside on an attractive bricked patio.

3 **CAFÉ PACIFICA** • *2424 San Diego Ave.; (619) 291-6666. Full bar service. Dinner nightly. Major credit cards; $$$. GETTING THERE: The café is in Old Town, between Arista and Conde streets.*

This bougainvillea-draped adobe building in Old Town contains—not another Mexican restaurant—but one of the city's better seafood havens. Café Pacifica is noted for fresh seafood lightly cooked and sometimes interestingly spiced. Examples are ahi tuna with shittake ginger sauce, griddled mustard catfish, garlic seafood fettuccini, broiled salmon with sweet peppers and shallots, and a very fine and busy *bouillabaisse*. The menu also lists a few steak and chicken dishes and it offers a good selection of wines by the glass, both white and red. The interior might be described as elegantly stark. The small cottage is divided into three dining areas with simple dark furnishings, beaded ceiling lighting and white walls hung with occasional paintings.

4 **THE CRAB CATCHER** • *1298 Prospect St., La Jolla; (619) 454-9587. Full bar service. Lunch through dinner daily. Major credit cards; $$$. GETTING THERE: The restaurant is in The Coastwalk complex in downtown La Jolla, just above La Jolla Cove, opposite Ivanhoe Street.*

A restaurant with a great view that's popular with tourists might be tempted to slack off in the kitchen, although we've had some quite decent meals at this Coastwalk installation. The rather straightforward menu lists mixed grill, cioppino, sesame crusted tuna, salmon with rosemary, crab-stuffed fish and assorted catches of the day. You can't beat the setting, with the main dining room practically hanging over the beach. It's an extensive complex, with separate wine and oyster bars and a very cozy patio. The main dining room is particularly eye-appealing, with comfortable wicker chairs, white nappery and impressionistic beach scenes on the walls.

5 **FISH MARKET and TOP OF THE MARKET** ● *750 N. Harbor Dr.; (619) 232-FISH. Full bar service. Lunch and dinner daily and Sunday brunch. Major credit cards; $$ for the Fish Market and $$$ to $$$$ for Top of the Market. GETTING THERE: The complex is on the edge of Tuna Fleet Park near the lower end of Harbor Drive. From downtown, take Broadway to the waterfront and turn left.*

Forget your visions of a noisy marketplace and great heaps of filleted fish on beds of ice. This deliberately handsome complex is a fish market in name only. You'll find a small counter of perfectly good fresh fish on the lower floor, although this facility is primarily a two-level seafood restaurant. The downstairs Fish Market is for us plebeians, with a homey maple furniture décor and quite reasonable prices. Top of the Market is the gourmet room, where the views and the prices are loftier. It has a rather clubby look, with wood paneling and white nappery. Both levels provide nice bay views.

Notwithstanding the harmless "fish market" ruse, these are both fine restaurants and they probably offer the largest seafood selection in town. The last time we checked the chalkboard out front, sixteen varieties of just-caught fish were listed. This extensive complex also has crab broilers, an oyster bar and sushi bar. A specialty here is mesquite charbroiled fish, particularly at the downstairs establishment. Entrées get dressier upstairs, with items such as fresh Cajun style catfish with scallion horseradish sauce, and yellowfin tuna with soy wasabi lime sauce. The upstairs menu changes frequently.

6 **PEOHE'S** ● *1201 First St., Coronado; (619) 437-4474. Full bar service. Lunch Monday-Saturday, dinner nightly and Sunday brunch. Major credit cards; $$$. GETTING THERE: It's at water's edge in the Ferry Landing Marketplace. Cross the Coronado Bridge from San Diego, turn right onto Orange Avenue, follow it a couple of blocks to its end, then turn right again onto First Street.*

It's difficult to take seriously a restaurant with fake rocks, indoor palm trees, waterfalls and Hawaiian music in the background. Despite its wacky Waikiki look, Peohe's serves a fine brace of well-prepared seafood. Even the Zagat guide, famous for putting down tourist traps, give it high marks. And you can't beat the view, through windowed walls across the bay to the San Diego skyline. In fact, much of the building sits on a pier, with an inviting outdoor deck over the bay. Some of the entrées are strange but tasty, such as halibut with bananas, macadamia nuts and frangelica. The less adventurous can opt for the New England lobster, garlic shrimp and assorted fresh fishes of the day.

7 **POINT LOMA SEAFOODS** • *2805 Emerson St.; (619) 223-1109. Wine and beer. Monday-Saturday 9 to 7 and Sunday noon to 7. No credit cards; $. GETTING THERE: Drive southeast on Rosecrans Street, turn left onto Emerson and follow it a few blocks to its terminus at the Municipal Sportfishing Pier.*

Local office workers, tourists and sports fisherpersons swarm this inexpensive takeout at noontime to load up on fried fish, calimari and seafood sandwiches. They carry their booty, with disposable plates and cutlery, to a large indoor dining area, to a pretty patio or to a string of dockside tables alongside the Municipal Sportfishing Pier. When all the seats are taken, they park their fannies on planter boxes and balance their paper plates on their knees. Point Loma Seafoods also is a large fish market, with a good selection of fresh seafood and an alarming assortment of smoked fish, including salmon, shark, tuna, swordfish and more. This casual seafood circus has been drawing 'em in since 1962.

8 **RED SAILS INN** • *2614 Shelter Island Dr.; (619) 223-3030. Full bar service. Breakfast through dinner daily. Major credit cards; $$ to $$$. GETTING THERE: To reach Shelter Island, head toward Point Loma on Rosecrans Street (State Route 209) and turn left onto Shelter Island Drive. Red Sails is near the entrance to the island, at the corner of Anchorage Lane.*

Most other local guidebooks ignore this venerable institution, which surprises us. The food is fine and not overpriced, the setting is pleasing, the view over an adjacent marina is great and it has certainly stood the test of time and taste. Red Sails Inn began in the 1930s at San Diego's old Fisherman's Wharf, which disappeared under harbor redevelopment. It then shifted to Shelter Island in 1957 and there it remains today, one of the most enduring restaurants in town. We've dined there often, in the main dining room trimmed with nautical artifacts, and on a fountain patio overlooking the marina. It offers a long list of fresh seafoods, seafood-steak combos, cioppino and scampi. Don't look for raspberry purée or air dried tomatoes here; look for ample servings of good seafood at fair prices.

9 **SALLY'S RESTAURANT** • *At the Hyatt Regency San Diego, 1 Market Place; (619) 687-6080. GETTING THERE: The Regency is near Seaport Village just off Harbor Drive, and the restaurant is on the hotel's harbor side, adjacent to the village.*

Severely modern is the best description for this trendy restaurant, with black exposed heating ducts, black and dark green furnishings, lots of riffles and curves and tiny drop lamps suspended from slender wires. If all this overwhelms, you can take a table outside. Equally overwhelming is Sally's large selection of seafood—braised mahi-mahi, roasted swordfish, Maine lobster, sautéed shrimp, a spicy seafood paella, arctic char, grilled tuna and the list continues. The kitchen also features saddle of lamb, beef tenderloin and chicken. For an interesting—if somewhat pricey—dining experience, sign up for one of the Chef's Table dinners at Sally's demonstration kitchen. You and half a dozen or so others will sit family style while the chef presents a multi-course dinner, with the proper wine to match each course.

10 WORLD FAMOUS • 711 Pacific Beach Dr., Pacific Beach;

(619) 272-3100. Full bar service. Breakfast through dinner daily with weekend brunch. Major credit cards; $$. GETTING THERE: Its famous location is right beside the beach promenade, near Mission Boulevard at the end of Pacific Beach Drive.

This large fish house is famous mostly for drawing in the tourists, who come for the view of the ocean, which is practically splashing right outside the large picture windows. For an even closer encounter, you can dine on a patio beside the beachwalk. While not awesome, the food is fair, with five or six fresh catches of the day available, and you can ask that your filet of whatever be lightly cooked, if that's your preference. (It couldn't hurt to ask; some Midwestern tourists like their fish cooked to the consistency of an artgum eraser.) Other than fresh fish, World Famous offers shrimp scampi, potato crusted crab cakes, and sesame jumbo shrimp. Dark woods, captains chairs and a few fishy ornaments give the place a proper nautical look.

THE TEN BEST MEXICAN RESTAURANTS

This city founded by Spaniards who—after a revolution—became Mexicans, naturally has an abundance of Hispanic restaurants. In selecting the Ten Best, we ignored franchises operated by restaurant management school graduates (sorry about that, Chevy's) and focused on local places. They range from stylish restaurants to hole-in-the-wall mom and pop taco parlors. Not surprisingly, many are in or about Old Town San Diego State Historic Park, since that's where the city's Spanish and Mexican roots began.

1 ACAPULCO • 2467 Juan St.; (619) 260-8124. Full bar serv-

ice. Lunch and dinner daily plus Sunday brunch. Major credit cards; $$. GETTING THERE: Acapulco is part of the Hacienda Hotel at Juan and Harney streets, immediately northeast of Old Town San Diego State Historic Park.

Although Acapulco is part of a southern California chain of Mexican restaurants, you can trust the food to be authentic. It has been twice picked as the best Mexican restaurant by *La Opinion*, southern

California's leading Spanish language newspaper. We like its cheerful interior with lots of Spanish arches, painted floral patterns on the walls and tile floors. Diners also can adjourn to a sun porch or a patio, and many dining areas have city views. The menu features typical Hispanic cookery, and if you're really hungry, try one of the *muy grande* platters. These hefty dinners include a main dish—shrimp, halibut-shrimp combo or chicken—plus several side dishes. One of our favorites, although not really traditional Mexican, is Yucatan roasted chicken in cilantro orange marinade.

2 *ALFONSO'S* • *1251 Prospect St., La Jolla; (619) 454-2232. Full bar service. Lunch through late evening daily. MC/VISA, AMEX; $$. GETTING THERE: Alfonso's is in the heart of La Jolla between Ivanhoe and Cave streets.*

The food is Hispanic, although the ambiance is definitely La Jollan. Alfonso's offers Mexican dining for La Jolla's well-heeled residence and for tourists who like to sit on the patio and watch other tourists stroll along Prospect Street. That doesn't mean the food isn't good; it's just more expensive than at more humble Mexican restaurants. However, it's rather inexpensive compared with other La Jolla diners. It's a rather informal place for this stylish town; Alfonso likes to mingle with his regulars and greet out-of-towners. His shrimp, beef and chicken dishes are dressed up with some interesting sauces. Try the shrimp Mercedes with a touch of garlic; no, it's named for his wife, not his car. The restaurant's interior is cozily intimate, with comfortable booths, low ceilings, dim lighting and curved brick arches.

3 *CASA DE BANDINI* • *2660 Calhoun St.; (619) 297-8211. Full bar service. Mid-morning through dinner daily. Major credit cards; $$ GETTING THERE: It's just northeast of the Plaza in Old Town State Historic Park.*

This is perhaps San Diego's most elaborately dressed Mexican restaurant. Housed in an Old Town adobe dating from the 1820s, Casa de Bandini is an imposing double-balconied structure surrounding a central courtyard. Its several dining rooms are wonderfully overly decorated with heavy carved beams holding up the ceilings, floral paintings on whitewashed walls and massive wrought iron chandeliers. The courtyard is a virtual jungle of an outdoor dining area, busy with trellises, arbors and fountains. Mariachis stroll inside and out to complete this picture of Mexican dining excess.

While the food isn't awesome, it's quite good, and the usual smashed beans and rice menu has been expanded to include interesting California-Mexican fare such as a spicy chicken and beef dish, plus several seafood entrées. The portions here are large enough to sink your *barca.*

4 CAFÉ COYOTE • *2461 San Diego Ave.; (619) 291-4695. Wine and beer. Lunch and dinner daily. MC/VISA; $$. GETTING THERE: Coyote is just below Old Town State Historic Park at the corner of Conde Street.*

This is one of Old Town's hot spots—a lively café with a teal blue and salmon Southwest look and a menu that steps beyond tortilla-wrapped things to offer several tasty seafood dishes. Among Coyote's entrées are fresh fish sautéed in tomatillo jalapeño sauce with jack cheese; and tequila lime shrimp with cilantro and garlic. If you must have something wrapped in a tortilla, try the fish fajitas or burritos. The menu also lists an assortment of pork, beef and chicken dishes, including a tasty margarita chicken. Tequila aficionados can choose from eighty different varieties—probably the largest selection in town. Coyote's dining room is quite appealing, with comfy booths and cheerful *Latino* murals on the walls. *Al fresco* diners can choose from sidewalk seating or a more sheltered patio between two buildings.

5 CHILANGO'S MEXICO CITY GRILL • *142 University Ave.; (619) 294-8646. Mexican regional; no alcohol. Lunch and dinner daily. No credit cards. GETTING THERE: It's in the Hillcrest District, between Second and Third avenues.*

This tiny storefront restaurant serves some of the tastiest and least expensive Mexican food in town. Although it has the usual smashed beans and rice dishes, it also serves exceptionally tasty Mexican regional fare. Chilango's specialty is chicken, beef or rice dishes in a *poblana* sauce—a mix of six different chilies and molé. And no, it isn't hot; it's a bit on the sweet side. Another tasty item is *memelas*, a *masa* cake covered with chicken or pork and smothered with sauce. Our favorite is *pollo asado*—grilled chicken with *poblana*. The interior is both spartan and cheerful, with Spanish tile floors and warm orange walls hung with a few Mexican ornaments. It has eight tables inside and two on the sidewalk.

6 EL INDIO MEXICAN RESTAURANT & CATERING • *3695 India St.; (619) 299-0385. Mexican takeout; no alcohol. Breakfast through dinner daily. No credit cards. GETTING THERE: El Indio is at India near Winder Street, part of the India Street's restaurant row. Take any of several off-ramps from parallel I-5 or follow one-way India Street from downtown. NOTE: Because it's one way, to return downtown you must continue on India to Washington, go left under the freeway and left again onto Kettner. There are several I-5 on-ramps along the way.*

If you want remarkably filling Mexican food at remarkably cheap prices, head for this busy take-out at the upper end of India Street. It's almost always busy with residents of the surrounding Middletown neighborhood—mostly Gringos, actually—so expect to stand in line if you arrive at lunch time. The place is cheerfully decorated with Mexican murals and dangling piñtas. You can take your fare to an outdoor patio, which is oddly located on a traffic island between India Street and an I-5 on-ramp. Don't expect either the café or the patio to be quiet during lunch and dinner hours. The fare is typical—tacos, burritos, enchiladas, chimichangas, tamales and fajitas. Jalapeño poppers are a specialty.

7 EL TECOLOTE • *6110 Friars Rd.; (619) 295-2087. Full bar service. Lunch and dinner Monday-Saturday, dinner only on Sunday. Major credit cards; $$. GETTING THERE: Head north on Freeway 163 from downtown and, as you cross under I-8, take the westbound exit to Friar's Road. The restaurant is about a mile and a half down on your right, in a bright red building in La Cumbre Square, at the junction of Via Las Cumbres. It's opposite River Valley Golf Course and just beyond a condo complex called The Bluffs.*

El Tecolote is a suburban version of Alfonso's—a Mexican restaurant popular with the Baby Boomer set. It's located in an upscale residential area about a mile west of Fashion Valley mall. However, it has a much livelier look than Alfonso's, busily decorated with Mexican trappings and photographs of personalities who have dined here. There's a patio out front and a full bar and pool room to one side. El Tecolote issues typical Hispanic fare, dressed up a bit for its suburban clientele. Entrées include chicken breast *poblana* (a mix of chilies and molé), meat enchiladas with molé sauce, carne asada and the full range of things encased in tortillas.

8 OLD TOWN MEXICAN CAFÉ AND CANTINA • *2489 San Diego Ave.; (619) 297-4330. Full bar service. Breakfast through late dinner daily. Major credit cards; $$. GETTING THERE: It's just below Old Town State Historic Park between Conde and Harney streets.*

A favorite of locals and winner of several restaurant association awards, Old Town is a no-nonsense café without the elaborate Latin décor of its neighbors. This noisy and crowded place is chopped into several dining rooms with high backed booths and just a few doo-dads to remind patrons that it's a Mexican restaurant. The menu is reminder enough. It's busy with fajitas, enchiladas, tostadas, burritos and such. House specialties include Mexican style ribs, spicy pork carnitas and shrimp in garlic butter.

9 RANCHO EL NOPAL • *In Old Town at 4016 Wallace St.; (619) 295-0584. Full bar service. Lunch and dinner daily. Major credit cards; $$. GETTING THERE: It's located just outside the entrance to Bazaar del Mundo.*

We found several reasons to like this large Old Town restaurant. It features Southwest as well as Mexican specialties, it has both handsomely decorated dining rooms and a large garden dining area, and it issues really big margaritas. Try the *camerones y carne asada,* shrimp sautéed in butter, garlic and green sauce, served with a thinly sliced charbroiled steak. Another specialty is chilies *poblanos*—mild, charbroiled peppers stuffed with chicken and served with *poblano* sauce. Sizzling fajitas are a feature here as well.

10 *MIGUEL'S CUCINA* • *2912 Shelter Island Dr., Point Loma, (619) 224-2401; and 1351 Orange Ave., Coronado, (619) 437-4237. Full bar service. Lunch and dinner daily. Major credit cards; $$. GETTING THERE: The Point Loma restaurant is near the corner of Shelter Island Drive and Rosecrans Street; turn bayward off Rosecrans and it's on your left. For the Coronado café, cross the San Diego-Coronado Bay bridge and go left on Orange Avenue several blocks to the downtown area.*

Although both versions of Miguel's are in serious tourist areas, they're popular with locals as well. These are inviting places, dressed up with painted murals, *lantilla* (tree branch) ceilings and cheerful *Latino* artifacts. The Point Loma version has a small outdoor deck overlooking adjacent Shelter Island, while the Coronado edition is among the little shops in the downtown area. The fare at both places is predictably Mexican and well prepared. In addition to the full range of tacos, burritos, flautas and such, the restaurants serve boneless breast of chicken with lime and orange juice marinade, jalapeño shrimp with bell peppers and mushrooms, and jumbo shrimp enchiladas with avocado garnish.

THE TEN BEST OTHER ETHNIC RESTAURANTS

It is said that everyone and everything coming to America is, at least to some degree, Americanized. This is certainly true of ethnic cuisine, in San Diego and elsewhere in our fair land. Mexican fare has been diluted by Chevy's and—gasp!—Taco Bell. Many Italian places produce designer pizzas that would make a Neapolitan blink, and California avocados have crept into Japanese sushi. Even most Chinese restaurants, almost always owned by Chinese, have been influenced by American tastes and by the lack of availability of ethnic vegetables. It's difficult to find hairy melons growing in the nearby Imperial Valley.

Despite such dilutions and limitations, San Diego has a rich variety of restaurants that are ethnic in principle. In fact, it has too many varieties. Since our format is limited to Ten Best, we must offer apologies to the Afghani, Cuban, Polish and other ethnic restaurant types that failed to make the cut.

1 CHINESE: **Taste of Szechuan** • *670 University Ave.; (619) 298-1638. Wine and beer. Lunch through late night. MC/VISA; $$. GETTING THERE: It's in the Hillcrest District northwest of Balboa Park, between Sixth and Seventh avenues.*

San Diego has several larger and more elaborate Chinese restaurants, with the requisite garish gold trim and red tussled lanterns. However, this pretty little café in the Hillcrest area serves the tastiest Chinese food in town, and the atmosphere is pleasing and relaxing. Call it austere elegance. Although it's family owned, Taste of Szechuan isn't a typical mom and pop Asian café with formica tables and golden dragons. It's done in soft mauve, from its comfortable booths with dainty floral designs to its ceramic tile trim, which is vaguely Spanish. Soft classical music plays in the background and votive candles flicker on each table.

Although the Szechuan name implies peppery Mandarin fare, the menu features a nice balance of both mild and spicy dishes. Further, the Szechuan fare doesn't sizzle your tongue; the chilies are applied with discretion. The food is faultlessly fresh and carefully prepared and the café is spotlessly clean, right down to the hermetically sealed fortune cookies at the end of the meal. ("You have a kind and generous nature.") Our favorite entrée is Szechuan garlic chicken, subtly spiced and—an odd thing for poultry—crunchy.

2 FRENCH: **La Próvence** • *708 Fourth Ave.; (619) 544-0661. Country French; wine and beer. Lunch and dinner daily. MC/VISA; $$. GETTING THERE: This bit of rural France is in Gaslamp Quarter, at the corner of G Street.*

Local culinary eyes will probably roll at our choice for San Diego's best Gaelic restaurant, since this isn't formal French but southern country French. However, rural French cooking is our preference. We've never been fond of the rich, heavy sauces of the more formal fare. And if so-called *nouveau* touches are added, the food is no longer French. You'll be charmed by the look of La Próvence, with its muted colors, French windows, potted plants and a trickling fountain in one corner.

The fare is of the countryside—*coq au vine*, bullfrog legs, mushroom veal stew, grilled seafood with aioli sauce, salmon pomegranate with scallions, shrimp brochette, and rack of lamb with a touch of cognac. An added bit of charm: Daily specials are written on a chalkboard on an outside wall. This Gaslamp Quarter café naturally has an outside dining area. Small tables, set off by a wrought iron rail, allow one to sip wine, enjoy a fine lunch or dinner and watch the passersby. La Próvence certainly does, as a small sign says, reflect *z' esprit du soleil,* the spirit of the sun.

3 GERMAN: **Kaiserhof** • *2253 Sunset Cliffs Blvd., Point Loma; (619) 224-0606. Wine and beer. Lunch and dinner daily except Monday. Major credit cards; $$$. GETTING THERE: Kaiserhof is near the corner of West Point Loma Boulevard, on the outer edge of Point Loma.*

This is as close as San Diego gets to an authentic German restaurant, and it's close enough, with lots of schnitzels on the menu and an outdoor *biergarten.* The kitchen creates the usual wienerscnitzels, saurbratens and bratwursts, plus slightly creative items such as wild boar goulash, roast duck with apple raisin stuffing and boneless chicken *zigeuner* with paprika sauce, peppers and onions. The dining room features carved wood paneling and a few heraldic medallions to give it that proper old European feel.

4 GREEK: **Athens Market Taverna** • *109 W. F St.; (619) 234-1955. Full bar service. Breakfast and lunch Monday-Saturday, dinner nightly. Major credit cards; $$. GETTING THERE: It's in Gaslamp Quarter, between First Avenue and Front Street, opposite the Mervyn's side of Horton Plaza.*

Although the name suggests a lively Greek tavern with undulating belly dancers, this attractive Gaslamp Quarter restaurant is quite prim in its décor, with French windows, white nappery with flower vases, and framed pictures of Greece on soft beige walls. The dancers do wriggle their tummies on Friday and Saturday evenings, creating festive moments in this rather refined setting.

However, most people come not for undulating navels but for the food, which is traditional Greek—*moussaka* (eggplant, zucchini and ground sirloin), *kotopoulo* (baked chicken with lemon, olive oil and oregano), and *dolmas* (grape leaves stuffed with rice and meat, served at Athens Market Taverna with an egg-lemon sauce). We like to ask for the one thing we can pronounce—Athens Market Special. It's a combination of four typical Greek dishes.

5 INDIAN: **Bombay Restaurant** • *3975 Fifth Ave.; (619) 298-3155. Wine and beer. Lunch and dinner daily. Major credit cards; $$$. GETTING THERE: It's in a shopping complex called Village Hillcrest between Washington Street and University Avenue in the Hillcrest District.*

Not your typical East Indian restaurant busy with multi-colored tapestries and brasswares, Bombay is a contemporary looking place with crisp white nappery on tables indoors and out. The main dining room is accented by a textured "fountain wall" with water seeping through its contours. Outdoor dining is just off the Village Hillcrest patio. The menu focuses on *tandoori* (Indian barbecue) fare, such as boneless chicken breast marinated in herbs, spices and yogurt; lamb *tika* in spices, lemon sauce and yogurt; plus several vegetarian dishes.

6 *ITALIAN:* **Busalucchi's Ristorante** • *3683 Fifth Ave.; (619) 298-0119. Sicilian; full bar service. Lunch weekdays and dinner nightly. Major credit cards; $$. GETTING THERE: This pasta palace is in the lower Hillcrest District, at the corner of Pennsylvania Avenue. The easiest way to reach it is to take one-way Fifth Avenue from downtown.*

Although more subtle northern Italian cooking is currently in vogue, this long-established café focuses on the spicier, red sauce and garlic oriented Sicilian cooking. Specialties include chicken Parmesan, veal Marsala and scaloppine, and calimari steak piccata with capers and wine. Perhaps the best dishes are the house-made pastas rich with spicy sauces and enough garlic to threaten a good marriage. Missed by most visitors although easy to find, the restaurant occupies an old Hillcrest District house. Cozy interior dining areas are tucked into several rooms. The décor is a bit dressy—as are the waiters—yet the atmosphere is casual and informal. Our favorite dining area is a canvas-roofed terrace over the street.

7 *JAPANESE:* **Sushi Ota** • *4529 Mission Bay Dr., Pacific Beach; (619) 270-5670. Wine and beer. Lunch Tuesday-Friday; dinner nightly. MC/VISA; $$$. GETTING THERE: You'll find your sushi tucked into the elbow of a small L-shaped shopping complex at the corner of Mission Bay Drive and Bunker Hill. Take the Grand/Garnet Avenue exit from I-5, which puts you on Mission Bay Drive; the restaurant is just ahead on your right.*

One local dining guide gives this spartan little sushi place a "D" for value, while the Zagat San Diego restaurant guide gives it the highest food rating of any of its listings. So who's right and how good can raw fish be? Having spent two years in Japan and being married to an Asian lass with a palate much better than mine, I agree with Zagat; the food is outstanding. Sushi, of course, is more than raw tuna; it includes a variety of seafoods, raw or cooked, often with interesting wrappings. Further, Ota goes beyond sushi to offer quite tasty tempura, teriyaki and fried soft-shell crabs. The place is austere in a crisp Japanese sort of way, done in gray and white with dark tables and a single large silk painting on one wall. Although it's hard to find, many people do, so reservations are essential.

8 *POLYNESIAN:* **Bali Hai** • *2230 Shelter Island Dr.; (619) 222-1181. Full bar service. Lunch and dinner daily, plus Sunday brunch. Major credit cards; $$ to $$$. GETTING THERE: To reach Shelter Island, head toward Point Loma on Rosecrans Street (State Route 209) and turn left onto Shelter Island Drive. Follow it to Shelter Island, spin around a traffic circle and drive a short distance northeast to the restaurant.*

The full name of this establishment is "Sam Choy's Hawaii at the Bali Hai" and that tells us a lot. Sam Choy is a Chinese-Polynesian from Hawaii who operates three other restaurants on the islands. He has written several Polynesian cookbooks, including one with a great title—*The Choy of Cooking*. Sam likes to blend flavors and techniques of Chinese cookery with traditional Polynesian recipes and we like most of his results. Start with one of those silly tropical drinks with little umbrellas, such as mai tais, Navy grog or planter's punch, accompanied by a puu puu platter—an appetizer tray of smoked chicken bits, tiny spareribs and nachos.

For the main course, try one of Sam's Chinese style wok specialties such as shrimp in lobster sauce, teriyaki lamb or cashew chicken. Among more traditional Polynesian dishes are coconut shrimp and macadamia nut chicken. One of our favorites is barbecued shrimp with ginger, cilantro and papaya-pineapple marmalade. The restaurant, built to suggest a giant tiki hut with heavy tree trunks holding up a conical ceiling, predates Sam by several decades. It was the first restaurant built here after Shelter Island was formed in the 1950s and it has weathered several ownerships. With glass window walls facing San Diego Bay and the city skyline, Bali Hai has one of the best dining views in southern California.

9 SPANISH: Café Sevilla ● *555 Fourth Ave.; (619) 239-5979. Full bar service. Dinner only, plus* tapas *bar snacks. Major credit cards; $$ to $$$. GETTING THERE; The café is in Gaslamp Quarter, between Market and Island streets.*

Visually, this is one of the more appealing cafés in San Diego. Step inside and you'll be transported to Seville at night, with subdued lighting, brick arches, cozy booths, sexy little blue drop lamps and a barrel-arched black-painted starry ceiling. Spanish cuisine is much more complex and less tortilla-oriented than that of Mexico. Feta, olives and other Mediterranean based foods are common ingredients. Specialties here include halibut with salsa and goat cheese, roasted lobster flambéed with Spanish brandy, and the popular *paella*—bits of clams, mussels, calimari, shrimp, sausage and roasted chicken in Spanish saffron rice. The adjacent bar, with a beautifully ornate backbar, is a favorite cocktail gathering place, where locals and visitors sip sangria and nibble *tapas,* small hors d'oeuvre plates of *paella,* meatballs in sherry sauce and other spicy specialties. Flamenco dancers and other entertainments ensure that nights in this lively café will transport patrons to its namesake city.

10 SOUTHEAST ASIAN: Karinya Thai Cuisine ● *825 Garnet Ave., Pacific Beach; (619) 270-5050. Wine and beer. Lunch Tuesday-Friday and dinner nightly. MC/VISA; $ to $$. GETTING THERE: Take the Grand/Garnet Avenue exit west from I-5, which puts you on*

Mission Bay Drive. Continue north about half a mile, then turn west (left) onto Garnet. The restaurant is the SeaCoast Square shopping complex at Garnet and Mission Boulevard, a block from the beach and Crystal Pier.

This exceptionally pretty restaurant serves the full range of Thai cuisine, plus several vegetarian dishes. Brocaded sashes are draped across white tablecloths, and the walls are adorned with select Thai artifacts and artwork. Some tables are done in classic Thai fashion, with seating benches and brightly colored pyramid-shaped leaning pillows.

Kitchen specialties include tamarind fish, crispy fried shrimp with tamarind-ginger sauce, a mixed seafood claypot and grilled beef with broccoli and garlic sauce. A specialty is Volcano Chicken, a Cornish game hen deep fried and served with peas and carrots in a sweet butter sauce. Many of the Thai dishes are quite hot, although you can ask to have them toned down.

Part of the secret of success in life is to eat whatever you like and let the food fight it out inside.
— **Mark Twain**

Chapter four

SAVORING
SOMETHING SPECIAL
RESTAURANTS WITH AN ATTITUDE

California's second largest city offers an interesting variety of dining experiences. The listings in this chapter focus on places that are specialized by their designer theme, location or menu. The first list contains a mixed bag—the Ten Best restaurants with a particular decor or food specialty. We then follow with categories for the Ten Best breakfasts, the Ten Best outdoor dining areas and the Ten Best view restaurants.

While the focus is more on specific styles of restaurants, we haven't sacrificed food quality in making our selections. All of our nominees serve interesting and reasonably well-prepared grub.

As in the previous chapter, we use dollar signs to indicate the price of a typical dinner with entrée, soup or salad, not including drinks, appetizers or dessert: *$* = less than $10 per entrée; *$$* = $10 to $19; *$$$* = $20 to $29; *$$$$* = $30 and beyond.

THE TEN BEST SPECIALTY RESTAURANTS

Since these selections don't relate to one another, they're listed in no particular order.

1 THE BEST BACK TO THE FIFTIES CAFÉ: Corvette

Diner • 3946 Fifth Ave.; (619) 542-1001. American; full bar service. Lunch and dinner daily. Major credit cards; $$. GETTING THERE: It's between University and Washington in the Hillcrest District.

Well of course it's contrived—from the white, black and pink tile floors to the Elvis posters and the old advertising signs—but it's fun. You're greeted by lots of noise and a gleaming 1958 Corvette as you step into the happy bedlam of this place. A live disk jockey spins platters and the short-skirted waitresses, wearing "Don't be a weenie" badges on their ample bosoms, occasionally break from their chores to do a kind of funky chicken line dance. Aging Baby Boomers needn't be shy about entering this place, since the deejay plays tunes familiar to them, from Dino ballads to Beatles rock. The menu is what you'd expect—chicken fried steak, liver and onions, grilled Reubens and assorted hamburgers. Our "Hawaii 5-O" burger with pineapple and teriyaki sauce fell far short of awesome, although the fries were good and—like—we dug the noisy ambiance.

2 THE BEST BARBECUE: Kansas City Barbecue • 610 W.

Market St.; (619) 231-9680. American barbecue; wine and beer. Lunch and dinner daily. MC/VISA; $ to $$. GETTING THERE: You can find your ribs near the waterfront at Market and Kettner, off Harbor Drive.

Your little barbecue café is featured in a "sleazy bar scene" in the 1985 epic *Top Gun* and suddenly, customers are beating a path to your ribs, right? Well, almost. Quite by chance, the location director for the naval aviation epic starring Tom Cruse stopped by Kansas City Barbecue for an afternoon beer. He liked the place and asked owners Martin and Cindy Blair if his studio could use it for a bar scene. (Most of the movie was filmed at nearby Marine Corps Air Station Miramar, where Navy and Marine Corps jet jockeys really are trained as "top guns.") The bar, as you saw in the film, is wildly decorated with military artifacts, ladies panties and bras, truckers' caps, personalized license plates and whatever. The Blairs aren't shy about the bar's its role in the movie. Signs proudly proclaim this to be the site of the Top Gun "sleazy bar scene." However, we didn't come here to drink were Tom Cruse drank. We came for the ribs and they're the best in town. The straightforward menu features beef and pork ribs, barbecued chicken and assorted combos thereof. Why Kansas City in San Diego? Because that's where the owners are from and K.C. is noted for its stockyards and great slow-cooked barbecue.

3 *THE BEST BRITISH GRILL:* **Shakespeare Pub & Grille** • *3701 India St.; (619) 299-0230. British and American; wine, beer and Scotch malts. Lunch and dinner daily. MC/VISA, AMEX; $. GETTING THERE: Shakespeare is at India and Winder, part of the restaurant row at the northwest end of India Street. Take any of several off-ramps from parallel I-5 or follow one-way India Street from downtown. NOTE: Because it's one way, to return downtown you must continue on India to Washington, go left under the freeway and left again onto Kettner. There are several I-5 on-ramps along the way.*

A long way from the merry old sod, this appealing grill occupies a cottage perched atop an ivy-covered wall above India Street. The interior is properly pub-like, with wooden chairs and tables, plank floors, a central bar and a few British prints and beer label logos on the walls. There's also an outdoor dining deck. The fare is essential Brit and quite inexpensive—fish and chips, steak and mushroom pie, bangers and mash, and ploughman's plate. (For those deprived of the distinction of British Isles ancestry, bangers and mash is pork sausage with mashed potatoes and peas; ploughman's plate consists of slices of cheese, pickled onions and a "Scotch" egg which is hard-boiled with sausage meat and bread crumbs.) Out of deference to its southern California location, the pub also offers a fish taco and hamburgers.

4 *THE BEST WILDLY DECORATED CAFÉ:* **Planet Hollywood** • *197 Horton Plaza; (619) 702-7827. American; full bar service. Lunch and dinner daily. Major credit cards; $$. GETTING THERE: This errant planet is downtown, on the Broadway side of Horton Plaza.*

Create an absolutely bizarre place that suggests a cross between a Hollywood horror sci-fi and the gloomy forest scene from *Snow White* and the people—particularly younger ones with disposable income— will come running. Planet Hollywood, whose cafés do seem to be from another world and possibly from another universe, is enjoying immense success with its grotesque décor and hip music. The food is pretty ordinary—the usual 'burgers, pastas, fajitas, pizzas, chicken 'n' ribs. However, in a place decorated with a mannequin of a badly mauled robotic Arnold Schwarzenegger from *Terminator II* and a shriveled walking mummy, who expects gourmet?

5 *THE MOST STYLISH CAFÉ:* **Palomino Euro Bistro** • *In the Aventine at 8990 University Lane Center, La Jolla; (858) 452-9000. Mediterranean fare; full bar service. Lunch weekdays and dinner nightly. Major credit cards; $$ to $$$. GETTING THERE: Take the La Jolla Village Drive exit from I-5, about nine miles north of the I-8 interchange, go east for a mile to Lebon Drive and turn right. The Aventine is a shopping and business complex opposite the Hyatt Regency.*

This trendy place is as appealing to the eye as to the palate—an *art moderne* space with Tuscan oxblood red columns, mauve and orange curtains, curving laminated ceiling beams and marble topped tables. A large outdoor patio is an inviting place to sit and watch the passing parade of the Aventine. From the demonstration kitchen with its blazing open firepit emerges savories such as roast sea bass with sweet pepper and tomato ragout, mahi mahi with cinnamon *cous cous*, spit roasted pork loin with roasted onion relish, and assorted thin-crust designer pizzas. The adjacent lounge is equally stylish and inviting—a lively extension of the restaurant.

6 **THE BEST DELI RESTAURANT:** *Samson's* • *8861 Villa La Jolla Dr., La Jolla; (858) 455-1461. Assorted ethnic and deli fare; wine and beer. Breakfast through dinner daily. Major credit cards; $ to $$. GETTING THERE: Samson's is in La Jolla Village Center. Follow I-5 north about eight miles from the I-8 interchange, take the Nobel Drive exit and go briefly west over the freeway. The shopping center is at Nobel and Villa La Jolla Drive and Samson's is in the northwest corner, beside a multi-screen theater complex.*

We'll begin by saying that we found no great Jewish delis in the San Diego area—nothing on the order of those grandly cluttered and aromatic places in New York and San Francisco. Samson's, while a bit too orderly to be a classic deli, will do if you seek something kosher. It serves the usual *knishes* and smoked fishes, kosher short ribs, stuffed cabbage rolls and such. It also has a remarkable variety of other foods—bakery items, sausages, sandwiches, buffalo wings, Swedish meatballs and mozzarella sticks. The bakery boasts a hundred items, from *challah* bread to pastries, cookies and cheesecakes. And yes, you can order a Bar Mitzvah cake. With all this variety, it has a rather small deli case and specialty foods area. Most of the space is taken up by the restaurant, and it has patio dining.

7 **THE BEST HAMBURGER CAFÉ:** *Boll Weevil* • *Local chain with about ten outlets. Those in or near San Diego are at 2743 Shelter Island Drive near Rosecrans Street, (619) 224-0444; 5826 Mission Gorge Road near Fairmount Avenue, (619) 282-4660; Pacific Highway at Elm, (619) 234-2464; and 7777 Fay Ave., La Jolla, (858) 459-4541.*

Beef may be out of fashion but not at this local chain. Boll Weevil's flagship cholesterol carrier is a half-pound hamburger, served on an equally large sesame bun. Other offerings include cheeseburgers, bacon cheese burgers, barbecue burgers and chili size, plus hot dogs and assorted other sandwiches. These aren't inexpensive; the half-pound "Steer Burgers" are over $3. However, they're prepared as a proper burger should be—cooked to your liking and served on a toasted bun to avoid sogginess. As soon as you take a seat and before you give your order, a large condiment tray arrives with relish, crisp red onion rings, mustard, catsup, hot yellow peppers, dill pickles and Tabasco sauce. The burger is served open faced and naked; you add your own accessories. Fries are extra and worth the added cost; they're the shoestring variety, crisp, piping hot and lightly salted. The Bolls Weevil are simple places, most with a kind of Formica rural café look, although the one at Shelter Island suggests a distressed tropical cottage.

8 *THE BEST PIZZA PARLOR: Pizza Nova* • *5120 N. Harbor Dr. (in Point Loma between Nimitz and Scott), (619) 226-0268; and 3755 Fifth Ave. (in Village Hillcrest between University and Washington), (619) 296-6682.*

We aren't great fans of the new designer pizzas such as smoked duck sausage and—good grief!—Mexican lime chicken. However, you may be, so we sought a place that issues both. Nova's wood-fired pizzas arrive on a thin and crunchy crust, and you can order the *nouveau* gimmick varieties, or a classic Italian cheese and tomato pizza. Or you can build your own, choosing from a list of thirty-five different items. The combination pizza—by which we always judge pizza parlors—is excellent, nicely spiced and heavily laden with pepperoni, sausage, mushrooms, black olives, and green and yellow peppers. Anchovies are available on request, although that is a disgusting thing to do to a pizza. Pizza Nova also offers pastas, lasagna, roasted chicken and for you vegans, eggplant Parmesan. A couple of meatless pizzas also are available.

These pizza places are sleekly attractive, with salmon colored walls, mauve booths, black tables and chairs, and busy open kitchens. The wine, a necessary accouterment to pizza, is a bit pricey although the pizzas themselves are no more expensive than those at franchise establishments.

9 *THE BEST SUNDAY BRUNCH: Chez Loma* • *1132 Loma Ave., Coronado; (619) 435-0661. Continental; full bar service. Brunch Sunday and dinner nightly. Major credit cards; $$$ for brunch. GETTING THERE: Cross the Coronado Bridge, turn left onto Orange Avenue and follow it about a mile to the traffic circle in downtown Coronado. Chez Loma is on the right, in an old Victorian house at the corner of Loma and Orange.*

Buffet style brunches are not uncommon San Diego, with the usual spreads of everything from salads to mussels to steam table hot dishes. We prefer the elegance of Chez Loma's Sunday brunch, featuring individually prepared entrées. Among the selections are frittatas, eggs Benedict, quiche, grilled chicken and several designer omelettes. Brunch includes fresh fruit, croissants, preserves and honey butter. Guests are served individually in the restaurant's charming French country style dining room.

10 THE BEST VEGGIE RESTAURANT: The Vegetarian

Zone • *2949 Fifth Ave.; (619) 298-7302. Asian and American vegetarian; wine and beer. Lunch through dinner Monday-Saturday and breakfast through dinner on Sunday. MC/VISA, DISC; $ to $$. GETTING THERE: The Zone is just west of Balboa Park, at the corner of Quince Street. The easiest way to get there from downtown is to follow one-way Fifth Avenue.*

Have you had your tofu today? This large operation includes a restaurant, deli and environmentally correct gift shop where you can buy spiritually soothing CDs and tapes, items that make social statements, herbal teas and incense. The restaurant is remarkably cute, with planter sconces, flower paintings on the walls and cheerful floral table coverings. The menu lists chickenless "chicken loaf" and meat-free meatloaf, Greek spinach pie, layered tofu, vegetarian lasagna and other entrées made from things that grow from the soil. There's an inviting landscaped patio out front and naturally the restaurant is run by solar energy.

SUNNYSIDE UP: THE TEN BEST BREAKFAST CAFÉS

To qualify for our list of Ten Best Breakfast Cafés, an establishment must start serving at least by 7 a.m. and feature a good selection of wake-up fare. Naturally, it must offer plenty of hot, strong coffee to get one's heart started. Being latté fanatics, we tilt toward restaurants that serve specialty coffees. However, our number one choice isn't exactly cappuccino country.

1 PERRY'S CAFÉ • *4610 Pacific Hwy.; (619) 291-7121.*

American; no alcohol. Breakfast to midafternoon. MC/VISA, DISC; $. GETTING THERE: Take Pacific Highway north about three miles from downtown to a traffic light where Rosecrans and Taylor streets come together, opposite Old Town. Go through the signal and Perry's is on your left, surrounded by a large parking lot.

San Diego's best breakfast café looks right out of the sixties, from its chubby geometric roof outside to its long serving counter and Naugahyde booths inside. Apron-clad waitresses write out your order on little pads and the first thing they ask when you step through the door is: "Coffee, dearie?" Glass sugar shakers and stainless steel creamers sit on the counter and on the tables. The menu features every kind of breakfast you can think of, and a specialty is the *frittata,* an Italian omelette served with a side of beans and tortillas, potatoes, baked apple or mixed fruit. Another menu page is filled with Mexican breakfasts, from the ubiquitous *huevos rancheros* to Mexican eggs Benedict and breakfast burritos. The American side has several omelettes and other egg dishes, smoked pork chops, biscuits and gravy, pancakes, waffles and French toast. This isn't one of those cutesy places that offers you a little lazy susan with six syrup varieties. You get a small stainless steel tub of syrup and blob of butter. However, you can mess up your pancakes, waffles or French toast with fruit topping and a huge dollop of whipped cream. Expect the truckers in the next booth to giggle if you order it that way.

2 *BIG KITCHEN* • *3003 Grape St.; (619) 234-5789. American; no alcohol. Breakfast to midafternoon. No credit cards; $. GETTING THERE: From downtown, take Broadway or Market Street east to 30th, go north about a mile to Grape and turn right; it's a couple of doors down on the right. (Thirtieth jogs to the right, briefly becoming Fern Street, but keep bearing north and you'll intersect Grape.)*

"Small world, big kitchen," says a flower-trimmed sign out front. This funky café seems transplanted from San Francisco's Haight Ashbury, with its basic yet eclectic décor, window boxes and ceiling fans, and a kind of existentialistic aura. It's popular with residents of this slightly weathered North Park neighborhood. They line up for hefty breakfasts of thick French toast, eggs and chorizo, tofu omelettes and in-house muffins. The vaguely holistic menu also features black bean chili, falafel and spinach lasagna for lunch. If you dined here in 1974 and peeked into the Big Kitchen's kitchen, you might have seen a handsome young black woman washing dishes. She went on to greater pursuits, although her name is still scrawled on one of the restaurant walls: Whoopi Goldberg.

3 *THE BROKEN YOLK* • *1851 Garnet Ave., Pacific Beach; (619) 270-YOLK. American; wine and beer. Breakfast through midafternoon daily. Major credit cards; $. GETTING THERE: Take the Grand/Garnet Avenue exit from I-5, go several blocks north then turn left onto Garnet Avenue. The restaurant is about eight blocks down, between Lamont and Kendall Streets, across from the Pacific Plaza II Shopping Center.*

They say you can't make an omelette without breaking a few yolks, and they break plenty at this airy café. It has an imposingly long list of omelettes, such as a "John Wayne" with chili and American cheese and the "Cabrillo" with bell pepper, onion and salsa. Other items include waffles, hotcakes, a "Western Benedict" with avocado, and Mexican accented fare such as *machata* (scrambled eggs with shredded beef, bell peppers and salsa) and that old standby *huevos rancheros*. Early risers can get one of several breakfast specials for under $4. It's a relatively attractive place with ceiling fans, drop lamps and cane-back chairs.

4 *CHAZ'S SUNSET CAFÉ* • *4535 Ocean Blvd., Pacific Beach;* *(619) 270-6980. American; wine and beer. Breakfast served through noon. MC/VISA; $. GETTING THERE: Take Mission Boulevard through Pacific Beach and turn beachward onto Feldspar and follow it a block to the end. Chaz's is just to the left.*

This cheerful little beach shack is handy for breakfast if you plan to play in the surf and sand off Pacific Beach. It has a good assortment of omelettes, including the spicy "Zorro's Famous," served with salsa and a tortilla. Other breakfast fare ranges from the usual pancakes, waffles, bacon 'n' eggs to eggs Benedict, which is issued with the traditional ham or with seafood. A wind-sheltered, windowed patio offers views of the beach and the adjacent Ocean Front Walk.

5 *CITY DELICATESSEN* • *535 University Ave.; (619) 295- 2747. American and ethnic; wine and beer. Breakfast through late night. MC/VISA; $ to $$. GETTING THERE: It's at University and Seventh avenues in the Hillcrest District.*

Despite its name, this isn't a full-scale delicatessen; it's a Forties-Fifties style restaurant with a small deli case. We like the pleasing décor and the extensive selection of breakfast offerings. You can go for a short stack or waffle for very little money, or try various omelettes and the usual assortments of bacon, sausage and eggs. If you really need fueling, order the Hobo Breakfast of two eggs, two pancakes and two slices of bacon or sausage. Our favorite is a tasty blend of bacon, tomatoes, mushrooms, lox and onions.

6 *D.W. RANCH FAMILY RESTAURANT* • *2440 Hotel Circle North; (619) 297-3393. American; full bar service. Breakfast through dinner daily. Major credit cards; $ to $$. GETTING THERE: The restaurant is off I-8, just beyond Motel 6. Take the Hotel Circle exit.*

Opening its doors at 6:30 a.m., this simple family style diner is handy for visitors staying at one of the lodgings in Mission Valley's Hotel Circle. It features an alarming assortment of omelettes plus the usual eggs, flapjacks and waffles. And if you like spice in your breakfast, try one of several Mexican specialties, such as *chorizo* with scrambled eggs, shredded beef with onions and spices, *huevos rancheros* or a Southwest style breakfast burrito.

7 *HOB NOB HILL* • *2271 First Ave.; (619) 239-8176. American; wine and beer. Breakfast through dinner daily. Major credit cards; $. GETTING THERE: Take one-way First Avenue west from downtown; it's on the corner of First and Juniper Street.*

We selected this venerable establishment as the best locals' restaurant in the previous chapter (page 54). It's also one of the Ten Best Breakfast Cafés in town, serving substantial and tasty fare such as homemade beef hash, smoked pork chops with eggs, and eggs Benedict or Florentine. Other fare includes thick French toast, waffles with pecans, flapjacks and assorted omelettes. This old fashion restaurant has been filling up San Diegans since 1944.

8 OLD TOWN MEXICAN CAFÉ AND CANTINA • *2489 San Diego Ave.; (619) 297-4330. Mexican; full bar service. Breakfast through late dinner daily. Major credit cards; $ to $$. GETTING THERE: It's just below Old Town State Historic Park between Conde and Harney streets.*

If you want to lend a Mexican accent to your breakfast, try this locally popular spot. Opening its doors at 7 a.m., it's one of the few Old Town restaurants that serves breakfast. Naturally, it features *huevos rancheros* and Spanish omelettes. Among other Hispanic-accented breakfasts are pork carnitas hash, corn tortillas with fried eggs and beans, and Mexican sausage with eggs, rice and beans. Another specialty is a scrambled egg, cilantro and onion taco. If you must, however, the café serves a "Gringo breakfast" of eggs with bacon, ham or sausage.

9 THE MENU • *3784 Ingraham St., Pacific Beach; (619) 370-9999. American; wine and beer. Breakfast through midafternoon daily. MC/VISA; $. GETTING THERE: Take Ingraham through Mission Bay Park to Pacific Beach; the cross street is La Playa Avenue.*

This place claims—in very large letters—to have the best breakfast in San Diego. It certainly has some of the most substantial, with hefty entrées such as steak and eggs, pork chops and eggs and chicken fried steak and eggs. Other items include eggs Benedict, assorted omelettes and the usual flapjacks and waffles. It's a simple, vaguely prim little place with flowered oilcloth tables, bentwood chairs and a few prints on the walls.

10 RED SAILS INN • *2614 Shelter Island Dr.; (619) 223-3030. American, mostly seafood; full bar service. Breakfast through dinner daily. Major credit cards; breakfast $. GETTING THERE: Head toward Point Loma on Rosecrans Street (State Route 209) and turn left onto Shelter Island Drive. Red Sails is at the entrance to Shelter Island, at the corner of Anchorage Lane.*

This is one of the few area seafood restaurants that also focuses on breakfast. It's a great place to start a warm day, since its wakeup fare can be served on a fountain patio beside a marina. Red Sails is one of the oldest restaurants in town, dating back to the 1930s when it was at the now-defunct Fisherman's Wharf. Perhaps in honor of the sailors and Marines who have eaten here through the decades, one of its breakfast specialties is chipped beef on toast. Any former serviceman can tell you that it has a much more colorful name. Other specials are shrimp omelettes, broiled fish and eggs, corned beef hash and the always popular *huevos rancheros*.

FOOD AL FRESCO: THE TEN BEST OUTDOOR CAFÉS

Because of San Diego's balmy weather, sidewalk cafés are quite prevalent. Nearly all restaurants in its two most concentrated dining areas, Gaslamp Quarter and Old Town, have outdoor tables. Some, in fact, have more tables outside than in. We considered two factors in choosing our *al fresco* cafés. First of course, they must have an appealing outdoor dining area. And second, in the interest of variety, we sought out restaurants with varied ethnic persuasions.

1 CASA DE BANDINI • *In Old Town at 2660 Calhoun St.; (619) 297-8211. Mexican; full bar service. Mid-morning through dinner daily. Major credit cards; $$. GETTING THERE: The restaurant is just northeast of the Plaza in Old Town State Historic Park.*

Readers of the *San Diego Union* recently chose Casa de Bandini as the restaurant with the best dining patio and we agree. Surrounded by a large two-story adobe dating back to the 1820s, the courtyard dining area is a lush jungle, busy with trellises, arbors and fountains, made even brighter and cheerier by colored lights and strolling mariachis. Even chilly evenings can be comfortable since the garden is kept cozily warm by heat lamps. And the food is quite good. Several seafood and California-Mexican entrées dress up the traditional Mexican menu of things tucked into tortillas.

2 CALIFORNIA CAFÉ BAR & GRILL • *Fifth level at Horton Plaza; (619) 238-5440. American regional; full bar service. Lunch through dinner daily. Major credit cards; $$. GETTING THERE: Horton Plaza is downtown, rimmed by First and Fourth avenues, Broadway and G Street.*

An attractive outdoor deck at this Horton Plaza café provide shoppers with an opportunity to take a break from credit card abuse. They can enjoy some contemporary California cuisine or perhaps a cooling drink. The café's interior is pleasing as well—a trendy mix of dark woods, geometric colors and open space. The menu is proper for a place called California Café, with entrées such as chicken-vegetable stir fry, garlic-rubbed breast of chicken and grilled Atlantic salmon.

3 CASA DE PICO • *In Old Town at 2745 Calhoun St.; (619) 296-3267. Mexican; full bar service. Mid-morning through dinner daily. Major credit cards; $$. GETTING THERE: It's in the middle of Bazaar del Mundo at the western end of Old Town San Diego State Historic Park.*

If you like outdoor dining and you don't mind being on display for other Bazaar del Mundo visitors, this is your place. Casa de Pico's large courtyard is surrounded by shops and shoppers in this colorful Mexican bazaar. It has a small indoor dining area, although most the cafe is beneath the sun, with umbrella tables and heat lamps. Cheerful and gaudy, it doesn't pretend to be a traditional Mexican restaurant. Traditional tourist Mexican restaurant, yes. However, in addition to its usual smashed beans and rice dishes, it has a health-conscious side to its menu, with several vegetarian items.

4 THE KING AND I • *620 Fifth Ave.; (619) 238-2328. Thai; wine and beer. Lunch weekdays, dinner nightly. Major credit cards; $ to $$. GETTING THERE: This Thai restaurant is in Gaslamp Quarter, near the corner of Market Street.*

The King and I features a cozy little sidewalk patio accented by wrought iron trim. The interior is attractive as well, with golden statues of pretty, bowing maidens and bright Southeast Asian artifacts. The fare is typically spicy Thai—charcoal broiled pork on green cabbage and cilantro, broiled chicken with Thai spices and curry, beef satay in coconut milk and curry powder with peanut sauce, plus several vegetarian dishes.

5 LA STRADA • *702 Fifth Ave.; (619) 239-3400. Italian and American; full bar service. Lunch and dinner daily. Major credit cards; $$. GETTING THERE: La Strada is in Gaslamp Quarter near G Street.*

This trendy, noisy Italian bistro spills onto the Gaslamp sidewalks with a large green wrought iron-rimmed seating area. Clear plastic curtains drop down to protect *al fresco* diners during San Diego's infrequent rainstorms. Housed in one of the Quarter's fine old buildings, it has a high-ceiling dining room with lots of brick. The décor is sort of medieval-goes-modern, with period Italian murals, white nappery and an open kitchen. The Italian menu has picked up some Southwest accents on its way to San Diego. Polenta, smoked salmon and other *nouveau*-correct fare appears on an otherwise Tuscan menu.

6 THE LIVING ROOM • *1010 Prospect St., La Jolla; (858) 459-1187. Light entrées and deli fare; no alcohol. Breakfast through late evening. MC/VISA; $. GETTING THERE: This Living Room is in downtown La Jolla at the corner of Prospect and Girard.*

The sidewalk patio of this little bistro walk-up is a great place for watching the passage of La Jolla's beautiful people and halter-topped tourists. Step inside to place your order, then pick up a newspaper or magazine and adjourn to the outside tables. They're cordoned from the sidewalk by a decorative wooden fence. The Living Room offers eggs, smoked salmon, bagels and other breakfast fare, and baked brie, chicken pie, quiche, croissant sandwiches and soups for lunch and dinner. It also features speciality coffees and teas and a good selection of cakes and tarts.

7 *POINT LOMA SEAFOODS* • *2805 Emerson St.; (619) 223-1109. Wine and beer. Monday-Saturday 9 to 7 and Sunday noon to 7. No credit cards; $. GETTING THERE: Drive southeast on Rosecrans Street toward Point Loma, turn left onto Emerson and follow it a few blocks to its terminus at the Municipal Sportfishing Pier.*

This casual takeout is a great place for dining *al fresco*. After your number is called, pick up your paper plate piled high with fried seafood or fish and chips and adjourn to an attractive patio or to a row of tables alongside the Municipal Sportfishing Pier. While seagulls, pigeons and possibly pelicans eye your food hungrily, you can watch the action of the marina as commercial and charter fishing boats and whale-watching boats cruise in and out. Beyond their masts, you'll have a nice view of the bay and distant San Diego skyline.

8 *RANCHO EL NOPAL* • *4016 Wallace St.; (619) 295-0584. Full bar service. Lunch and dinner daily. Major credit cards; $$. GETTING THERE: It's in Old Town, just outside the entrance to Bazaar del Mundo.*

Do you like to people-watch as you dine? Rancho el Nopal occupies a key corner opposite the Old Town Plaza, near the entrance to Bazaar del Mundo. This dining garden is particularly appealing, with thick vegetation, umbrellas, heat lamps and—a really nice touch for evening dining—kerosene lanterns suspended over the tables. The fare is what you'd expect, with lots of things wrapped in tortillas, fajitas, combination Mexican dinners and margaritas the size of fishbowls.

9 *SAMMY'S CALIFORNIA PIZZA* • *770 Fourth Ave.; (619) 230-8888. Pizza and pasta; wine and beer. Lunch and dinner daily. Major credit cards; $$. GETTING THERE: Sammy's is in Gaslamp Quarter between F and G streets.*

If you like pizza as your *al fresco* entrée, Sammy's has one of the most inviting outdoor seating areas in Gaslamp Quarter. Window boxes and wall-sconce clay planters add pleasing patches of green to its brick patio. It features curious designer pizzas such as garlic chicken, pineapple and Canadian bacon and Jamaican shrimp. You can get more straightforward pepperoni and sausage if you must. The pasta side of the menu also has culinary oddities, such as Thai chicken linguine and chicken tequila fettuccini.

10 SCULPTURE GARDEN CAFÉ • *Off El Prado in Balboa Park; (619) 696-1990. Light American fare; wine and beer. Lunch through midafternoon Tuesday-Sunday; closed Monday; $ to $$. GETTING THERE: It's near the San Diego Museum of Art at the northwest corner of Plaza de Panama.*

This small walkup has sun-bathed tables just off Plaza de Panama and sheltered tables under a canopy for those rare rainy days. It's a pleasant place for sitting, sipping wine and watching the human parade along El Prado. The fare, light and a bit pricey, includes sandwiches, salads and designer coffees. One of its more interesting creations is an artichoke sandwich with olives, daikon sprouts and provolone.

VITTLES WITH A VISTA: THE TEN BEST VIEW RESTAURANTS

You can't eat scenery, so we won't send you to a restaurant that offers great views but has mediocre food and sullen service. Some of our selections have earned listings elsewhere in this book for their food quality and/or general ambiance. Our choices range from elegant restaurants such as our number one selection to simple little takeouts, where you can pick up your fried fish and adjourn to an outdoor table that provides fine views of the waterfront.

1 MR. A'S • *2550 Fifth Ave.; (619) 239-1377. American-continental; full bar service. Lunch weekdays and dinner nightly. GETTING THERE: The restaurant is located on the 12th floor of the Fifth Avenue Center near the corner of Laurel Street, just below Balboa Park. Take Laurel from I-5 or one-way Fifth from downtown.*

Since Mr. A's sits atop the top floor of a building that sits on a hill, it offers an imposing panorama of San Diego, its harbor, Mission Bay, the downtown highrises and beyond. And if the view is great, so are the ambiance and the food. We rate it as one of San Diego's Ten Very Best Restaurants in the previous chapter; see page 53 for details.

2 THE BAY CAFÉ • *1050 N. Harbor Dr.; (619) 595-1083. Light fare; mostly fried seafood; wine and beer. Midmorning through late afternoon; hours vary with the seasons; $. GETTING THERE: The café is part of the San Diego Harbor Excursion complex, on the Embarcadero below downtown, near the base of Broadway.*

Calling this a café is almost an overstatement, since it's a small takeout. However, it provides some of the best views in town. After picking up your fish and chips, calimari or fried seafood platter from the take-out window, you can pack it up to a rooftop dining area, sit in plastic chairs and enjoy the sea breezes. The second-story perch has unfettered views of San Diego Bay, waterfront activity and the nearby downtown skyline.

3 CRESCENT SHORES GRILL • *In Hotel La Jolla at 7955 La Jolla Shores Dr.; (858) 459-0541. Contemporary American; full bar service. Lunch weekdays, brunch weekends and dinner nightly. Major credit cards; $$$. GETTING THERE: The hotel is a short distance above downtown La Jolla, at the junction of Torrey Pines Road and La Jolla Shores Drive.*

It's difficult not to find a nice view in La Jolla, and this eleventh floor grill provides fine vistas of the red tile rooftops of tree-shrouded neighborhoods, and the ocean beyond. When you're not gazing out the window, admire the smart interior done up in light colors with drop lamps over comfortable booths. Crescent Shores Grill also is good place for a scenic drink; small tables in the adjacent bar hug big picture windows. The restaurant's menu is contemporary American, featuring fare such as breast of free-range chicken (that's a cluck that's not cooped up), grilled swordfish with melon salsa, mesquite grilled salmon with roasted fennel and linguine, and barbecued babyback ribs with sweet potato purée. Sundown's a great time to be up here, and the restaurant offers a three-course "Sunset Gourmet Menu" to herald that event.

4 THE FISH MARKET and TOP OF THE MARKET • *750 N. Harbor Dr.; (619) 232-FISH. American, mostly seafood; full bar service. Lunch and dinner daily and Sunday brunch. Major credit cards; $$ for the Fish Market and $$$ to $$$$ for Top of the Market. GETTING THERE: The complex is on the edge of Tuna Fleet Park near the lower end of Harbor Drive. From downtown, take Broadway to the waterfront and turn left.*

This dual restaurant is perched on a peninsula extending into San Diego Bay to maximize the views. Both the downstairs and upstairs dining rooms have window walls; they're nice places to sit and watch the boats work and play on the bay. Some cruise practically beneath the windows, since a commercial fishing fleet shares this manmade peninsula. The downstairs dining room is rather casual, with a small fresh fish counter to justify calling itself The Fish Market; upstairs is more clubby and attractive, with higher prices. We review this dual restaurant in greater detail, as one of the Ten Best Seafood places in Chapter Three, page 60.

5 GEORGE'S AT THE COVE • *1250 Prospect St., La Jolla; (858) 454-4244. American, mostly seafood; full bar service. Lunch and dinner daily. Major credit cards; $$$. GETTING THERE: You'll find George in a shopping complex above La Jolla Cove.*

We selected George's as San Diego's very best restaurant in the previous chapter, agreeing with *Bon Appétit* that it's "a seaside showplace that also serves superb food." And it certainly qualifies for our Ten Best View list. It has two dining areas providing nice vistas of La Jolla Cove. The upstairs Ocean Terrace is open to the cove and the sea beyond, with nothing between diners and the view except a low glass partition. The enclosed and more formal downstairs dining room has a virtual glass wall facing the sea. For more on George's, see page 49.

6 KONO'S SURF CLUB CAFÉ • *704 Garnet at Ocean Front Walk, Pacific Beach; (619) 483-1669. American; wine and beer. Breakfast through late afternoon; $. GETTING THERE: Go west on Garnet Avenue from Mission Bay Drive and follow it to the end. Kono's is across Ocean Front Walk from Crystal Pier and the view seating is on the pier.*

This popular take-out has indoor and outdoor seating on the inland side of Ocean Front Walk. It earns a spot on our view list because of an "extension" dining area—a small deck fused into Crystal Pier, across the walk and right above the beach. The routine here is to stand in line at the café, get your food and carry it across the promenade to the deck, which is beside a shell and curio shop. The view up and down the beach is great. It's very popular in summer and on weekends so get there early if you want a seat. The food's not fancy, consisting of breakfast burritos, burgers, quesadillas and other light fare.

7 MARINE ROOM • *2000 Spindrift Dr., La Jolla Shores; (858) 459-7222. American, mostly seafood; full bar service. Lunch Monday-Saturday, dinner nightly and Sunday brunch. Major credit cards; $$$$. GETTING THERE: From downtown La Jolla, head north on Prospect until it blends into Torrey Pines Road, go about a third of a mile, then turn left onto Spindrift. The restaurant is about a third of a mile down.*

La Jolla's legendary Marine Room has such a closeup view of the surf that on two occasions in the past half century, the sea entered the dining room. Certainly the view is grand, since the restaurant sits practically on the beach, in a pretty little cove. It's not unusual at high tide for the incoming surf to lap at the windows. The Marine Room is a very handsome place with an excellent kitchen, and it earned a spot as one of our Ten Very Best Restaurants in the previous chapter (page 52). The dining room is dressed in floral carpeting, brocaded chairs and scallop wall sconces. However, the most impressive decorator item is the seaward wall of glass.

8 *PEOHE'S* • *1201 First St., Coronado; (619) 437-4474. Full bar service. Lunch Monday-Saturday, dinner nightly and Sunday brunch. Major credit cards; $$$. GETTING THERE: It's at water's edge in the Ferry Landing Marketplace. Cross the Coronado Bridge from San Diego, turn right onto Orange Avenue, follow it a few blocks to its end, then go right again onto First Street.*

If you want a splendid dining view of the San Diego skyline, this is the place. Sitting at the edge of the water on Coronado—partially on a dock, in fact—Peohe's has a great downtown vista. Even with the nice view, the restaurant is curiously overdressed, regaling its patrons with fake rocks, indoor palm trees and waterfalls. Despite its touristy décor, Peohe's is a serious seafood restaurant, earning high marks from local critics, and it's on our Top Ten Seafood list in Chapter Three, page 60.

9 *TOP O' THE COVE* • *1216 Prospect St., La Jolla; (858) 454-7779. French-continental; full bar service. Lunch and dinner daily. Major credit cards; $$$$. GETTING THERE: This is one of several restaurants in downtown La Jolla Cove that overlooks the cove.*

Although the view from here is splendid, you may find yourself distracted by the fine old European décor. It's much more opulent than the restaurant's name suggests, with fabric booths, candlelit tables and wood paneling graced by classical art. There is that view, however, and the dining room is terraced to maximize it. Several tables sit before window walls and if you call far enough ahead, the maitre d' will reserve one for you. The fare is mostly French, with a few continental variations and an occasional contemporary American touch. Although the menu changes, you might encounter pan-seared tuna with soy wasabe vinaigrette, medallions of elk with Pinot Noir shallot sauce, tenderloin of beef with green peppercorn cognac and cream sauce over herb fettuccine, and filet mignon with Burgundy wine sauce and smoked bacon. The restaurant has an outstanding wine cellar.

10 *TRATTORIA ACQUA* • *1298 Prospect St., La Jolla; (858) 454-0709. Italian and seafood; full bar service. Lunch weekdays, weekend brunch and dinner nightly. Major credit cards; $$ to $$$. GETTING THERE: Acqua is in the Coastwalk above La Jolla Cove.*

This establishment boasts of "Italian cuisine with a Mediterranean view." The best vantage point is a covered terrace perched just above La Jolla Cove. Interior views through window walls are nice as well. Trattoria Acqua doesn't rest on its vista laurels; it recently was voted the best San Diego Italian restaurant. With this imposing view, you can partake of jumbo shrimp scampi, osso buco, or a seafood pasta of shrimp, mussels, clams and calimari over black and white linguine. You also can get order interesting designer pizzas.

Being poor is no disgrace, but it's no great honor, either.   —**Will Rogers**

Chapter five

PROUD PAUPERS
A BUDGET GUIDE

San Diego is relatively inexpensive when compared with other major California cities such as San Francisco and Los Angeles. It's currently suffering a surplus of hotel and resort rooms, so you can find some good buys. However, the better hotels and resorts still go for well over $100 a night, and entrées at the finer restaurant are in the high teens to twenties.

This chapter is for folks on a budget, who are seeking out the *really* inexpensive places to play, dine and sleep. It begins with freebies—the city's Ten Best attractions that cost not a penny.

FRUGAL FUN: THE TEN BEST FREE ATTRACTIONS

Who says you can't get something for nothing? Some of San Diego's best lures are free—notably Old Town State Historic Park, several attractions at Balboa Park, and that great aquatic playground called Mission Bay.

1 **BALBOA PARK** • *The park Visitor Center is in the northwest corner of the House of Hospitality, off Plaza de Panama, across from the San Diego Museum of Art; (619) 239-0512. GETTING THERE: Take the Laurel Street exit from I-5 and go uphill, or go north on Fifth Avenue from downtown and turn right onto Laurel, which becomes El Prado (The Promenade) as it enters the park.*

Balboa Park is home to most of the city's museums and the world famous San Diego Zoo, and we reviewed these in detail in Chapter Two. Although these places have admission fees, you can have a great day in Balboa Park without a cent in your Levi's. Not only are the lawns, the lush landscaping, the play areas and picnic areas free, so are many of its attractions.

Our favorite freebie is the Botanical Building at 1550 El Prado; (619) 235-1110 or 235-1122. It's open daily except Thursday 10 to 4; with free horticultural tours Saturdays at 10. Created for the 1915 Panama-California International Exposition, this large domed building is constructed entirely of redwood laths. We like to relax on a bench beside a trickling garden fountain and admire the more than 500 tropical plants inside this imposing structure. It is impressive outside as well, fronted by a reflection pond whose reflections are roiled by a flotilla of happy ducks. (It's supposed to be a lily pond, although ducks greatly outnumber the pads.)

If you like art, stop by the excellent Timken Museum of Art at 1500 El Prado; (619) 239-5548. Hours are Tuesday-Saturday 10 to 4:30 and Sunday 1 to 4:30; closed Mondays and the month of September. It's not only one of San Diego's better art museums, it's free. While the collection is small, it's versatile, including select works of European masters and noted American artists, plus a large exhibit of Russian religious icons. For more on the museum, see Chapter Two, page 36.

Also free are the park's five formal gardens. The best of these are Alcazar Garden, off El Prado and adjacent to the Mingei International Museum; and the Japanese Friendship Garden at 2215 Pan American Road. Entertainment is gratis in Balboa Park as well. Catch one of the organ concerts at the Spreckels Organ Pavilion at 2211 Pan American Road, every Sunday from 2 to 3, plus Monday evenings at 8 in July and August; see details below. Finally, you can even get around this huge 1,400-acre park at no cost. A tram hauls visitors to key spots throughout the grounds, daily from 9 to 5:15. Pick up a park map marked with tram stops at the Visitor Center.

2 **BELMONT PARK** • *3146 Mission Blvd. (at Mission Bay Drive) in Mission Beach; (619) 491-2988. Park open all day. Rides operate Sunday-Thursday 11 to 10 and Friday-Saturday 11 to 11 in summer, then Sunday-Thursday 11 to 5 and Friday-Saturday 11 to 9 the* *rest of the year. Grounds admission free; various prices for rides. GET-TING THERE: Take I-8 west to Mission Bay Park and follow West Mission Bay Drive through the park to Mission Beach; it blends into Ventura Place at the amusement center's parking lot.*

Although there are modest fees for the rides—ticket books are available at a booth near the roller coaster—it costs nothing to stroll about the grounds of this fine old beachside amusement park. Also free are wrought iron tables and chairs where you can sit in the sun and watch others stroll about, while listening to the riders scream on the Giant Dipper. One of the few beachside amusement zones left on the West Coast, Belmont Park was built by sugar magnate John D. Spreckels in 1925 as the New Mission Beach Amusement Center. It's owned and operated by the City of San Diego and it was completely renovated in the late 1980s.

3 **CHICANO PARK** • *Beneath the San Diego anchorage of the San Diego-Coronado Bay Bridge. GETTING THERE: Follow Harbor Drive from the Embarcadero to the bridge anchorage and turn left up Crosby Street, then right onto Newton Avenue.*

Well of course parks are free, although this one's different. It's a virtual outdoor museum of brilliantly colored murals done by San Diego's Hispanic community. When the San Diego-Coronado Bay Bridge was built in the 1960s, its stanchions were planted smack dab in the middle of the Barrio Logan, one of the city's older Mexican neighborhoods. Since several homes had to be uprooted, residents worked with the city to create a park around this anchorage. Through the years, community artists have been covering the stanchions with murals. Subjects range from historic Mayan scenes to contemporary lifestyles to political commentary. You'll also see some large murals on a couple of buildings at the corner of Harbor Drive and Crosby Street.

4 **HERITAGE PARK** • *Harney and San Juan streets; (619) 694-3049. GETTING THERE: The park is immediately northeast of Old Town State Historic Park.*

This eight-acre park on an upslope above Old Town preserves seven historic buildings that were disassembled and moved here to save them from demolition. All have been immaculately restored and the park is operated by the San Diego County Department of Parks and Recreation. Buildings include a modest 1896 cottage, an Eastlake style home built in 1887, the Italianate style Bushyhead House owned by a founder of the *San Diego Union,* the 1889 Temple Beth Israel, and an 1889 Queen Anne Victorian.

Although not all the buildings are open to the public, they can be admired and photographed from the outside. Temple Beth Israel is open to visitors and the 1889 Queen Anne is now a bed & breakfast inn; see Chapter Six, page 110. One of the structures, the 1893 Victorian revival Burton House, has a gift shop and coffee parlor.

5 *LA JOLLA COVE and ELLEN BROWNING SCRIPPS PARK* • *Off Coast Boulevard in downtown La Jolla. GETTING THERE: As you approach downtown La Jolla from San Diego on Prospect Street, fork to the left onto Coast Boulevard.*

When we asked our El Cajon friends Larry and Sharon Ihle to recommend the best free attractions in the San Diego area, La Jolla Cove was at the top of their list. And why not? The cove is a wave-sculpted enclave just below this upscale community's downtown area. The air and the sea are free, and so is the small beach tucked into the cove's wind-and-wave-sculpted sandstone bluffs. It's popular for snorkeling and skindiving, although the water can get rough outside the cove's shelter. The small Ellen Browning Scripps Park, a patch of green covering the cove's low headland, is one of the prettiest little city parks in California. It's decorated by several trees that have been twisted by the wind into giant bonsai. Benches and picnic tables invite one to linger and admire this most dramatic of coastal vistas.

Just north of the cove and the park are the **La Jolla Caves**. These small grottoes can be reached via a wooden stairway. There's a modest admission charge, collected at an adjacent shell shop. (However, the shop was closed when we last passed through.)

6 *MARINE CORPS RECRUIT DEPOT AND MUSEUM* • *Between the Pacific Highway and San Diego International Airport. Museum hours are Monday-Wednesday and Friday 8 to 4, Thursday 8 to 5, Saturday noon to 4; closed Sunday; (619) 524-6038. Visitors can pick up a walking tour map of the base at the museum. GETTING THERE: Take the Pacific Highway northwest from downtown and follow signs indicating the Marine base and museum; entry is through Gate Four and the museum is just ahead and on the right.*

A military base may seem an odd choice as a free tourist attraction, although this one is quite interesting, and it's open to the public. It's the oldest Marine Corps installation in western America, dating from 1911, and many of its mustard colored Spanish colonial style buildings are listed on the National Register of Historic Places. They were designed by Bertram Grosvenor Goodhue, who also fashioned the structures for San Diego's 1915 Panama-California Exposition in Balboa Park. Particularly impressive is a half-mile-long arcade linking a series of Spanish style buildings along the huge parade ground.

Fans of military history and particularly former Marines will enjoy the large, professionally done museum on the east side of the parade ground. Displays concern the history of the Marine Corps in San Diego and the many wars in which Leathernecks have fought, from the American Revolution through Desert Storm. Exhibits include weapons, uniforms, dramatic combat photos and paintings, a World War I Ford ambulance and a classic Jeep used in World War II and the Korean Conflict. Particularly interesting is a small bronze three-dimensional replica of history's most famous combat photo—the Iwo Jima flag raising on Mount Suribachi during World War II. It was sculpted by Felix de Welden, who also created the larger-than-life version at Arlington National Cemetery in Washington, D.C.

7 *MISSION BAY PARK* • *Northwest of downtown above the I-5 and I-8 junctions; park headquarters is at 2581 Quivira Court; (619) 221-8900. GETTING THERE: Take Mission Bay exit from I-5 and go toward the ocean or follow I-8 west and take West Mission Bay Drive northwest.*

It costs nothing to enjoy the many miles of beaches, walking and biking trails and swimming bays in this 4,600-acre recreation area. Mission Bay was a swampland until reclamation began in the 1950s to create this fine aquatic park. Half the park is land—mostly landscaped—and the other half is water. Even with developments such as Sea World and several resort complexes, seventy-five percent of Mission Bay Park is open space. For more on this area, see Chapter Two, page 27.

8 *OCEAN FRONT WALK* • *Between Mission Beach and Pacific Beach. GETTING THERE: Drive through Mission Bay Park on West Mission Bay Drive; the route ends in Mission Bay at the corner of Mission Boulevard and Ventura Place.*

A three-mile-long promenade called Ocean Front Walk stretches along the Pacific shore between Mission Beach and Pacific Beach. It cuts a convenient concrete corridor between the sandy shore and beachfront homes, vacation rentals and businesses. On any sunny day, it offers the best free show in town. Like the more famous Venice boardwalk near Los Angeles, Ocean Front Walk is a pulsing parade of cyclists, rollerbladers and skaters, swimmers still wet from the surf, strollers and runners, and people who just like to hang out. On most summer days, several beach volleyball games will be underway, surfers will be lolling on their boards like lazy seals just offshore, couples with furrowed brows will sit with chess boards balanced on their knees and a few folks my be dancing to the music of a ghetto blaster.

9 *OLD TOWN SAN DIEGO STATE HISTORIC PARK* • *(619) 220-5422. Park visitor center and historic buildings open daily 10 to 5. Various hours for other Old Town facilities. GETTING THERE: Take the Old Town exit from I-5 or I-8 northwest of the city.*

This most historic section of San Diego deserves a spot on our list of frugal fun places, as well as earning a niche as one of the city's Ten

Best Attractions in Chapter Two, page 28. There is no park admission charge, and entry to the main museum and several historic buildings is free as well. One can spend many hours in this state park without spending a peso. Of course, if you do want to spend money, that's relatively easy. In addition to the historic exhibits, Old Town has a large shopping complex called Bazaar del Mundo, several restaurants and all sorts of specialty shops.

10 *SPRECKELS ORGAN PAVILION CONCERTS* • *In Balboa Park at 2211 Pan American Rd.; (619) 702-8138. Public concerts every Sunday from 2 to 3, plus Monday evening concerts at 8 in July and August. The pavilion also is used for special concerts. GETTING THERE: Take the Laurel Street exit from I-5 and go uphill, or go north on Fifth Avenue from downtown and turn right onto Laurel, which becomes El Prado (The Promenade) as it enters the park. The organ pavilion is just south of Plaza de Panama.*

When you hear this magnificent 4,500-pipe organ fill the air with music, you'll agree that it's one of San Diego's ten best free attractions. These pipes range from thirty-two feet long to the size of pencils. The world's largest organ, it was given to the city in late 1914 by two very sweet guys—sugar magnates Adolph and John Spreckels. It was used to open the Panama-California International Exposition the following year. The Pavilion is particularly impressive during the Christmas holidays when it becomes the site of a life-size Nativity scene, with special Yuletide concerts.

THE TEN BEST CHEAP EATS

We define "cheap eats" as places where you can get a filling entrée and at least one side dish—soup or salad—for less than $7.50. We're talking about dinner, not a light lunch. We do *not* include the popular franchise fast food joints, despite the fact that most of them can fill you up with greasy burgers and over-salted fries for well under our price ceiling. Eating at MacDonald's or Taco Bell isn't a dining experience; these places are more into marketing than offering healthy food to their customers. (I've never cared much for plastic dinosaurs or Beanie Babies with my meal.)

Most of our Ten Best selections are ethnic—particularly Asian. San Diego has dozens of simple Chinese, Thai and Vietnamese cafés where you can get a filling meal within our price limit. More than a dozen are in the "Asian Triangle" on Convoy Street between I-805 and Freeway 16; see page 95. Since most Asian restaurants are family owned, they can save on labor costs to keep prices down; daughter helps serve the customers before and after school while son sweats in the kitchen. However, our grand prize winner is a Mexican café, and it's a far cry from a basic smashed beans and rice place:

1 CHILANGO'S MEXICO CITY GRILL • *142 University Ave.;
(619) 294-8646. Mexican regional; no alcohol. Lunch and dinner daily.
No credit cards. GETTING THERE: It's in the Hillcrest District, between
Second and Third avenues.*

This tiny storefront café also earned a spot on our Ten Best Mexican Restaurants list in Chapter Three, page 64. It's a true rarity—an inexpensive diner that serves excellent food. It specializes in dishes with *poblana* sauce—a mix of six different chilies and molé. Five *poblana* dinner specials fit within our $7.50 limit and they include beans and rice with corn kernels, salsa and chips, hot tortillas and a drink. Another tasty and inexpensive item is *memelas*, a *masa* cake covered with chicken or pork and smothered with sauce. Our favorite is *pollo asado*—grilled chicken with *poblana*. Chilango's interior is spartan and cheerful with tile floors, warm orange walls and a few Mexican ornaments. It has eight tables inside and two on the sidewalk.

2 ALEXI'S GREEK CAFÉ • *3863 Fifth Avenue; (619) 297-1777. Greek; wine and beer. Lunch and dinner daily. Major credit cards.
GETTING THERE: It's between University and Robinson in the Hillcrest
District.*

Just the two of you? This small, tidy café serves a special dinner for two for under $12. The hearty meal includes chicken kabobs, *spanakopita*, *gyros*, soup, salad, fries and pita bread. Alexi also features daily specials within our $7.50 price range, such as meat loaf, stuffed cabbage rolls and chicken.

3 BALIAN'S CAFÉ • *1039 Fourth Ave.; (619) 238-4134.
Greek, Armenian and American. Lunch and dinner daily. MC/VISA. GETTING THERE: It's in the heart of downtown San Diego, between Broadway and C Street.*

This small multi-national walk-up features several special plates well within our range—chicken, *spanakopita*, *dolmas*, *moussaka*, *hummus* and combinations thereof. The entrées include pita bread and a Greek salad. All of this is served in a cozy if rather austere café with a few ethnic photos and the traditional blue and white colors of Greece.

4 CHINA KING • *1041 Fourth Ave.; (619) 233-3389. Chinese;
beer. Lunch and dinner daily. GETTING THERE: It's beside Balian's Café,
between Broadway and C Street.*

Most small Asian cafés can fill you up with a single entrée and a bowl of rice for less than $7.50. However, China King has a complete buffet for well under that price, both for lunch and dinner. Items may include sweet and sour pork, chicken, Shanghai egg rolls, wonton soup, broccoli beef, vegetarian chow mein, plus a salad bar and Jello for dessert. China King is a cavernous, old fashioned diner with rows of Naugahyde booths and spartan décor.

5 *DUMPLING INN* • *4619 Convoy St., Kearny Mesa; (619) 268-9638. Chinese and Korean; wine and beer. Lunch and dinner daily. MC/VISA. GETTING THERE: Follow Freeway 163 about eight miles north of downtown and go west on Balboa Street (State Route 274) about half a mile to Convoy Street. Turn right on Convoy and go right again into First Korean Market Center.*

The neighborhood we call the "Asian Triangle" is in a commercial area on Kearny Mesa north of the city, where you'll find more than a dozen Chinese, Japanese, Korean, Thai and Vietnamese restaurants. Many are quite inexpensive and most can fill you up within our price range. Our favorite is a cute little place with a mirrored wall, drop lamps and potted plants. Its "house specialty stir fries" are available either as typical mix-and-match entrées, or as one-item dinner–size servings with rice and tea. These are full meals and several—kung pao chicken, Szechuan pork and bean curd, and sweet and sour pork—are within our budget. For about the same price, you can get several meat, chicken or shrimp rice dishes as a small plate, with hot Korean kim-chee (pickled cabbage) for a side dish.

6 *LA SALSA MEXICAN GRILL* • *Several in the San Diego area, including 1360 Orange Avenue at Dana Place in Coronado, (619) 435-7778; Horton Plaza food court downtown, (619) 234-6906; at 8750 Genesee Avenue northwest of Freeway 163, (619) 455-7229; and 1010 University Avenue at Tenth, (619) 543-0777. Mexican; no alcohol. Lunch and dinner daily. MC/VISA.*

La Salsas aren't funky little family cafés. They're rather attractive franchise operations, and they are several cuts above Taco Bell. The food is cooked to order, and you can get five different combination meals for less than $7.50. They include black beans, rice, salad, chips and salsa. The choices include a pair of soft tacos, taquitos, quesadil-las, a burrito or pollo asado. For seasoning, you can select from five different salsas. Most of these cafés have tables inside and out.

7 *MRS. GOOCH'S* • *711 University Ave.; (619) 294-2800. Eclectic; wine and beer. Breakfast through late dinner daily. Major credit cards. GETTING THERE: It's in the Whole Foods Market at Seventh and University in the Hillcrest District.*

Part of the Whole Foods Market, yet operated as a separate café, Mrs. Gooch's is an appealing split-level place with cathedral ceilings, drop lamps and comfy booths. Its busy menu features specialty coffees, fruit smoothies and juices, Italian grilled sandwiches, rice bowls and rotisserie chicken. Not all of its offerings are bargain-priced although it features several full meals within our range. Among them are breast of chicken with two side dishes, rice bowl with meat, and a daily blue plate special, which is usually a meat dish with soup or salad.

8 *POINT LOMA SEAFOODS* • *2805 Emerson St.; (619) 223-1109. Wine and beer. Monday-Saturday 9 to 7 and Sunday noon to 7. No credit cards. GETTING THERE: Drive southeast on Rosecrans Street, turn left onto Emerson and follow it a few blocks to its terminus at the Municipal Sportfishing Pier.*

This place just keeps cropping up—as one of the Ten Best seafood venues, one of the Ten Best outdoor cafés and now as one of the ten cheapest places in town. Most of its seafood plates are within our price limit, and these include fries and coleslaw. Our favorite is fish and chips, with three large chunks of Alaskan cod cooked to order. Other choices include shrimp Louis, fish Louis and a fish taco plate with re-fried beans. Never mind that you dine with plastic forks and disposable plates; the food's fine and the views down here are great.

9 *SAFFRON* • *3731 India St.; (619) 574-0177. Thai; no alcohol. Lunch and dinner daily. MC/VISA. GETTING THERE: Saffron is part of the restaurant row at the northwest end of India Street. Take any of several off-ramps from parallel I-5 or follow one-way India from downtown. NOTE: Because it's one way, to return downtown you must continue on India to Washington, go left under the freeway and left again onto Kettner. There are several I-5 on-ramps along the way.*

This strung-out storefront café features a variety of grilled chicken dishes with salad and jasmine rice for well under our minimum. Among other inexpensive entrées are Muslim chicken curry with potatoes, roasted peanuts and jasmine rice; and chicken, beef or pork Thai soup with rice. Saffron is a simply attired, family-run place with indoor and outdoor tables.

10 *SOUP EXCHANGE* • *1840 Garnet Ave.; (619) 272-7766. American; wine and beer. Lunch and dinner daily. MC/VISA. GETTING THERE: Follow I-5 about four miles north of the I-8 interchange and take the Grand/Garnet Avenue exit, which puts you on Mission Bay Drive. Continue north just over half a mile on Mission Bay, turn left on Garnet and follow it a mile west. The Soup Exchange is in the Pacific Plaza II shopping complex, at Garnet and Lamont.*

This large, airy restaurant offers all-you-can eat lunch and dinner buffets. They're similar to those pigouts in Las Vegas casinos, although with fewer food choices. The dinner buffet pushes the upper limits of our $7.50 maximum and may exceed it by the time you arrive, but it's well worth the price, particularly for those with big appetites. A single fee gets you several hot dishes such as lemon pepper chicken and beef ribs, plus pizza, several kinds of soups and salads, bakery goods and other desserts, including soft ice cream. Beer and wine are available for an extra charge.

THE TEN BEST CHEAP SLEEPS

As our criteria for budget lodging, we sought motels with high season rates of $55 or less per couple. We chose only those that were well-maintained and clean, and in or near San Diego. (We didn't request freebies; we posed as innocent tourists and asked to inspect the rooms.) We found only a few suitable places in this price range that were close to the city. Of course, rooms are cheaper if you're willing to drive fifteen or more miles to the suburbs. Most of our selections are members of budget chains. Many of the independent motels we checked were rather scruffy, so we didn't select them.

Of course, these prices may be higher by the time you arrive. Also, room availability at the lowest rates may be limited, so make reservations as early as possible. The motels we chose are within a few minutes' drive of downtown, although you might want to avoid the morning and evening commute hours.

San Diego's main motel row is along El Cajon Boulevard between La Mesa and University Heights above Balboa Park. (The boulevard blends into Washington Street.) There's not a heavy concentration of lodgings along this route; many have closed during the past several years. The best motel seeking places these days are obvious—near freeway off-ramps.

1 GOOD NITE INN • *4545 Waring Rd., San Diego, CA 92120; (800) NITE INN or (619) 286-7000. GETTING THERE: Go east about seven miles on I-8 and take the Waring Road exit. It curls under the freeway and goes past the motel. To reach it, turn right at a stoplight at Adobe Falls Road and backtrack.*

This is the nicest of the budget motels we found in the immediate San Diego area. It has large comfortable rooms with TV movies, tables and desks, coin laundry and a pool. A restaurant called Patch's Sports Bar and Grill is adjacent. Good Nite In is a relatively new motel chain, with fourteen units in California.

2 AZTEC BUDGET INN • *6050 El Cajon Blvd., San Diego, CA 92115; (800) 225-9610 or (619) 582-1414. Major credit cards. GETTING THERE: Go east on I-8 about eight miles from the I-5 interchange, take College Avenue a mile and a half south to El Cajon Boulevard and turn right; the motel comes up shortly on your right.*

Aztec is an old fashion single-level Spanish style motel with fair-sized, nicely maintained rooms. They have cable TV, phones, small vanities and tables.

3 GOOD NITE INN • *255 Bay Blvd., Chula Vista, CA 91910; (800) NITE INN or (619) 425-8200. Major credit cards. GETTING THERE: Drive about seven miles south of downtown on I-5, take the E Street exit and go west briefly to Bay Boulevard.*

This is another unit of the new budget chain, with large rooms, phones, TV movies and a pool.

4 HARVEY'S TOUR INN MOTEL • *7166 El Cajon Blvd., San Diego, CA 92115; (619) 463-5700. MC/VISA. Major credit cards. GETTING THERE: Go about nine miles east on I-8, take the Lake Murray/70th Street exit and turn south on 70th. Go left on El Cajon Boulevard and the motel is two blocks away, on your left between 71st and 72nd.*

This small independently-owned motel is quite nice, with fair-sized rooms, phones, TV and a swimming pool. Some units have small refrigerators and microwaves.

5 THE INN AT THE YMCA • *500 W. Broadway, San Diego, CA 92101; (619) 234-5252. MC/VISA. GETTING THERE: The "Y" is on lower Broadway, between India and Columbia streets.*

Forget your images of grim old YMCAs. Although it has dates from 1924, the Spanish colonial style Army-Navy YMCA has been spruced up and offers clean rooms at quite modest prices. It's run by a local group called Barone Galasso & Associates, which specializes in affordable housing. Rooms have TV and comfortable beds; none have private baths although some have sinks. Amenities—if we may use that word—include a laundry, barbershop, heated indoor pool and sauna. An adjacent modest-priced restaurant called Grand Central Café is open from breakfast through lunch. The "Y's" biggest plus is its location in the heart of downtown, and many rooms have views.

6 LAMPLIGHTER INN • *6474 El Cajon Blvd., San Diego, CA 92115-2645; (800) 545-0778 or (619) 582-3088. Major credit cards. GETTING THERE: Go east on I-8 about eight miles, take College Avenue a mile and a half south to El Cajon Boulevard and turn left. The motel is about half a mile east, on the left, opposite Seminole Drive.*

This AAA-rated motel has a few rooms under $55 in summer, although most are slightly above. It has TV movies, desks and phones, and a swimming pool.

7 **MOTEL 6** • *7621 Alvarado Rd., La Mesa, CA 91941; (800) 4-MOTEL 6 or (619) 464-7151. WEB SITE: motel6.com. Major credit cards. GETTING THERE: Drive about ten miles east on I-8, take the Fletcher Parkway exit and turn right. If you're westbound, take the 70th Street exit, turn left and left again onto Alvarado Road and go east less than a mile.*

This 51-unit Motel 6 has clean, basic rooms with TV movies and phones. The chain also has motels at 2424 Hotel Circle North near the I-8/I5 junction, (619) 296-1612; and near downtown at 1546 Second Avenue between Beech and Cedar (619) 236-9292. However, these are a bit more than $55 per couple.

8 **SAN DIEGO HOSTELS** • *521 Market St., San Diego, CA 92101, (619) 525-1531; and 3790 Udall St., San Diego, CA 92107, (619) 223-4778. GETTING THERE: The downtown hostel is in Gaslamp Quarter at the corner of Fifth and Market. The other is on Point Loma; follow I-8 to its western end, bear left onto Sunset Cliffs Drive, go left on Voltaire for about a mile (crossing over Nimitz Boulevard), then go right on Worden one block to Udall.*

These two American Youth Hostels offer the cheapest lodging in town, around $15 per person per night. The term "youth" is misleading. Folks of any age can and do stay at these places. They may be a little short on privacy since they're dorm style, although they're clean and well maintained.

9 **SUPER 8 MOTEL** • *4540 Mission Bay Dr., San Diego, CA 92109; (800) 800-8000 or (619) 247-7880. Major credit cards. GETTING THERE: From southbound I-5, take the Grand/Garnet Avenue exit and continue south through four signals; the motel is on the right. Northbound on I-5, take the Grand/Garnet exit and go straight through two signals; it's on the left.*

Rates were nudging our $55 limit when we last checked this motel, although it's in a good location, near Mission Bay Park and Mission Beach. The 116-unit facility has TV movies and room phones, a pool and airport courtesy van. Rates include continental breakfast.

10 **SUPER 8 MOTEL** • *425 Roosevelt Ave., National City, CA 91950; (800) 800-8000 or (619) 474-8811. Major credit cards. GETTING THERE: Drive about four miles south of downtown San Diego on I-5, take the Main Street/National City Boulevard exit, turn left under the freeway then make an immediate right onto Roosevelt.*

This 59-unit motel has a pool and spa, and fair-sized rooms with phones and TVs. Some have microwaves and small refrigerators.

A great hotel is like a duck swimming—composed and serene above the water, but paddling like hell underneath — **Hotel executive Tim Carlson**

Chapter six

PILLOW TALK
LISTS OF BEST LODGINGS

This book isn't intended to be a detailed lodging guide; there is an abundance of such publications available. However, in keeping with our Ten Best theme, we have selected some of San Diego's more impressive places of repose—its most elegant hotels, most expansive resorts and coziest bed & breakfast inns.

With such selections, this obviously isn't a budget directory. For that, you'll need to retreat to the previous chapter. Since our choices are primarily in the luxury category, most rooms are $100 per night or more. We use dollar-sign codes to indicate price ranges, based on summer rates: *$* = a standard two-person room for $99 or less; *$$* = $100 to $149; *$$$* = $150 to $199; and *$$$$* = $200 or more.

This city of sunshine, which draws more than fourteen million visitors a year, is noted for its seaside and bayside resorts. It also has several first class hotels downtown, such as the opulent Westgate, Wyndham Emerald Plaza and the historic U.S. Grant. Then of course, there are properties that cross the line, functioning both as resorts and business hotels. The Marriott and Hyatt Regency near the bayfront come to mind. Both are highrises near the convention center, popular with business travelers, so we've placed them in our hotel category, although they certainly have extensive resort amenities.

THE TEN BEST RESORTS

Most San Diego-area resorts are on Coronado, Mission Bay, Harbor and Shelter Islands, in La Jolla and inland in Mission Valley.

1 *HOTEL DEL CORONADO • 1500 Orange Ave., Coronado, CA 92118; (800) 468-8262 or (619) 435-6611. WEBSITE: www.hoteldel.com. Luxury resort with 692 rooms, several restaurants, pool, spa, sauna, tennis courts, gift shop and other amenities. Major credit cards; $$$. GETTING THERE: Cross the Coronado Bridge from San Diego, turn left onto Orange Avenue and follow it a little more than a mile.*

The great red-roofed "Del" has been an institution since it opened in 1888, and it still draws the rich and famous, and anyone who can afford room rates starting around $200 per couple. It is the complete retreat, with twenty-six acres of lushly landscaped grounds, several restaurants, a fitness center, shops, tennis courts, a large swimming complex and a great sandy ocean beach adjacent. (See separate Prince of Wales restaurant review in Chapter Three, page 53.) The Del even has its own history gallery, and guided docent tours can be arranged through the concierge.

If this grand dame of resorts doesn't show her age, it's because she's had frequent face lifts. Wooden structures—and this is one of the world's largest—require a lot of upkeep. Lowe Enterprises, which bought the property in 1997, is investing $50 million in renovation. Midwest businessmen Elisha Babcock and H.L. Story spent only a million to build and furnish the hotel more than a century ago. Their opulent beach hideaway became a quick hit. Through the decades, the Del has hosted fourteen U.S. presidents, celebrities such as Charles Lindbergh, the Duke of Windsor and *The Wizard of Oz* author Frank Baum, who supposedly patterned his Emerald City after the hotel. Dozens of movies and TV shows have been filmed here, from *Some Like It Hot* with Marilyn Monroe to *Baywatch*. *Gourmet* magazine recently listed Hotel del Coronado as one of the top five resorts in America.

2 *CORONADO ISLAND MARRIOTT RESORT • 2000 Second St., Coronado, CA 92118; (800) 228-9290 or (619) 435-3000. A full-service 300-unit resort; rooms have TV movies, refrigerators and microwaves. Facilities include three swimming pools, restaurant, bistro and bar, complete spa and tennis courts. GETTING THERE: Cross the Coronado bridge and take an immediate right onto Glorietta Boulevard; the resort is within half a mile at Second Street and Glorietta.*

This large, low-rise facility sprawls gently over several acres along the San Diego Bay side of the Coronado waterfront. Guests are greeted by a flock of flamingos strutting about a fountain pool at the entrance. Inside, the large lobby and room-width corridors and done in soft beige and peach, set off by wooden columns, with potted blooming ginger plants and modern art adding dashes of color. L'Escale Restaurant, overlooking a courtyard garden with San Diego Bay beyond, serves American and continental fare. For quick bites and live evening entertainment, pause at La Provence, a bistro and lounge off the lobby.

3 GLORIETTA BAY INN • *1630 Glorietta Blvd., Coronado, CA 92118; (800) 283-9383 or (619) 435-3101. A 100-unit resort with TV movies, refrigerators and data ports in the rooms. Guest facilities include a small pool, spa tub and coin laundry. MC/VISA, AMEX; $$$. GETTING THERE: Cross the bridge to Coronado, go left on Orange Avenue and follow it a bit more than a mile through downtown to Glorietta Boulevard; the inn is opposite Hotel del Coronado.*

Built in 1908 as the summer home of sugar baron John D. Spreckels, this Edwardian mansion has been fashioned into one of the area's coziest inns. We like its simple elegance, with muted colors, subtle Italian renaissance *rococo* accents and wicker lobby furniture. A bougainvillea-entwined arbor adds a splash of color to the nicely landscaped grounds. Several rooms and suites occupy the original mansion while others are in two-story wings. Most have patios or balconies and some have kitchen facilities.

4 HILTON AT JOLLA TORREY PINES • *10950 N. Torrey Pines Rd., La Jolla, CA 92037; (800) 762-6160 or (858) 558-1500. Low-rise resort with 400 large rooms and suites with TV movies, honor bars and data ports. The complex includes a workout room, sauna, night-lighted tennis courts and putting green. Torrey Pines Golf Course is adjacent. Major credit cards; $$$$ GETTING THERE: Take the Genesee exit from I-5 about eleven miles north of San Diego and go west about a half mile; the route curves to the right and becomes North Torrey Pines Road. Follow this another mile and turn left at Science Park Road into the hotel complex.*

The Hilton is in the Golden Triangle, a once thinly populated hilly area that has become home to the University of California, upscale residential and shopping areas and office towers. The hotel is in a particularly inviting spot, sitting above the famed Torrey Pines Golf Course and on the edge of the university campus. Approaching from North Torrey Pines Road, the low-rise resort is almost unnoticed. From the eighteenth fairway, however, it's a rather imposing terrace of luxury rooms bunkered into a hillside and cradling an attractive swimming complex. Virtually all the rooms have golf course views. Equally imposing is the view of the swimming pool and golf course from the curved, two-story lobby. The inviting Torreyana Grille downstairs from the lobby and above the pool complex serves upscale American-continental fare, while lighter bites are available at a poolside café.

5 *HUMPHREY'S HALF MOON INN & SUITES* • *2303 Shelter Island Dr., San Diego, CA 92106; (800) 345-9995 or (619) 224-3411. Low-rise tropical resort with 182 rooms and suites, swimming pool and spa. Units have TV movies and refrigerators. Humphrey's Restaurant featured in Chapter Three, page 56. Major credit cards; $$$. Rates include continental breakfast. GETTING THERE: To reach Shelter Island, head toward Point Loma on Rosecrans Street (State Route 209) and turn left onto Shelter Island Drive. Humphrey's is opposite a traffic circle.*

This Polynesian style facility is our favorite among the Shelter Island hideaways. The two-story residence wings enclose a large, nicely landscaped pool area, providing a feeling of isolation on the busy island. The poolside bar is a great place to relax, drink in hand, and listen to piped in music that successfully mutes the air traffic from nearby San Diego International Airport. Many rooms and suites—cheerfully furnished in bright Polynesian prints—have patios on the pool complex. One side of the pool garden area opens onto one of Shelter Island's marinas.

6 *LOEWS CORONADO BAY RESORT* • *4000 Coronado Bay Rd., San Diego, CA 92118; (800) 815-6397 or (619) 424-4000. A 438-room facility with two restaurants, lounges, pool, spa, sauna and other amenities. Major credit cards; $$$$. GETTING THERE: Loews is about five miles south of downtown Coronado on Silver Strand, opposite Silver Strand State Beach.*

Loews occupies its own personal peninsula on the bay side of Silver Strand, opposite a marina and upscale waterfront complex called Coronado Keys. It's a sleekly modern resort with a Spanish-California look. The lofty lobby is accented by a sweeping dual stairway that leads to a mezzanine level and the resort's highly regarded Azzura Point restaurant (reviewed in Chapter Three, page 50). An alcove on the mezzanine is a nice place to relax and admire the view of San Diego Bay and the distant city skyline. Loews has a large landscaped swimming complex, plus hot tubs and saunas. Particularly appealing is the gift shop area off the main lobby, fashioned as a country market, with specialty foods in addition to giftwares. It leads to a casual café that's open for breakfast through dinner.

7 *SAN DIEGO HILTON BEACH & TENNIS RESORT* • *1775 E. Mission Bay Dr., San Diego, CA 92109; (800) 221-2424 or (619) 276-4010. WEB SITE: www.hilton.com. A high-rise facility on eighteen acres of waterfront in Mission Bay Park with 357 rooms, tennis courts, a* boat dock and marina, main swimming pool and kids' wading pool, full service spa and three restaurants. Major credit cards; $$$$. GETTING THERE: The Hilton is on the east side of Mission Bay Park. To reach it, take the East Mission Bay Drive exit from I-5. Or follow Sea World Drive to East Mission Bay Drive if you're coming from the Point Loma area.

Fashioned as a Mediterranean style retreat with imposing columns, orange tile roofs and Spanish tile accents, the Hilton is Mission Bay's most attractive resort. Accommodations include bungalows with patios and tower rooms with view balconies. The Hilton has a single large swimming pool and it's an impressive one—the focal point of a landscaped complex with rock gardens, cascading waterfalls and trees. A Mission Bay beach walk is just beyond. At the hotel marina, a little paddlewheeler called the *Hilton Queen* takes periodic cruises about the bay. For dining, the Hilton offers Cavatappi, serving Italian fare; Café Picante, with dining indoors and out, featuring Southwest décor and entrées; and the poolside Banana Cabana. (To rhyme, it should be spelled Banaña Cabaña.)

8 SAN DIEGO PARADISE POINT RESORT ● *1404 W. Vacation Rd., San Diego, CA 92109; (800) 344-2626 or (619) 274-4630. WEB SITE: www.paradisepoint.com. A low-rise resort in Mission Bay Park with rooms and bungalows, including some studios and kitchen units. Facilities include an elaborate lagoon complex, six swimming areas, tennis courts, 18-hole putting course, fitness center, marina with boat rentals and three restaurants. Major credit cards; $$. GETTING THERE: The resort occupies Vacation Isle in the middle of Mission Bay Park. To reach it, take Ingraham Street through Mission Bay and turn west onto Vacation Road.*

The most striking feature of this 44-acre facility is a meandering lagoon complex with islands, fountains, lush landscaping and swimming pools. The main pool, off a large fitness center, has lap lines for those serious about working out in the water. For a great view of this facility, and of the entire San Diego countryside, climb eighty-one steps up an observation tower beside the lagoon. The resort's main restaurant, Café Aqua, has a tropical-nautical look with turquoise and salmon décor and a high ceiling held up by *faux* pier-piling posts. In serves American entrées, plus lighter fare such as pizzas and sandwiches. A gazebo off the main dining area is a cozy place to eat, with views of the lagoon.

9 SHELTER POINTE HOTEL & MARINA ● *1551 Shelter Dr., San Diego, CA 92106; (800) 566-2524 or (619) 221-8000. Low-rise 206-unit resort with two pools, spa, tennis courts, fitness center, restaurant and lounge. Major credit cards; $$. GETTING THERE: Take Rosecrans Street (State Route 209) south on Point Loma to Shelter Island Drive and turn right; the resort is about a mile down the island.*

This Spanish style complex is one of the more affordable full service retreats in the San Diego Area. It provides easy access to the island's walking and biking trails, fishing pier and its many restaurants. Boaters will like this place, since it borders Marina Kona Kai, with more than 500 slips and a large guest dock. Two-story lodging wings are built around a nicely landscaped courtyard, creating an appealing and quite retreat. The courtyard's pool deck is open to the marina. AJ's American Grill is a spacious, circular restaurant with a marina view, serving what the chef describes as "bold American food," another way of saying American *nouveau*.

10 TOWN AND COUNTRY RESORT AND CONVENTION CENTER

● *500 Hotel Circle North, San Diego, CA 92108; (800) 77-ATLAS or (619) 291-7131. Large 964-unit facility with nicely decorated rooms, four swimming pools, spas, five restaurants and other amenities. Major credit cards; $$. GETTING THERE: From either direction on I-8, take the Hotel Circle North exit; the hotel is just east of the River Walk Golf Course.*

Mission Valley has been home to several vacation retreats for decades although many are now outclassed by glitzier new resorts elsewhere. However, the well-maintained Town and Country has kept pace, and it's less expensive than most of the newer properties. Spread over thirty-two landscaped acres, it's one of the city's largest resorts, with nearly a thousand rooms and suites. Some are in a low-rise garden area and others occupy a new highrise.

Dining options include the Trellises, an indoor-outdoor garden grill serving California *nouveau* fare, Kelly's Steakhouse, Lanai Coffee Shop and Sunshine Deli. We like Town and Country's location, within walking distance of San Diego's light rail system and Fashion Valley mall. A pedestrian bridge across what's left of the San Diego River links the hotel to both.

THE TEN BEST HOTELS

Most of San Diego's finest hotels are focused in the downtown area and the adjacent waterfront. They range from the stylish new highrise Marriott and Hyatt to historic hostelries that speak of a gentler era.

1 WESTGATE HOTEL SAN DIEGO

● *1055 Second Ave., San Diego, CA 92101; (800) 221-3802 or (619) 238-1818. WEBSITE: www.westgateotel.com. Downtown hotel with 223 rooms and suites, two dining rooms and cocktail lounges, gourmet shop, health club and complimentary transportation. All rooms have TV/VCRs and refrigerators. Le Fontainebleau is reviewed in Chapter Three, page 52. GETTING THERE: The Westgate is just off lower Broadway in the heart of downtown.*

Although the Westgate doesn't have an imposing exterior—looking more like an apartment building than a hotel—it's stunning within. Step into the lobby and you may think you've entered the Palace of Versailles, with its Baccarat crystal chandeliers, Flemish and French tapestries, scalloped drapes, Persian carpets and European antique furnishings. Le Fontainebleau on the mezzanine level is perhaps the city's most opulent restaurant. Equally ornate although smaller and thus cozier is the Westgate Room restaurant to the rear of the ground floor lobby; see Chapter Nine, page 141. Across the corridor, the Plaza Bar is an elegant French Provincial style retreat with beaded chandeliers, wall sconces, tapestries and a black marble bartop.

2 *HORTON GRAND HOTEL* • *311 Island Ave., San Diego, CA 92101; (800) 542-1886 or (619) 544-1886. WEB SITE: www.horton-grand.com. Victorian style hotel with 132 individually decorated rooms and suites, plus a lobby bar and restaurant. Major credit cards; $$. GETTING THERE: The hotel is in Gaslamp Quarter, between Third and Fourth avenues.*

This wonderfully elegant brick hotel with its elaborate carved wood bay windows appears to have been in Gaslamp Quarter for more than a century. It's actually a skillful merger of two 1890s hotels that were disassembled and reconstructed here in 1986—the Grand Hotel and the Brooklyn, where famous lawman Wyatt Earp once stayed. The Horton is the most attractive Victorian style hotel in San Diego. Step inside its lush filigreed lobby and admire the print wallpaper and matching upholstered chairs, the wainscotting, Tiffany style lamps and white wicker furniture. This is a virtual museum, with historic photos on the walls and assorted artifacts from the past. They include a 17th century Chinese sedan chair (since Chinatown once occupied this area), and a full-sized *papier mache* horse with a saddle that was made by the Kahle Saddlery, which was on the ground floor of the Brooklyn Hotel. The Horton's central courtyard is particularly appealing—a landscaped Victorian garden with white wrought iron chairs, umbrella tables and white miniature lights that add evening sparkle. Back inside, Ida Bailey's Restaurant and the cozy Palace Bar continue the Victorian theme, with wainscotting, print wallpaper and—in the Palace—a daring nude painting. However, the bar does make one concession to the present—a large screen TV set.

3 *HYATT REGENCY LA JOLLA* • *3777 La Jolla Village Dr., La Jolla, CA 92122; (800) 233-1234 or (619) 552-1234. Stylish sixteen-story hotel with 419 rooms and suites; swim complex, pool and sauna, tennis courts and gift shop. Major credit cards; $$$$. GETTING THERE: Drive about nine miles north of San Diego on I-5, take the La Jolla Village Drive exit, go east through the first traffic light, then turn right and uphill into the hotel complex.*

Towering high above the Golden Triangle, the Hyatt Regency is a post-modern creation with a curving roof that suggests a highrise airplane hangar. Inside, however, you'll encounter the typical marble-clad Hyatt Regency elegance, done here in a Roman theme, with several statues gracing the upper lobby. In the more dramatic lower lobby with an atrium ceiling, a marbled Poseidon points the way to the large swimming pool and a huge health spa called the Sporting Club. Diners can choose from the Barcino Grill off the lower lobby, with California fare; Michael's, a clubby lounge with light fare; and Japengo, serving Asia-Pacific cuisine.

Opposite the Hyatt's courtyard is the Aventine, an upscale shopping and dining area.

4 *HYATT REGENCY SAN DIEGO* • *1 Market Place, San Diego, CA 92101; (800) 233-1234 or (619) 232-1234. Luxury highrise hotel with 875 rooms and suites, two restaurants, pool and outdoor spa, sauna, steam room, health club, tennis courts and business center. Sally's Restaurant listed in Chapter Three, page 61. Major credit cards; $$$$. GETTING THERE: The Regency is adjacent to Seaport Village just off Harbor Drive.*

One of the tallest buildings in San Diego, the Hyatt is a bit austere from the outside, with its offset square towers that taper to a peak. However, it's quite appealing from within, featuring a three-story lobby and an airy European-California décor. Spacious corridors, serving almost as extensions of the main lobby, offer comfortable seating areas, bars and shops. For more shopping, one merely continues out the hotel's harbor side to adjacent Seaport Village. The Hyatt provides stellar views of city and waterfront, particularly from its fortieth-floor Top of the Hyatt and—for those who just want a brief look—the elevator lobby View Lounge. The hotel is popular with traveling professionals, featuring a large business complex, in-room FAX machines and computer modems.

5 *LA VALENCIA HOTEL* • *1132 Prospect St., La Jolla, CA 92037; (800) 451-0772 or (858) 454-0771. Historic hotel with 100 rooms and suites, two restaurants, pool, spa and sauna. Major credit cards; $$$$. GETTING THERE: La Valencia is in downtown La Jolla, between Herschel and Ivanhoe streets.*

Anyone who has ever driven through La Jolla will recognize La Valencia as that wonderful pink stucco and tile-roofed building with a Moorish dome. It has been a landmark since 1928 and renovations through the decades have kept it impeccably maintained. La Valencia is pure delight—an old world retreat in the heart of La Jolla's shopping and dining district. Walk past the Mediterranean colonnade into the lobby and you've slipped from one world into another. There is a hushed elegance about this place, with its warm décor, monumental ceiling beams and corbels, Spanish mosaics, wrought iron crown chandeliers and its tasteful yet cheerful floral fabric furnishings. Rooms are large and luxurious and most have ocean views. Dining options include the landscaped outdoor Tropical Patio and the Mediterranean Room with views of the Pacific. The Whaling Bar, off the lobby, is an enticing clubby retreat, with dark woods and rose carpeting.

6 *MARRIOTT SAN DIEGO MARINA* • *333 W. Harbor Dr., San Diego, CA 92101; (800) 228-9290 or (619) 234-1500. WEBSITE: www.sdmarriott.com. Downtown hotel with 1,354 rooms, six restaurants, a marina, fitness center, shops and other amenities. Major credit cards; $$$$. GETTING THERE: The Marriott is on the waterfront at Harbor and Front Street.*

This is the most striking structure in San Diego—twin towers of glittering glass rising above the waterfront. One is oval and the other is concave, as if they were once joined and then drifted apart, like the continents of Africa and South America. All guest rooms have views either of the bay or city and many have balconies. Despite its striking exterior, the lobby is surprisingly modest. The overall complex is quite extensive, with a large landscaped free-form pool, tennis courts, a shopping arcade and a harborside walk. Just beyond is the 446-slip Embarcadero Marina. The hotel is adjacent to the San Diego Convention Center.

7 *PACIFIC TERRACE HOTEL* • *610 Diamond St., Pacific Beach (San Diego), CA 92109; (800) 344-3370 or (619) 581-3500. WEB SITE: www.pacificterrace.com. Oceanfront hotel off the Pacific Beach promenade with seventy-three rooms, a swimming pool and spa. Major credit cards; $$$$. GETTING THERE: Pacific Terrace at Diamond and Mission Boulevard. From I-5, take the Grand/Garnet Avenue exit, which puts you on Mission Bay Drive. Continue north briefly and take either Grand or Garnet about two miles to Mission Boulevard and go north a few blocks to Diamond. From Mission Bay Park, take West Mission Bay Drive to Mission Beach, then follow Mission Boulevard north to Diamond.*

Although small, this is a particularly inviting hotel since it sits right on Ocean Front Walk, a beach promenade that stretches from Pacific Beach to Mission Beach. From poolside or from its west-facing rooms with their distinctive curved balconies, one can watch the passing parade on the promenade and see breakers rolling over the beach just beyond. Its public areas have a cheerful tropical floral décor, which carries into the large, beautifully decorated guest rooms. All units have refrigerators and many have spa tubs, bathroom TV sets and kitchen units. All have balconies and most face the beach.

8 *SHERATON SAN DIEGO HOTEL & MARINA* • *1380 Harbor Island Dr., San Diego, CA 92101-1093; (800) 325-3535 or (619) 692-2200. WEB SITE: www.sheraton.com/sandiegomarina. Highrise resort with 1,045 rooms featuring modern California décor, with TV movies, modems and other amenities. Facilities include a small boat dock, lighted tennis courts, pool, spa and three restaurants. Major credit cards; $$$$. GETTING THERE: The Sheraton is at the entrance to Harbor Island, which can be reached via Harbor Drive from downtown. Or take any airport exit from I-5, since Harbor Island is opposite San Diego International Airport.*

The twin towers of the Sheraton San Diego, one of the largest hotels in the area, dominate Harbor Island. Its rooms offer fine views of downtown, Point Loma, Coronado and much of the rest of the greater San Diego area. A second mid-rise tower is about half a mile farther west on Harbor Island. Called the West Tower, it's a former Ramada Inn. The main hotel's lobby is quite impressive, with huge columns supporting laminated curved wooden arches, marble floors and big planters. A large aquarium creates a nice backdrop for the concierge desk. Quinn's Mooring, a spacious nautical style lobby bar, overlooks the marina and pool at the rear of the complex. Spouting seahorse fountains help keep that pool filled. Harbor's Edge, the large main dining room, is laid out in a sweeping arc, with windows on Mission Bay; it serves contemporary American fare. The cute little Aroma Café serves light fare, and it has a couple of tables set up for computer internet access. Swimmers and sunbathers can get light bites at the cheerfully decorated Waterworks café.

9 *U.S. GRANT HOTEL* • *326 Broadway; (800) 237-5029 or (619) 232-3121. Historic 280-room downtown hotel with restaurants, fitness center and business center. The Grant Grill is listed in Chapter Three, page 51. GETTING THERE: The Grant is in the heart of downtown, bounded by Third and Fourth avenues.*

Although it could use a tuck here and there, San Diego's second most historic hotel—after the "Del"—deserves a spot in our Ten Best list. In an era when chrome and glass are the hallmarks of luxury hotels, we like this renaissance hostelry, with its imposing marble lobby with beaded chandeliers and warm wood paneling. The legendary Grant Grill and its adjacent bar have that proper clubby look. The hotel's exterior is federalist Gothic with square shoulders and four American flags fluttering in the breeze. A casual observer might mistake the Grant for a government building, until they step into that elegant lobby. And no, Ulysses S. Grant never slept here, although a dozen other presidents have, from Cleveland to Bush. When the hotel was built in 1910, one of the partners was President Grant's son, and he named it in honor of his father.

The old fashioned hotel has had to make some compromises in recent years. It gained national attention in 1967 when several local women staged a sit-in to protest its policy of excluding ladies from the Grant Grill until after 3 p.m. And currently, it suffers the indignity of having its front corners leased out to a Togo sandwich shop, Baskin Robbins and Bruegger's Bagels. Still, it remains a most elegant and peaceful retreat from the chaos of lower Broadway just outside—particularly when high tea is served in the afternoons.

10 *WYNDHAM EMERALD PLAZA HOTEL • 400 W. Broadway, San Diego, CA 92101-3505; (800) WYNDHAM or (619) 239-4500. WEB SITE: www.wyndham.com. A 436-room highrise hotel with TV, mini-bars, writing desks and other amenities. Facilities include a pool, spa, gift shop, guest laundry and two restaurants. Major credit cards; $$$. GETTING THERE: The Wyndham is on lower Broadway downtown, between State and Columbia streets.*

The Wyndham Emerald Plaza makes the most dramatic statement in the city's downtown skyline; it's a multi-terraced cluster of seven hexagonal glass towers. The hotel shares these imposing structures with a highrise office complex. If the Wyndham is striking in profile, it is equally dramatic from within, with the most impressive hotel lobby in San Diego. This seven-story skylighted atrium, with glass elevators clinging to its walls, is accented by monumental glass, plastic and brass hanging sculptures and beveled mirrors. Climb to the one of several terraced mezzanine levels for an imposing view back down to the lobby area. The Grill Restaurant, open to the lobby, features California cuisine while the Atrium Lounge lobby bar serves light fare. Jazz trios perform here on Friday and Saturday nights.

THE TEN BEST BED & BREAKFAST INNS

San Diego is not a major B&B venue. We found fewer than twenty listed, and some of these were individual rental cottages or single room units. We selected the ten best inns that have two or more guest rooms. Some are in fine old nineteenth century homes while others are in more contemporary structures, and one is a floating "boat and breakfast." Our top selection occupies a handsome Victorian mansion that was saved from the wrecker's ball and moved to Heritage Park near Old Town.

For a list of area B&B's, contact the Bed & Breakfast Directory for San Diego, P.O. Box 3292, San Diego, CA 92103; (619) 297-3130.

1 *HERITAGE PARK BED & BREAKFAST • Near Old Town at 2470 Heritage Park Row, San Diego, CA 92110; (800) 995-2470 or (619) 299-6832. WEB SITE: www.heritageparkinn.com; E-MAIL: inn-*

keeper@heritageparkinn.com. Twelve units with phones and private baths; full breakfast. Major credit cards; $$ to $$$$. GETTING THERE: The inn is part of Heritage Park, a collection of early San Diego buildings on an upslope just above Old Town State Historic Park.

This beautifully detailed Queen Anne Victorian with a distinctive corner tower was built in 1889 by wealthy businessman Harfield Timberlake Christian. Each of the twelve rooms and suites is individually decorated, featuring elaborate Victorian furnishings, although modern amenities such as showers and spa tubs have been added. A formal breakfast is served by candlelight, guests are invited to afternoon tea on the veranda and vintage films are shown each evening.

2 BEARS AT THE BEACH BED & BREAKFAST • *1047 Grand Ave., San Diego (Pacific Beach), CA 92109; (619) 272-2578. Two units with TVs; one private and one adjacent bath; full breakfast. $. GETTING THERE: Take the Grand/Garnet Avenue exit from I-5, continue north half a mile on Mission Bay Drive, then go left on Grand for about two miles. The inn is between Dawes and Cass streets.*

These beach bears live in a modest, affordable B&B about four short blocks from the ocean. Several stuffed Teddies serve as a decorator theme in this comfortable 1950s cottage, sharing the place with wicker furniture and ceiling fans. The sounds of adjacent Grand Avenue are muted by a walled garden, where breakfast, and afternoon and evening snacks are served on warm days.

3 BED & BREAKFAST INN AT LA JOLLA • *7753 Draper Ave., La Jolla, CA 92037; (800) 582-2466 or (858) 456-2066. WEB SITE: www.innlajolla.com. Fifteen units with phones and private baths; some room TVs; full breakfast. MC/VISA, AMEX. $$ to $$$$. GETTING THERE: The inn is near downtown La Jolla, at the corner of Draper and Prospect.*

This opulent inn, housed in a 1913 mansion and an annex, is furnished with Victorian and American antiques. Some rooms have ocean views, fireplaces and mini-bars. Breakfast and afternoon wine and cheese are served in a dining area, or on a patio or sun deck. The inn is within a short walk of tennis courts, La Jolla Cove, the Museum of Contemporary Art and downtown La Jolla shops and restaurants.

4 BLOM HOUSE BED & BREAKFAST • *1372 Minden Dr., San Diego, CA 92111; (800) 797-2566 or (619) 467-0890. Two rooms and a two-bedroom suite, with private baths; full breakfast. $. GETTING THERE: Go north on Freeway 163, cross I-8 and take Friars Road briefly west. Head north about a quarter of a mile on Ulric Street, then turn right onto Lindbrook Drive, right onto Babette Street and right again on Minden.*

This old fashioned cottage with high ceilings and hardwood floors has been nicely restored and furnished with antiques. Amenities include TV/VCRs, refrigerator and phones. The inn is located in a residential area on the upslope of Mission Valley, not far from the Fashion Valley mall.

5 *CAROLE'S BED & BREAKFAST • 3227 Grim Ave., San Diego, CA 92104; (800) 975-5521 or (619) 280-5258. Eleven units with TV and phones; some private and some shared baths; continental breakfast. Major credit cards; $; two-bedroom apartment $$$. GETTING THERE: Take I-805 north from downtown San Diego, go west on University Avenue five blocks to Grim, turn left and go south six blocks to Thorn Street. From I-5, take Pershing Drive northeast through the Balboa Park Golf Course, go east on Redwood Street for five blocks, then north on Grim for one block.*

Carole's inn occupies a turn-of-the-century Craftsman style home furnished with American antiques. It once was the abode of San Diego mayor Frank Frary. Amenities include a pool, spa and landscaped tropical and desert gardens. The inn is located in the North Park District, just to the east of Balboa Park.

6 *ELSBREE HOUSE BED & BREAKFAST • 5054 Narragansett Ave., San Diego, CA 92107; (619) 226-4133. Five rooms with private baths; continental breakfast. $ to $$; three-bedroom condo with kitchen $$$$. GETTING THERE: Follow I-8 to its western terminus then continue southwest onto Point Loma on Sunset Cliffs Boulevard. After a mile, turn right onto Narragansett, headed toward the ocean.*

This Cape Cod style inn is right at home in this attractive Point Loma residential area overlooking the Pacific Ocean; the beach is within half a block. The large, comfortable complex is done in oak and wicker, cheered by floral prints. Some of the units have private balconies or patios.

7 *HARBOR HILL GUEST HOUSE • 2330 Albatross St., San Diego, CA 92101; (619) 233-0638. Six units with private baths; carriage house with a kitchen; continental breakfast. MC/VISA; $. GETTING THERE: Take the Laurel Street exit from I-5, go uphill on Laurel about five blocks to Albatross, and go right for two blocks.*

Terraced into steep slopes below Balboa Park, this 1920s guest house offers fine views of San Diego Bay and surrounding neighborhoods. The three-level inn has kitchen facilities on each floor, and a sun deck and garden with bay vistas. Rooms have TV and phones and some have views. Furnishings are a comfortable mix of traditional contemporary.

8 *SAN DIEGO YACHT AND BREAKFAST CO.* • *1880 Harbor Island Dr., San Diego, CA 92101; (800) 922-4836 or (619) 297-9484. WEB SITE: www.yachtdo.com; E-MAIL: yachtdo@yachtdo.com. Six berthed yachts and harborside villas with phones, TV and private baths; full breakfast. Major credit cards; $$$$. GETTING THERE: The firm is at Marina Cortez on Harbor Island, off Harbor Drive opposite San Diego International Airport.*

Several fully furnished yachts are available as B&B rentals, along with two "villas"—floating dockside houses. Each has a main salon or living area, galley, staterooms, TV/VCRs and stereo units. They sleep from four to six. Adjacent facilities include a swimming pool, recreation areas, biking and walking paths and small boat rentals.

9 *SANDCASTLE BED & BREAKFAST* • *3880 Bayside Walk, Mission Beach, CA 92109; (619) 488-3880. WEB SITE: www.beachandbay.com. Two units with TV and private baths; continental breakfast. Major credit cards; $$. GETTING THERE: The home is on the shoreline of Mission Bay Park. Take West Mission Bay Drive through Mission Bay to Mission Beach, turn right (north) onto Mission Boulevard and follow it just over a mile to Vanitie Court, then go right again to Bayside Walk.*

This modern home on the Mission Beach sandspit between Mission Bay and the Pacific has been fashioned into a two-unit bed & breakfast. The Rooftop unit is on the third floor, with a large deck and impressive views of Mission Bay and the Pacific. The Garden suite is at ground level with a bay view garden deck and hammock; it has a living room and two sleeping areas.

10 *VILLA SERENA BED & BREAKFAST* • *In Point Loma at 2164 Rosecrans St., San Diego, CA 92106-1972; (800) 309-2778 or (619) 224-1451. WEB SITE: www.inn-guide.com/villaserena; E-MAIL: kschrei468@aol.com. Three units with private baths; full or expanded continental breakfast. MC/VISA, DISC; $$. GETTING THERE: Take the Rosecrans exit (State Route 209) from I-5 and drive about two miles out Point Loma; the inn is between Udall and Voltaire streets.*

Occupying a restored 1930s Italian walled villa with a courtyard, this B&B is on the Point Loma peninsula, within minutes of Shelter and Harbor islands and the airport. Two bedrooms are upstairs and can be converted into a family unit; a larger suite is on the ground floor, with a fireplace. Furnishings are a mix of rural Italian and contemporary American. A tropical garden has a pool, spa and *koi* ponds.

I am a great friend to public amusements, for they keep people from vice.
— **Samuel Johnson**

Chapter seven

DIVERSIONS AFTER DARK
THE BEST NESTS FOR NIGHT OWLS

San Diego offers a full range of nighttime pursuits, including a city symphony and opera company, comedy clubs, a couple of dinner theaters and several amateur and professional theater groups, including the famous Old Globe in Balboa Park.

To find out what's happening where and when, pick up a Thursday edition of the San Diego *Union-Tribune.* Its tabloid insert, *Night & Day* thoroughly covers the local entertainment scene. Within its sixty or more pages, you can discover the hottest jazz clubs and dance spots, learn who's live onstage and find out where your favorite flick is flickering. It also reviews local restaurants and even offers commentary on the newest music videos, handy in case you have to spend a restless night in your hotel or motel room.

Another useful source is a booklet called "What's Playing?" available free at most visitor centers. Produced by the Performing Arts

League, it lists nearly every performing arts group and theater in the county. You can get a year's subscription by calling (619) 238-0700. The *Restaurant & Nightlife Guide*, part of *San Diego Magazine*, lists dozens of nightclubs and other live entertainment venues. The SRH Info Hotline at (619) 973-9269 will tell you what's happening where.

GETTING TICKETED ● Ticketmaster is the largest ticket agency in San Diego, accepting phone orders for most cultural and sports events; (619) 220-TIXS. For discounted tickets, usually on the day of the performance, call Arts Tix at (619) 497-5000. Several other agencies are listed in the San Diego Yellow Pages under "Ticket sales."

THE TEN BEST PERFORMING ARTS GROUPS

Much of what happens culturally in San Diego occurs at the Civic Theatre complex in the San Diego Concourse on First Avenue between A and C streets; (619) 570-1100. Part of the ambitious Centre City redevelopment project of the 1970s, this performing arts center includes the 3,000-seat Civic Theater, 4,000-seat Golden Hall and—up the street at Seventh Avenue and B streets—Copley Symphony Hall. These are venues for San Diego's symphony, ballet and opera companies. The theaters also host traveling shows ranging from on-the-road Broadway productions to Celtic dance groups. Although rather drab outside, the Civic is quite regal within, particularly the Beverly Sills Grand Salon, named for the *diva* who frequently performed with the San Diego Opera Company. The city's other serious theater venue, which ranks at the top of our list, is the Old Globe complex in Balboa Park.

1 OLD GLOBE THEATRE ● *1363 Old Globe Way; (619) 239-2255. WEBSITE: www.oldglobe.org. GETTING THERE: The Old Globe Theater is just north of El Prado in Balboa Park. The easiest approach is via Laurel Street from I-5, since it becomes El Prado as it enters the park.*

It began simply enough, with the San Diego State College production of Shakespeare's *Twelfth Night* in 1947. Since then, the Old Globe has become one of the nation's leading repertory companies, doing contemporary, *avant garde* and classic Shakespeare in its three-theater complex. The Globe won a Tony Award in 1984 for "notable achievement and continuing dedication to theater artistry." It's the oldest professional theater company in California and the second oldest in the West, after the Oregon Shakespeare Festival in Ashland, founded in 1935. In addition to the 581-seat Old Globe, the complex includes the outdoor Lowell Davies Festival Theatre and the more intimate Cassius Carter Centre Stage. Old Globe's season begins in early February and extends through the fall. Its busiest months are July through September, when it presents a mix of Shakespeare and contemporary works in its three theaters.

2 *CALIFORNIA BALLET COMPANY* • *8276 Ronson Rd.; (619) 560-2741.*

Founded in 1968 by Robert and Maxine Mahan, this is one of the largest ballet operations in western America, with performances at the Lyceum Theater in Horton Plaza, the Civic Theater at 202 C Street and in other San Diego County locations. It's *Nutcracker* at the Civic is an important part of the city's Christmas celebration. Maxine, a fifth generation San Diegan, also runs a large ballet school, with branches in Poway and El Cajon.

3 *CORONADO PLAYHOUSE* • *1775 Strand Way, Coronado; (619) 435-4856. GETTING THERE: Cross the San Diego-Coronado Bay Bridge, go left on Orange Avenue through the downtown area, past Hotel del Coronado to Silver Strand; the theater is on the left, near the Coronado City Hall.*

Another longtime local theater group, the Playhouse dates from 1950. It presents comedies, dramas and musicals in an intimate cabaret theater setting, with dinner show packages available on weekends.

4 *GASLAMP QUARTER THEATRE COMPANY* • *Horton Grand Theatre, 444 Fourth Ave.; (619) 234-9583. GETTING THERE: Horton Grand Theatre is in Gaslamp Quarter, between Island Avenue and K Street.*

This lively company presents upbeat comedies, mysteries and dramas in the handsomely refurbished Victorian era 250-seat Horton Grand Theatre. The theater also is used by other performing arts groups.

5 *LA JOLLA PLAYHOUSE* • *Mandell Weiss Center for the Performing Arts at the University of California at San Diego, 2910 La Jolla Village Dr.; (858) 550-1010. GETTING THERE: Go north on I-5 about nine miles from San Diego and take the La Jolla Village Drive exit west about a mile to Expedition Way and go right into the campus.*

One of southern California's most honored legitimate theaters, the La Jolla Playhouse was established in 1947 by no less luminaries than Gregory Peck, Dorothy McGuire and Mel Ferrer. Regular visitors to La Jolla, they wanted a place where they and other Hollywood stars could do live theater. In the decades that followed, the Playhouse honor roll has listed Robert Ryan, Eve Arden, Lee Marvin, James Mason, Olivia de Havilland, Charlton Heston and—good grief!—Dame Mae Whitty.

The playhouse closed its downtown La Jolla theater in 1964 then reopened in 1983. Its home is now in the Weiss Center for the Performing Arts on the University of California campus. Performances are held in the Weiss Theater and the more intimate Weiss Forum. The Playhouse's current focus is on innovative and experimental theater and it still attracts film stars wanting to work before the footlights.

6 *LAMB'S PLAYERS THEATRE* • *1142 Orange Ave., Coronado; (619) 437-0600. GETTING THERE: Cross the San Diego-Coronado Bay Bridge, go left on Orange Avenue about a mile to the theater in the heart of the downtown area, on your right.*

This year-around repertory company presents musicals, dramas and comedies at its small theater in downtown Coronado.

7 *SAN DIEGO OPERA* • *Performances in the Civic Theatre; (619) 232-7636 or (619) 570-1100 for tickets. GETTING THERE: The theater is in the San Diego Concourse downtown, on First Avenue between A and C streets.*

In addition to presenting the classics of Puccini, Verdi and Wagner, the San Diego Opera Company stages contemporary works, such as a recent musical adaptation of John Steinbeck's *Of Mice and Men*. It presents five operas a year, from December through April. It has drawn some of the opera world's greatest operatic voices, such as Joan Sutherlin and Beverly Sills (who appeared together in 1980), and Placido Domingo.

8 *SAN DIEGO REPERTORY THEATRE* • *Performances at the Lyceum Theater in Horton Plaza; (619) 544-1000. GETTING THERE: The theater is at 79 Horton Plaza, ground level, off Broadway Circle.*

A struggling young actress who paid her rent by washing dishes at San Diego's Big Kitchen was one of the founders of the San Diego Repertory Theatre in 1974. She appeared in several of its early productions, then went on to gain fame in Hollywood, with an Academy Award nomination for her role in *The Color Purple*. Whoopi Goldberg doesn't do the "Rep" anymore, although other wanna-be stars perform here, hoping to follow her footsteps. San Diego Repertory Theatre produces quality dramas and comedies throughout the year.

9 *SAN DIEGO SYMPHONY* • *Performances in Copley Symphony Hall, 750 B Street; (619) 235-0804. GETTING THERE: Copley Symphony Hall is downtown, at the corner of Seventh Avenue.*

Established in 1926, this is the oldest performing arts group in the city, initially called the Philharmonic Orchestra of San Diego and then the San Diego Civic Orchestra. It presents an ambitious series of concerts through most of the year, from classics to pops. Definitely not a stuffy organization, it offers theme concerts such as the Connoisseur

Series featuring the classics; the Light Bulb Series, focusing on musical themes or eras; and Family Festivals, with a mix of light classic and contemporary music. Our favorite is the Rush Hour Series, upbeat early evening concerts to lure weary workers away from commuter traffic jams.

10 *STARLIGHT MUSICAL THEATER* • *Starlight Bowl in Balboa Park; (619) 544-7827. GETTING THERE: The bowl is just south of Pan American Plaza, adjacent to the Aerospace Museum in Balboa Park.*

Dating from 1946 and originally called the Starlight Opera, this company doesn't do operas, although it's first production was Gilbert and Sullivan's operetta *The Mikado*. The present company, Starlight Musical Theater, presents several Broadway musicals in Balboa Park Bowl from mid-July through late September. Sitting under the stars in this amphitheater is one of San Diego's more pleasing pastimes. However, both audience and performers suffer one drawback: The bowl is just beneath the final approach to San Diego International Airport, and jets rumble overhead every few minutes. The company uses a spotter to signal performers with a red light when a plane is approaching. The effect goes something like this: "Some enchanted evening, you may see—pause, rumble, rumble, rumble, pause—a stranger, across a crowded room..."

THE TEN BEST NIGHTCLUBS

If you like your amusements live as well as lively, San Diego is your kinda town. More than fifty clubs, pubs and restaurants feature live entertainment one or more nights a week. Offerings range from jazz and swing to pops and rock. Much of this action is concentrated downtown, particularly in Gaslamp Quarter. Some of the area's major resorts feature club entertainment as well.

1 *CAFÉ SEVILLA* • *555 Fourth Ave.; (619) 239-5979. Full bar service. GETTING THERE: The café is in Gaslamp Quarter, between Market and Island streets.*

At this lively nightspot, salsa is a dance as well as a spicy dip. You'll find little *fado* here. The bar adjacent to Café Sevilla features upbeat entertainment nightly, with dancing, flamenco guitarists and other Spanish style amusements. This café and bar, with its sparkly black ceilings, brick Moorish arches and Spanish carved woods, will transport you to Seville and possibly even Barcelona. (What's a *fado*? It's sad and melancholy song, usually performed in dimly lit nightclubs in Spain.)

2 CANNIBAL BAR • *At the Catamaran Resort Hotel, 3999 Mission Blvd., Pacific Beach; (619) 488-1081. GETTING THERE: The Catamaran is on the northern edge of Mission Bay Park at Santa Rita Place, between Mission Beach and Pacific Beach. Take West Mission Bay Drive north through Mission Bay, swing right onto Mission Boulevard and continue about a mile to Santa Rita; the Catamaran is on your right.*

This popular Mission Beach-Pacific Beach club features live music most nights of the week, ranging from jazz, swing and blues to contemporary rock. The tropic style Cannibal Bar is in the rear of Catamaran Resort, just off Mission Bay.

3 THE CASBAH • *2501 Kettner Blvd.; (619) 232-4355. GETTING THERE: The Casbah is in the Middletown area, on the east side of Kettner at Laurel Street. Take the Laurel Street exit from I-5.*

Don't expect belly dancers in this club, despite its name. The music tilts toward rock, with live groups nearly every night of the week. Local groups and performers such as Jivewire, Rip Carson & the Twilight Trio and A.K. Skurgis are featured.

4 THE COMEDY STORE • *916 Pearl St., La Jolla; (858) 454-9176. GETTING THERE: This store of mirth is near Fay Street in downtown La Jolla.*

For the price of a couple of drinks, you can laugh at the stand-up antics of up-and-coming comedians, along with an occasional established performer. And if you think you might be the next Robin Williams, Sundays are open mike nights.

5 CROCE'S RESTAURANT & JAZZ BAR • *802 Fifth Ave.; (619) 233-4355. GETTING THERE: Croce's is in Gaslamp Quarter, between E and F streets.*

In addition to being a popular restaurant (Chapter Three, page 55), Croce's offers a lively entertainment scene. Ingrid Croce, widow of folksinger Jim Croce, books jazz and rhythm and blues groups in two different clubs, the Jazz Bar and the New Orleans style Top Hat Bar and Grill. It's a family affair, since one of the headliners often is musician A.J. Croce, Jim and Ingrid's son.

6 HARMONY ON FIFTH • *322 Fifth Ave.; (619) 702-8848. GETTING THERE: It's between J and K streets on the southern edge of Gaslamp Quarter.*

This sleek restaurant-lounge-supper club features nightly entertainment, including blues, jazz and assorted combos.

7 *HUMPHREY'S* • *2241 Shelter Island Dr.; (619) 224-3577. Full bar service. GETTING THERE: To reach Shelter Island, head toward Point Loma on Rosecrans Street (State Route 209) and turn left onto Shelter Island Drive. Humphrey's Half Moon Inn is just to the right of a traffic circle and the restaurant is a short distance beyond.*

This chic bar adjacent to Humphrey's Restaurant is the liveliest spot on Shelter Island. It features singers, musicians and combos most nights, a piano bar during the cocktail hour, plus music for dancing on its small dance floor.

8 *IN CAHOOTZ* • *5373 Mission Center Rd.; (619) 291-8635. GETTING THERE: Take the Mission Center Road exit from I-8 and go north through three traffic lights; In Cahootz is on the right.*

Musically, San Diego isn't major country country, leaning more toward pops, light rock and jazz. However, this foot-stompin' place more than fills the void, offering country entertainers, dancing and dance lessons. Want to master the cowboy two-step or line dance? This is the place. It's affordable, too, with nightly happy hours from 5 to 8 and inexpensive buffet dinners.

9 *LOEWS CORONADO BAY RESORT* • *4000 Coronado Bay Rd., Coronado; (619) 424-4000. GETTING THERE: Loews is about five miles south of downtown Coronado on Silver Strand, opposite Silver Strand State Beach.*

This modern Spanish-California style resort has two live entertainment venues. Musicians, combos and vocalists perform in the lobby bar most nights of the week, with the accent on light pops, jazz and blues. The second-level Azzura Point restaurant, offering great San Diego skyline views, also has live music in an adjacent piano bar.

10 *McP'S IRISH PUB & GRILL* • *1107 Orange Ave., Coronado; (619) 435-5280. GETTING THERE: Take the San Diego-Coronado Bay Bridge to Coronado and turn left onto Orange Avenue. McP's is about a mile away, in the heart of downtown on your left.*

You can get a pint 'o stout and some good Irish grub at this downtown grill and you also can enjoy live music several nights a week. However, it's more likely to be blues, pops or light rock than Celtic.

THE TEN BEST PLACES TO CATCH A FLICK

As in much of the rest of the country, most of San Diego's movie theaters are multiscreen operations, some with screens the size of bedsheets. However, those we've checked out have reasonably sized screens and they generally have one big-screen viewing room with ranks of stereo speakers with enough watts to blast the popcorn cup out of your lap. This is where they show their wide-screen epics. Generally, the better multi-screen theaters are in shopping malls.

Incidentally, local radio station KYXY 96.5-FM sponsors a free "movie locator" service. Dial (619) 444-FILM to learn what movies are playing where. You also can get live event and ticket information. The local AMC theater chain has an advance ticket ordering service by phone; call (619) 558-2AMC.

1 *GASLAMP ALL STADIUM 15* • *701 Fifth Avenue at G St.; (619) 232-0400. GETTING THERE: As the name obviously suggests, it's in Gaslamp Quarter.*

This is our favorite area theater complex because it has all stadium seating, it offers the current hits and it's conveniently located in the heart of Gaslamp Quarter, not far from Horton Plaza. The spacious atrium lobby is quite handsome with a kind of modern art deco look. The building itself looks right at home in the Gaslamp, clad in old brick with a turn-of-the-century façade.

2 *AMC FASHION VALLEY 18* • *Fashion Valley Mall at 7007 Friars Rd.; (619) 296-6400. GETTING THERE: Follow Freeway 163 about a mile north from I-8 and take Friars Road west; the mall is on your left. The theater complex is on the upper level, on the south side of the mall.*

One of San Diego's largest movie complexes, the AMC Fashion Valley 18 is marked by a large multi-colored tower. An outdoor patio, adjacent to the box office and near a food court, is a handy place to relax while waiting for your favorite flick to begin flicking.

3 *AMC LA JOLLA 12* • *In La Jolla Village Square; (858) 558-2234. GETTING THERE: Go north about eight miles on I-5 from the I-8 interchange, take the Nobel Drive exit, cross over the freeway and turn left into La Jolla Village Square. The theater complex is in the lower level of the main mall.*

The box office for this multi-screen theater is on your right beside Ray's Game Center, and the large lobby is the next level down. (It's easy to miss the box office and breeze ticketless into the lobby.)

4 *AMC MISSION VALLEY 20* • *In Mission Valley Mall at Mission Center Road and Camino del Rio. GETTING THERE: Go east about four miles on I-8 from the I-5 interchange and take the Mission Center Road/Auto Circle exit. Go north over the freeway, then east onto Camino Del Rio and turn north into the mall.*

This is the largest theater complex in the San Diego area, so the odds are that you'll find your current favorite. To find the theater, look for the towering modernistic marquee led aloft by painted pipes, like a worlds fair structure.

5 COVE THEATER • *7730 Girard Ave., La Jolla; (858) 459-5404. GETTING THERE: The Cove is between Silverado and Kline in downtown La Jolla, three long blocks up from Prospect.*

The Cove is a rarity—an old fashion single-screen theater. Although it lacks the classic wedge-shaped marquee, it occupies a fine old brick building, with the box office on the sidewalk. The Cove specializes in foreign and art films and independent productions.

6 GROSSMONT MALL THEATERS • *In Grossmont Mall at 5500 Grossmont Center Dr., La Mesa; (619) 465-7100. GETTING THERE: Go east on I-8 to La Mesa, take the La Mesa Boulevard/Grossmont Center Drive exit, to left under the freeway and turn left into the center, at the third stoplight. The movie complex is midpoint on the north side of the mall.*

Part of the Pacific Theaters chain, this facility has eight screens, although there may be more by the time you arrive. It was undergoing expansion when we last caught a film there.

7 HILLCREST THEATER • *3936 Fifth Ave.; (619) 299-2100. GETTING THERE: The theater is on the second level of Village Hillcrest at the corner of Fifth and Washington Street.*

A member of the Landmark theater chain, this modern five-screen facility features mostly independent productions, art and foreign films.

8 LA JOLLA VILLAGE THEATER • *8879 La Jolla Village Dr., La Jolla; (858) 453-7831. GETTING THERE: It's in La Jolla Village Center, which is across Nobel Drive from La Jolla Square; see directions for AMC La Jolla 12 above, then turn right off Nobel instead of left.*

Occupying a rather spartan white-painted brick building on the northwest side of shopping center, this four-screen theater is part of the Landmark chain. It focuses on art and foreign films and independent production, plus some mainstream movies.

9 MANN 7 THEATERS • *In Hazard Shopping Center, Friars Road at Freeway 163; (619) 291-7777. GETTING THERE: From I-8, go north about a mile on Freeway 163, turn left onto Friars Road, then left again onto Frazee Road. The theater complex is to the rear of the shopping center, on the lower level.*

This seven-screen theater has an appealing art deco look with a stylized marquee and a lobby trimmed by chrome accents and strings of white light bulbs. It shows first run films and a few independent productions.

10 UNITED ARTISTS 14 • *475 Horton Plaza; (619) 234-4661. GETTING THERE: The theater complex is on Level 4 of Horton Plaza, rimmed by First and Fourth avenues, Broadway and G Street.*

This multi-screen facility is convenient for downtowners. It has a large ultra-Dolby stereo theater for the big hits with those eardrum rattling soundtracks, plus the usual smaller screens.

Chapter eight

PUB CRAWLING
THE BEST PLACES TO SIT AND SIP SUDS

We aren't really serious bar types. For one thing, Betty doesn't drink; for another, I prefer my libations with my meals and that means wine. However, bars are an important fabric of a city, so when we research these guides, I indulge in a bit of pub-crawling while my wife and co-author follows more meaningful pursuits, such as finding interesting museums.

If your idea of a night out is to loaf in a grimy pool hall that smells of stale cigarette smoke and yesterday's spilled beer, you may disagree with most of our selections. (Of course, with California's rigid anti-smoking laws, bars are no longer smoky, although many still smell of sale beer.) I prefer brighter, livelier lounges.

While I'm certainly fond of comfortable old saloons with their mahogany planks and dusty moose heads, I'm also drawn to the cheerful new watering holes, where drinking is more of a social exchange than a melancholy ritual.

THE TEN BEST WATERING HOLES

San Diego has few straight drinking establishments. Most of its bars are extensions of restaurants, and they tend to be open and cheery, usually with outdoor seating areas in salute to the city's balmy weather. I found some of the city's best bars in its hotels.

1 GRANT GRILL LOUNGE • *U.S. Grant Hotel, 326 Broadway; (619) 232-3121. GETTING THERE: The Grant is across from Horton Plaza Park and bounded by Third and Fourth avenues.*

The venerable U.S. Grant Hotel is home to San Diego's best pub. This clubby yet lively bar is separate from the much more subdued Grant Grill and it's one of downtown's most popular cocktail hour retreats. The bar is quite handsome, with dark woods and thick paneled columns holding up a lofty ceiling. It's large enough to invite camaraderie while still offering quite corners for those who want to be alone. Stools at the main bar are comfortable, with upholstered backs. While neither a tavern nor sports bar, it has single elements from each—one pool table and one big-screen TV. Both are off in corners so as not to be intrusive.

2 ATRIUM LOUNGE • *In the Wyndham Emerald Plaza Hotel at 400 W. Broadway; (619) 239-4500. GETTING THERE: The Wyndham is on lower Broadway between State and Columbia streets.*

This is one of our favorite bars because it's part of the Wyndham's impressive seven-story atrium lobby. Relaxing at the bar counter or at a table, you can admire the monumental hanging sculptures and beveled mirror glass on terraced mezzanines that make this the most dramatic hotel lobby in town. It serves light snacks and features a pianist Wednesday and Thursday and a combo—usually a jazz trio—on Friday and Saturday nights.

3 THE BRICK TAVERN • *Columbia and B Street; (619) 702-7023. GETTING THERE: The tavern is in Old Columbia Square, three blocks up from Broadway in the downtown area.*

This pub is particularly appealing for its brick-walled open air patio shaded by flowering plum trees. The inside bar, with its carved wood backbar, high ceilings and exposed heating ducts, also is attractive. Further, the place has the proper number of TV sets for sports events. It has several brews on tap, including a powerful locally-concocted one called the Arrogant Bastard. The tavern offers light pub fare such as chicken quesadillas and burgers. It shares this large former warehouse building with a couple of walk-up food places, giving you a larger dining choice.

4 **CAFÉ SEVILLA** • *555 Fourth Ave.; (619) 239-5979. GET-TING THERE: This combination café and bar is in Gaslamp Quarter, be-tween Market and Island streets.*

The Spanish style bar sharing a fine old brick building with a Span-ish restaurant is one of the most appealing in San Diego, with a beauti-ful hand carved wooden backbar, glossy tile floors and brick accents. Patrons can sit at the long, polished bar or at cute little tables, where they can sip sangria and other Spanish specialty drinks and perhaps nibble *tapas*. These are Spanish style *hors d'oeuvres*, little plates of *pa-ella*, chicken or shrimp coquettes, or meatballs in sherry garlic sauce. They are served with crunchy French bread and red and white dips. During nightly happy hour from 5 to 7, you can get deep discounts on sangria and *tapas*. This thus is a very popular place for the Gaslamp Quarter after-work crowd.

5 **DW's PUB** • *In the Marriott San Diego Marina, 333 W. Har-bor Dr.; (619) 234-1500, extension 6789. GETTING THERE: The Marri-ott is on the waterfront at Harbor Drive and Front Street.*

This is a "dual bar" with twin personalities. The interior of this large pub is clubby and elegant with dark woods, an ornate chandelier and brass accents. The seating area spills out into a larger corridor where it takes on a cheerful tropical look with floral carpeting and bamboo style tables and chairs. The outer bar has fine views of the ho-tel's elaborately landscaped swimming pool area. This would be a great lobby bar, except that the lobby of this large hotel is about a block away.

6 **HANG TEN BREWING COMPANY** • *310 Fifth Ave.; (619) 232-6336. GETTING THERE: It's on the southern edge of Gaslamp Quar-ter, on the corner of K Street.*

Is it really true that "hang ten" means to move so far forward on your surfboard that all of your toes hang over? That's the legend told at this lively Gaslamp Quarter brewpub. The décor here is "old brick meets tropical beach shack." The bar is housed in a former warehouse building with exposed beam ceilings, and it has a kind of Beach Boys look with splashy surfing sketches and a couple of surfboards mounted on the walls. The music is upbeat, a mix of surfer and rock. Sippers can choose from about ten house brews, with names like Wipeout Stout, Wahine Wheat, Beach Blonde and—oh my—Mermaid's Milk. The main bar, also a restaurant serving pizza and barbecued things, is busy with long legged chairs and tables. If you seek a cozier area, you can adjourn to a lower rear bar away from the center of activity, with a few booths a pool table.

7 *HUMPHREY'S* • *At Humphrey's Half Moon Inn, 2241 Shelter Island Dr.; (619) 224-3577. GETTING THERE: To reach Shelter Island, head toward Point Loma on Rosecrans Street (State Route 209) and turn left onto Shelter Island Drive. Humphrey's Half Moon Inn is just to the right of a traffic circle and the bar is a short distance beyond.*

This modern, upbeat bar offers a nice view of a marina and Point Loma from its terraced seating area. It features live entertainment most nights and is appropriately decorated with musical notes and color photos of assorted performers. The lounge has a serious selection of domestic and international beers, plus wines by the glass. Although it's essentially a lounge and club, it serves light fare from lunch through late evening, such as salads and sandwiches. For more filling food, the highly-regarded Humphrey's restaurant is adjacent; see Chapter Three, page 56.

8 *PALOMINO* • *In The Aventine at 8990 University Lane Center, La Jolla; (858) 452-9000. GETTING THERE: Take the La Jolla Village Drive exit from I-5, about ten miles north of San Diego, go east a mile to Lebon Drive and turn right. The Aventine is a shopping and dining complex opposite the Hyatt Regency.*

This is the most *chic* drinking salon in the greater San Diego area. An extension of the Palomino restaurant, it's an eye-appealing blend of marble topped cocktail tables, a carved mahogany backbar, oxblood red columns, curving ceiling beams, hand blown glass chandeliers and marble topped tables. It features a dozen international beers on tap, more than that number of wines by the glass and the full range of other items for social sipping. Try the Palomino Palini, a frozen drink of champagne, peach nectar, lemon and cassis. It can be ordered in one of two sizes, depending on who plans to take advantage of whom later.

9 *PLAZA BAR* • *The Westgate Hotel San Diego, 1055 Second Ave.; (619) 238-1818. GETTING THERE: The Westgate is just off lower Broadway downtown; the Plaza Bar is on the ground floor.*

Like other areas of the Westgate (Chapter Six, page 105), the Plaza Bar is a study in French Provincial elegance, with beaded chandeliers, period furnishings, wall sconces, tapestries and a black marble bartop. Soft music emerges from some unidentified source. During some evenings, a pianist will be at the keyboard of a grand piano as you sip your single-malt Scotch. This is not only the San Diego area's dressiest cocktail lounge; it's one of the most opulent we've seen in western America. Enjoying a drink here is like having cocktails in a wealthy friend's drawing room.

10 *THE SPOT RESTAURANT AND TAVERN* ● *1005 Prospect Ave., La Jolla; (619) 459-0800. GETTING THERE: The Spot is in downtown La Jolla at the corner of Girard Avenue.*

A La Jolla landmark since 1916, the Spot is more restaurant than tavern, although it's a great place for a leisurely libation. And no, it doesn't offer an ocean view; people come here to sip and talk and eat. Sit at the long polished bar and admire the grand clutter of this place. Its wood paneled and exposed brick walls are covered with stuffed fish trophies, photos, paintings, prints and whatever else the owners managed to hang. The main bar is a comfortable perch since it has long-legged chairs instead of backless stools. There are small tables for those who prefer cozier seating, although they're sometimes occupied by diners at lunch and dinner. Sippers have a choice of several wines by the glass, plus the usual beers and other libations. This *the* La Jolla cocktail hour retreat. If you insist on treating it as a restaurant, food is served daily from lunch through late evening. The fare is essential American, including several steaks and a couple of chicken dishes for dinner, and omelettes and pizza for lunch.

THE TEN BEST "PERSONALITY BARS"

What's a personality bar? It's a watering hole with special character, either with a particular theme or attitude.

1 *THE BEST BEER PUB: Karl Strauss' Old Columbia Brewery* ● *1157 Columbia St.; (619) 234-2739. Lunch and dinner daily; MC/VISA. GETTING THERE: The pub is downtown between B and C streets.*

Local *brewmeister* Karl Strauss started San Diego's first brewpub a couple of decades ago and he's still going strong, with three outlets. This one is installed in an old brick building with beam ceilings, exposed heating ducts, wooden furniture and requisite other brewpub décor. Stainless steel brewing kettles are just off the main room and tours are available on request. Like most San Diego pubs, Old Columbia also is a restaurant, particularly popular with downtown nooners. The fare is typical—beer battered fried things, seafood gumbo, barbecued babyback ribs and such.

2 *THE BEST DELIBERATELY SCRUFFY BAR: Dick's Last Resort* ● *345 Fourth Ave.; (619) 231-9100. GETTING THERE: This alleged resort is in Gaslamp Quarter between J and K streets.*

Although this joint is a carefully orchestrated put-on, it looks like an over-the-hill resort, and maybe some of its employees have been at sea too long. It functions as a café, serving ribs, chicken, beef and burgers, although it's mostly a harmlessly rowdy bar. The Last Resort occupies a barn-like space that extends from Fourth Avenue through a brick-walled warehouse and a large patio to Fifth. To give it that properly disheveled look, scraps of paper are scattered on the warehouse floor and the furnishings are rudimentary plank tables and wooden chairs. The beer, the noise and the wisecracks flow freely. The bar sells "big-assed beers," the menu lists "salads and other roughage," and patrons are invited to buy "worthless junk," meaning logo T-shirts and caps. According to a sign out front, the resort serves "the kind of food your mom used to make when she was really mad at you."

3 THE BEST AND POSSIBLY ONLY PUB FROM DOWN UNDER: *The Australian Pub* • *1014 Grand Avenue, Pacific Beach; (619) 273-9921. MC/VISA. GETTING THERE: Take the Grand/Garnet Avenue exit from I-5 and go west on Grand to Cass Street. If you're in Mission Beach, go east two blocks on Grand Avenue from Mission Boulevard. The pub is in the elbow of a small L-shaped mall.*

While not a real Australian pub, this lively place is a good American imitation, with plenty of Fosters lager, walls coated with Aussie posters and advertising logos, and a bar menu featuring typical Australian food. This may be the only place in the San Diego area where you can get Vegamite, and after you taste it, you'll understand why. Other specialties from down under are fish and chips—yes, it's very big down there, served in newspaper cones—Aussie meat pie, steak and mashed potatoes and an "Aussie burger" with bacon, pineapple slice, beets, grilled onions and cheese. Whether or not you're a displaced Aussie, you'll find this to be a perfectly good neighborhood bar with lots of TV screens, pool tables, darts, shuffleboard and even foosball.

4 THE BEST GLORIA STEINHAM MEMORIAL BAR: *Hooters* • *410 Market St.; (619) 435-4668. GETTING THERE: Hooters is in Gaslamp Quarter at the corner of Fourth Avenue.*

"Delightfully tacky, yet noncompliant," reads a sign at this harmlessly outrageous bar. Noncompliant, indeed. Part of a national chain, Hooters is noted for nubile young waitresses wearing orange hotpants and scoop-neck T-shirts. Some years ago, the National Organization for Women tried to force the firm to hire male waitpersons. However, we were served by an attractive, amply endowed lass on rollerskates, not by a pouting male. Hooters offers a long list of draft beers and wines by the glass, in addition to the usual cocktails. The roller-skating waitresses serve food as well as beer and pretty smiles. The fare is light, such as spicy chicken wings, hamburgers and assorted other sandwiches. However, I don't think most guys come here for a gourmet dining experience. Hooters is popular as a sports bar, with a décor consisting of the girls and their pin-up photos, sports logos and many TV sets tuned to the latest games.

5 **THE BEST IRISH PUB: Patrick's II** ● *428 F St.; (619) 233-3077. GETTING THERE: Patrick's is just up from Horton Plaza in Gaslamp Quarter, between Fourth and Fifth avenues.*

Never mind that it has live blues and jazz several nights a week, instead of woeful Celtic ballads. This narrow, wood-floored drinking establishment is a proper Irish pub with dark woods, a dim interior and plenty of room to drink. There's a main bar where you can stand up with your pint o' stout (although there are stools) and a second bar across the room with just enough space for your glass and your elbows. Patrick's is decorated with a few shamrocks, "Irish Power" signs, an odd poster or two, and mostly with the Irish cheer of its patrons, no matter what their nationality.

6 **THE BEST BEACH BAR: Coaster Saloon** ● *744 Ventura Place, Mission Beach; (619) 488-4438. GETTING THERE: Take West Mission Bay Drive through Mission Bay Park to Mission Beach; the Coaster is beside the parking lot for Belmont Park.*

This serious drinking establishment is a bit on the scruffy side, but then, beach bars aren't supposed to be elegant. They're supposed to be light-hearted and perhaps a bit rowdy. This upbeat place, decorated mostly with noise and beer banners, is San Diego's closest thing to a good beach bar. It's not right on the beach although it's close enough—within a block and a half. It's a large place with an indoor drinking area, a couple of pool tables, a big tarp-covered patio and a few sidewalk tables. Out on the sidewalk, patrons clutching their sweaty beer bottles can actually see the beach. Don't come to the Coaster unless you like lots of noisy camaraderie. And don't bring the kids; this isn't a restaurant that pretends to be a bar. It's a saloon with a 21-year-old age limit. However, it does serve light food from morning through late night.

7 **THE BEST VIEW BAR: Top of the Hyatt** ● *Hyatt Regency San Diego, 1 Market Place; (619) 232-1234. GETTING THERE: The Regency is adjacent to Seaport Village just off Harbor Drive.*

Occupying the fortieth floor of the Hyatt, this lofty bar provides an imposing panorama of bayside San Diego, from Point Loma to Coronado and south to Mexico. It doesn't quite take in the full sweep of the area since the portion of the hotel's top floor facing downtown San Diego is occupied by luxury suites. However, the view is as high and wide as any you'll find in the city. The windows, of course, are floor to ceiling and the bar itself has a warm, clubby look with wood paneling and dark floral wall coverings. You can enjoy this view with lunch from noon to 2:30 from Wednesday through Sunday. The rest of the time, it functions as a cocktail lounge.

8 **THE BEST WINE BAR: The Wine Bar** • *823 Fifth Ave.; (619) 238-8010. GETTING THERE: This wine-sipping venue is in Gaslamp Quarter, between E and F streets.*

As its name states, this is *the* place for wine lovers. This cozy little bar in one of Gaslamp Quarter's venerable brick buildings serves more than forty different wines by the glass. Like any serious wine bar, it offers tastings in "flights." These are comparative tastings of a variety of wines with something in common—same vintner but different years, same variety but different vintners and so on. This slender tasting space looks like a wine cellar, with aging barrels standing about. It's dimly lit with grape clusters painted on its vaulted ceiling and winery scenes on the walls.

9 **THE BEST LOBBY BAR: Sheraton San Diego Hotel & Marina** • *(619) 692-2200. GETTING THERE: The Sheraton is at the entrance to Harbor Island, which can be reached via Harbor Drive from downtown. Or take any airport exit from I-5, since Harbor Island is opposite San Diego International Airport.*

This large lobby bar overlooks a marina and Mission Bay, sharing that view with the adjacent Harbor's Edge Restaurant. It has seating inside the spacious hotel lobby and on an outside deck. Bold dark wooden support beams add strong accents to the light, subtly tropical décor of the bar. Plush arm chairs and sofas provide inviting places to relax. This very attractive lobby bar is just to the left of the hotel's reception desk.

10 **THE BEST SPORTS BAR: Seau's** • *1640 Camino del Rio North in Mission Valley Center; (619) 291-7328. GETTING THERE: It's on the far eastern edge of Mission Valley Center, adjacent to Robinsons-May. Go east about four miles on I-8 from I-5 and take the Mission Center/Auto Circle exit. Drive north over the freeway, then east onto Camino Del Rio to the far end of the mall.*

When San Diego Charger all-pro tackle Junior Seau decided to build a sports bar, he wanted it to be a family place, complete with a kiddie's menu. In fact it's called Seau's: The Restaurant. However, on football weekends and baseball afternoons, this huge place with a lofty arched ceiling becomes so raucous that the little ones might scurry for cover. Send them to the videogame parlor in the adjacent Mission Valley Center, then settle down with a tall one and enjoy the game—or we should say games. You can choose from forty different TV monitors, including one that measures twelve by twelve feet. You won't be able to hear the soundtrack, although a true sports fan can figure out what's happening. (However, we had a little trouble with cricket, piped in on ESPN 2.)

Naturally the place is decorated with sports regalia. The menu is cleverly fashioned as a newspaper sports section with headlines such as: "Winning lineup of starters," and "Wood-fired pizzas that can take the heat." The basic burgers, sandwiches, quesadillas and salads probably won't win any culinary awards, but folks come here mostly for the jock camaraderie.

Sex has become one of the most discussed subjects of modern times. The Victorians pretended that it did not exist; the moderns pretend that nothing else exists.
— Fulton J. Sheen

Chapter nine

ROMANCE
AND OTHER PRIMAL URGES

Sunsets over the bay; surrey rides along the waterfront; candle-lit restaurants; hidden beaches; a climate that almost suggests the tropics. San Diego is certainly a romantic place.

Through the decades, it has had a reputation for being a bit naughty, as well. It has been a sailors' liberty town since the days of the hide trade, when vessels from around the world came to collect cowhides from the Mexican ranches. Richard Henry Dana wrote about this period in his epic *Two Years Before the Mast*. The U.S. Marine Corps has been here since 1911, and if anyone can raise more hell than a sailor ashore, it's a Marine ashore. The Navy came *en masse* in 1942 after the attack on Pearl Harbor, when the government moved its Pacific Fleet to San Diego Bay. During World War II, lower Broadway was lined with bars, bawdy houses and "locker clubs," and they spilled over into the rowdy area known as Stingaree.

All of that has changed now. Stingaree has become the gentrified Gaslamp Quarter and lower Broadway is home to fancy hotels and highrise office buildings. San Diego generally is regarded as a rather conservative city. It can still be a bit naughty, however.

THE TEN BEST PLACES TO SNUGGLE WITH YOUR SWEETIE

Can one find places to be alone together in the second largest city in California? Perhaps not completely alone—not in a city of a million people—although there are romantic spots where you can at least pretend that you're alone.

1 MOUNT SOLEDAD • *At the end of Mount Soledad Road in eastern La Jolla. Gates open from 8 a.m. to midnight. GETTING THERE: Two roads reach Mount Soledad. From La Jolla, turn inland onto Nautilus Street off La Jolla Boulevard, just over a mile south of the downtown area and drive uphill, following directional signs. Or follow I-5 north from San Diego and take the Grand/Garnet Avenue exit, which puts you on Mission Bay Drive. Continue north about half a mile on Mission Bay, go west (left) about a quarter of a mile on Garnet and turn right up Mount Soledad Road.*

More than 800 feet above the ocean, this is the highest point in La Jolla and the most romantic spot for sitting and admiring an expansive sweep of the greater San Diego area. Handy benches are provided for that purpose, or you can lie back on the grass or sit on the steps of a circular brick terrace that forms a base for the Soledad Mountain Easter Cross. Mount Soledad is a particularly romantic—although probably not deserted—spot at sunset, when you can watch Ole Sol dip into the Pacific while lights begin glittering from the surrounding communities.

2 THE BALI HAI "GARDEN" • *2230 Shelter Island Dr. GETTING THERE: To reach Shelter Island, head toward Point Loma on Rosecrans Street (State Route 209) and turn left onto Shelter Island Drive. Loop around a traffic circle and drive northeast to Bali Hai restaurant.*

Bali Hai restaurant (see below on page 138, and Chapter Three on page 69) occupies the second floor of a tiki-style building at the northeast end of Shelter Island. A charming little garden sits at water's edge just beneath the restaurant, with gurgling waterfall fountains, lush landscaping and a neat little Oriental moon bridge. Benches invite lovers to linger and admire the view of the San Diego skyline across the bay. And if you want to dine with that view and you like Polynesian food with Chinese accents, you need merely to adjourn upstairs.

3 IN A GLEAMING WHITE CARRIAGE • *Cinderella Carriage Company; (619) 239-8080. Seaport Village and Gaslamp Quarter. MC/VISA, AMEX.*

This operation allows you to snuggle while touring the scenic areas of San Diego. But of course you can ignore the scenery and the driver will discreetly ignore the two of you. The Cinderella Carriage Company operates pretty white horse-drawn surreys with tufted leather seats. Tours cover two areas—Gaslamp Quarter, starting at Fifth and F streets; and the Embarcadero, starting near Seaport Village. Give them a call and they'll pick you up at your hotel.

4 CRYSTAL PIER COTTAGES • *Crystal Pier Hotel, 4500 Ocean Blvd., San Diego (Pacific Beach), CA 92109; (800) 748-5894 or (619) 483-6983. GETTING THERE: Take the Grand/Garnet Avenue exit from I-5, go several blocks north then turn left onto Garnet Avenue and follow it about two and a half miles to the beach.*

Crystal Pier is one of the few privately owned wharfs on the West Coast and it's lined with charming little white and blue trimmed cottages—great places for snuggling with your sweetie while listening to the surf rumble below. Each has its own deck, where you can sit and watch the sunrise or sunset (and hope the neighboring tenants aren't doing the same). Accommodations range from studios with baths to one and two-bedroom units with full kitchens. Such coziness doesn't come cheap; rates begin at well over $100, although they're lower in the off-season.

5 ELLEN BROWNING SCRIPPS PARK AT LA JOLLA COVE • *Off Coast Boulevard in downtown La Jolla. GETTING THERE: As you approach downtown La Jolla from the south on Prospect Street, fork to the left onto Coast Boulevard.*

Ellen Browning Scripps Park is a small patch of green covering the La Jolla Cove's low headland. Benches invite lovers to sit beneath wind-twisted cypress trees and enjoy fine vistas out to sea. At the lower end of the park, you can watch seals play on nearby Seal Rocks. While hardly private, this popular park is one of the prettiest spots in the area. The only negatives here are glaring red and white signs telling visitors what they can't do: Build fires, bring dogs, carry glass containers, sleep overnight, climb the trees or drink from 8 p.m. until noon. At least, the signs don't forbid smooching.

6 EMBARCADERO MARINA PARK • *South end of the waterfront walk, alongside Harbor Drive. GETTING THERE: From downtown, take Broadway to the waterfront, turn left onto Harbor Drive, follow it about a mile south and then east, then go right on Kettner Boulevard for about a block.*

San Diego's waterfront walk extends from Spanish Landing across from the airport to Embarcadero Marina Park, opposite the San Diego Marriott. This extreme southern end is much less traveled than the upper portions. You can sit in relative privacy on one of the curved-back wooden benches in this attractively landscaped park. You have a choice of views—to the west over San Diego Bay, toward the Coronado Bridge and Coronado; or east across Embarcadero Marina to the dramatic twin glass towers of the San Diego Marriott. If you'd like to have a picnic in this little park, you'll find several tables.

7 PALM CANYON • *In Balboa Park, to the right of the Spreckels Organ Pavilion as you approach it from Plaza de Panama. GETTING THERE: Walk east toward the pavilion and watch on your right for a wooden sidewalk; it leads to a set of steps descending into the canyon.*

Balboa Park is cut by several shallow, thickly wooded canyons. This one, reached by wooden stairs, has several benches where you an sit and snuggle beneath the shade of palms and eucalyptus trees.

8 PRESIDIO PARK • *On Presidio Hill, above Old Town. GETTING THERE: Drive north through Old Town, turn right onto Taylor Street then right again onto Presidio Drive and follow signs to the Father Serra Museum. Continue just past the museum to Presidio Park.*

This pretty little patch of green, shaded by huge evergreens and eucalyptus trees, nestles into the southeast side of Presidio Hill. It's shielded from the sight and sound of freeways 5 and 8, which converge just below the Father Serra Museum. The park is rarely crowded, particularly on weekdays, since most visitors go no further than the museum. Spread out your wine and cheese on one of the tables and have a romantic picnic. Or just sit with your backs against one of those huge trees while contemplating this pleasant spot—and one another.

Walk across Presidio Drive and follow steps up to a thick eucalyptus grove at the top of the hill. Monuments here mark the site of Fort Stockton, an American bastion erected after San Diego was wrested from Mexico in 1846. If you're in a scholarly mood instead of a romantic one, historical markers will tell you about the Mormon Battalion that marched 2,000 miles across the country and stayed at the fort.

9 SAN DIEGO PARADISE POINT RESORT LAGOON • *1404 W. Vacation Rd. GETTING THERE: The resort occupies Vacation Isle in the middle of Mission Bay Park. To reach it, take Ingraham Street through Mission Bay and turn west onto Vacation Road.*

A large lagoon meanders through much of this Mission Bay Park resort and the main pond has three little gazebos built over the water. You can sit and snuggle and communicate with one another and the ducks, while listening to the romantic splash of the lagoon's fountains. These little gazebos are best visited after nightfall, when subdued lighting and the absence of other guests makes this place somewhat more romantic.

10 WINDANDSEA BEACH • *Southern La Jolla coast. GETTING THERE: The easiest approach is from the south (via Mission Beach and Pacific Beach) on La Jolla Boulevard, then turn beachward onto Nautilus Street.*

You won't find solitude here on most days; this spot below La Jolla's beautiful coastal homes is one of the most popular beaches in the San Diego area. Part of its popularity comes from the fact that it was featured in Thomas Wolfe's satirical novel, *The Pumphouse Gang,* which, we'll admit, doesn't sound very romantic. However, come here during the off-season, bring a bundling blanket and seek one of the many intimate coves, carved out of sandstone ridges. This is an absolutely grand place for watching the sunset as the lights of La Jolla and San Diego come alive like stationery fireflies.

THE TEN MOST ROMANTIC RESTAURANTS

Wouldn't it be romantic to take your significant other to a fine restaurant, clink your glasses over candlelight and enjoy a fine dinner? Of course. Many San Diego, La Jolla and Coronado restaurants offer fine cuisine and candlelight. To be truly romantic, however, they must be cozy and preferably dimly lit. We prefer booths to tables, particularly those in quiet corners.

To repeat our dinner price range listing from Chapter Three: **$** = less than $10 per entrée, not including, appetizers, drinks or dessert; **$$** = $10 to $19; **$$$** = $20 to $29; **$$$$** = $30 and beyond.

1 TOP O' THE COVE • *1216 Prospect St., La Jolla; (858) 454-7779. French-continental; full bar service. Lunch and dinner daily. Major credit cards; $$$$. GETTING THERE: It's in the heart of downtown overlooking La Jolla Cove.*

The management at the area's most romantic restaurant knows how to appeal to lovers. Several two-people tables are poised before walls of glass, offering grand views of La Jolla Cove when the two aren't looking into one another's eyes. Other tables-for-two are tucked into cozy corners, for those who seek more privacy as they dally over dessert. If you call ahead, the *maitre d'* will guarantee the table of your choice—window on the Pacific or intimate corner. Fine old European décor contributes to the restaurant's romantic setting, with candle-lit tables and warm wood paneling graced by classical art. For more detail on this fine establishment, see Chapter Four, page 87. Incidentally, it's one of only three restaurants picked both by the Zagat review and a recent *San Diego Union* readers' poll as one of the area's most romantic restaurants.

2 *BALI HAI • 2230 Shelter Island Dr.; (619) 222-1181. Full bar service. Lunch and dinner daily, plus Sunday brunch. Major credit cards; $$ to $$$. GETTING THERE: To reach Shelter Island, head toward Point Loma on Rosecrans Street (State Route 209) and turn left onto Shelter Island Drive. Spin around a traffic circle and follow the drive a short distance northeast to the restaurant.*

This is a conditionally romantic restaurant, depending on the cooperation of the *maitre d'*. Sam Choy's Hawaii at the Bali Hai is a rather airy Polynesian place that lacks our preferred cozy corners. However, it does have fine views of San Diego Bay and the city skyline—particularly impressive around sunset. The condition here is that you should insist on a window table, although they're set up for four people. The tables are well spaced, so you can hold private conversations while enjoying your tropical drinks with their cute little umbrellas, followed by coconut shrimp or macadamia nut chicken. For more on this restaurant, see Chapter Three, page 69.

3 *THE BELGIAN LION • 2665 Bacon St., Ocean Beach; (619) 223-2700. French-Belgian; wine and beer. Dinner Thursday-Saturday. Major credit cards; $$$ to $$$$. GETTING THERE: The Lion is at the corner of Bacon and West Point Loma Boulevard. The easiest approach is to follow I-8 to its western terminus, go southwest on Sunset Cliffs Boulevard, turn right onto West Point Loma and follow it two blocks to Bacon.*

This cozy French country cottage restaurant provides the ideal setting for an intimate dinner by candlelight, with its subdued lighting, brocaded furnishings and candelabra wall sconces. The interior, suggestive of a French manor house, is comfortably weathered, like a favorite easy chair. Soft music adds to an atmosphere of hushed elegance. The service is casually polite, with that European flair for discretion. Part of the Lion's intimacy is its limited hours. Since it's open only three nights a week, advance planning is required; and with planning comes anticipation. For more on this cozy cottage restaurant, see Chapter Three, page 50.

4 *GRANT GRILL • In the U.S. Grant Hotel at 326 Broadway; (619) 232-3121. American-continental; full bar service. Dinner nightly. Major credit cards; $$$ to $$$$. GETTING THERE: The U.S. Grant is in the heart of downtown, across a small park from Horton Plaza and bounded by Third and Fourth avenues. The Grill is just off the lobby on the Fourth Avenue side.*

This clubby, softly lit dining salon certainly qualifies as one of the more romantic spots in town. Ask for a soft curved-back booth with a candle-lit table in the rear, where you can snuggle close together while trying to decide between chicken linguine with prosciutto or pepper

crusted beef medallions. The tuxedo-clad waiters here are most attentive, yet will remain at a discreet distance when they know you want
to be alone. (For more on the Grill, see Chapter Three, page 51.)

5 **MARINE ROOM** • *2000 Spindrift Dr., La Jolla Shores; (858)*
459-7222. American, mostly seafood; full bar service. Lunch Monday-
Saturday, dinner nightly and Sunday brunch. Major credit cards; $$$$.
GETTING THERE: From downtown La Jolla, head north on Prospect un-
til it blends into Torrey Pines Road, go about a third of a mile, then turn
left onto Spindrift. The restaurant is on your left, about a third of a mile
down.

What could be more romantic than an intimate dinner with the
evening surf lapping just outside your window? At high tide, incoming
rolls have been known to rinse the windows of this opulent restaurant,
which sits right on the beach. When the two of you aren't watching incoming waves or one another, take note of the opulent dining room
with its floral carpeting, brocaded chairs and scalloped wall sconces.
Both the Zagat survey and *San Diego Union's* "San Diego's Best" readers
poll picked the Marine Room as one of the city's most romantic restaurants, and we certainly concur. We also selected it as one of San Diego's best restaurants overall; see Chapter Three, page 52.

6 **MARIUS** • *At Coronado Island Marriott Resort, 2000 Second*
St., Coronado; (619) 435-3000. French; full bar service. Dinner Tues-
day-Saturday; closed Sunday-Monday. Major credit cards; $$$ to
$$$$. GETTING THERE: Cross the Coronado bridge and go immediately
right onto Glorietta Boulevard; the resort is within less than half a mile
at Second Street and Glorietta.

This small dining room just off the lobby of the Coronado Island
Marriott is a perfect picture of cozy elegance, with lush French décor,
high ceilings and crisp nappery. The service at this stylish restaurant is
friendly and attentive yet unobtrusive. Marius is regarded locally as a
special occasion venue, but don't wait for an anniversary or birthday.
Dinner with your significant other at this restaurant is a special occa-
sion in itself. The Zagat survey rated Marius as San Diego's best French
restaurant and one of it's most romantic dining places. The fare ranges
from Parisian *haut cuisine* to *provençal* with contemporary accents. If
it's within your budget, put yourself in the chef's hands with a multi-
course *prix fixe* dinner with a wine suited to each course.

7 **MR. A'S** • *2550 Fifth Ave.; (619) 239-1377. American-conti-*
nental; full bar service. Lunch weekdays and dinner nightly. GETTING
THERE: The restaurant is located on the 12th floor of the Fifth Avenue
Center near the corner of Laurel Street, just below Balboa Park. Take
Laurel from I-5 or one-way Fifth from downtown.

This is the third restaurant that earned "most romantic" status from both the Zagat survey and a recent *San Diego Union* readers' poll. It's also the only dining room in town to merit AAA's rare four diamond award. We can't argue that Mr. A belongs on a select list, with its splendid view of the city, its cozy booths, plush carpeting, rich burgundy fabrics and scalloped drapes. Curiously, this elegantly romantic restaurant is perched atop an office building. Strolling arm-in-arm through the business-like elevator lobby, you'll have no clue about what you'll find twelve floors above. We also selected Mr. A's as one of San Diego's Ten Very Best Restaurants; Chapter Three, page 53.

8 *PRINCE OF WALES GRILL* • *Hotel del Coronado, 1500 Orange Ave., Coronado; (619) 435-6611. Continental; full bar service. Dinner only. Major credit cards; $$$. GETTING THERE: Cross the Coronado Bridge from San Diego, turn left onto Orange Avenue and follow it a little more than a mile.*

Hotel del Coronado is one of the area's most romantic spots, and its Prince of Wales Grill recently was selected as the most romantic restaurant by *San Diego Magazine*. We also picked it as one our Ten Best Restaurants; see Chapter Three, page 53. Set off a courtyard away from the bustle of the hotel, it offers intimate dining with pleasing ocean views. Recently remodeled, it no longer has that dark clubby look. The new décor features soft colors, gold accents and filmy scalloped drapes, creating a kind of pastel Valentine setting.

Even its name was inspired by a great romance. Edward Albert David, the Prince of Wales, stayed at the Del in 1920 and it was here that he may have first seen his future wife, Wallis Warfield Simpson. Several years later, after she was divorced and he was crowned king of England, they began seeing one another. His relationship with an American divorcée caused a proper British scandal. To put this turmoil to rest, he surrendered his crown to his young brother, announcing "I now quite altogether public affairs, and lay down my burden." They were married in France and spent their remaining years as the Duke and Duchess of Windsor. Edward never again lived in the country whose throne he surrendered for the love of a lady.

9 *TRATTORIA ACQUA* • *1298 Prospect St., La Jolla; (858) 454-0709. Italian and seafood; full bar service. Lunch weekdays, weekend brunch and dinner nightly. Major credit cards; $$ to $$$. GETTING THERE: Acqua is in the Coastwalk shopping complex in downtown La Jolla, just above La Jolla Cove.*

Acqua is bright and airy, yet intimate. It's divided into several small dining areas, most with great views of La Jolla Cove. Some of the tables are tucked into quiet corners. Good food of course is essential to a romantic dining experience and Acqua recently was voted by a local publication as the city's best Italian restaurant. Menu offerings include jumbo shrimp scampi, osso buco, and a seafood pasta of shrimp, mussels, clams and calimari over black and white linguine. It has a good wine list—another essential ingredient to a seductive dinner. Acqua earned a spot as one of our Ten Best View Restaurants in Chapter Four, page 87.

10 *THE WESTGATE ROOM* • *Westgate Hotel San Diego, 1055 Second Ave.; (619) 238-1818. Contemporary American and continental; full bar service. Dinner and Sunday brunch. Major credit cards; $$$ to $$$$. GETTING THERE: The Westgate is just off lower Broadway downtown; the Westgate Room is on the ground floor.*

The Westgate isn't the hotel's main restaurant. Both it and the main dining room, Le Fontainebleau, are quite opulent. The smaller Westgate Room is much more intimate, with just a few tables and booths. This stunning setting of soft peach colors, beaded chandeliers, candlelit tables with little flower vases, and scalloped drapes should stir a little romance in any relationship. The menu is as small as the setting, featuring a few select continental-California *nouveau* entrées such as Chilean sea bass, grilled sea scallops with roasted red pepper sauce, and New York steak with vegetable stir fry.

TEN NAUGHTY DIVERSIONS IN SAN DIEGO

As we noted at the beginning of this chapter, rather conservative San Diego still has its naughty side. What follows is a list of venues for harmless titillation. We don't endorse any of these listings; they are here—in a requisite list of ten—for the idly curious. The deadly threat of AIDS has taken the wind out of what's left of the sexual revolution in California and elsewhere, and we strongly advise against anyone seeking favors from unknown ladies or gentlemen of the evening.

1 *SHOP FOR SAFE SEX: Condoms Plus* • *1220 University Ave.; (619) 291-7400. Wednesday-Thursday 11 to midnight, Friday-Saturday 11 to 2 a.m. and Sunday 1 to 9. MC/VISA. GETTING THERE: This safe sex shop is in the Hillcrest District near the corner of University and Vermont Street.*

A cut above the typical porn shop, this little treasure trove of erotica features love-making potions, scented candles, sexy lingerie, and frisky greeting cards for both heterosexuals and gays. The paraphernalia in the front part of the shop would earn no worse than an "R" rating at the movies. As suggested by the store's name, it has a good selection of condoms, including some that glow in the dark. As a gift for the bored gent who has everything including a vivid imagination, buy the *Executive's Doodle Book* containing line drawings of women with essential features missing; he's expected to fill in the blanks. To reach the store's X-rated section, you need to step into a back room (adults only, please), where you'll find the usual porno videos and magazines and latex body parts.

2 BUY A NAUGHTY NEWSPAPER • *Available at news racks in various areas of San Diego.*

Have you ever wondered what's in those "adult newspapers" that you see in racks around town? Not much, really. Since anyone of any age with four quarters (the average going rate) has access to these tabloids, they've been toned down in recent years, with no nudies in the provocative ads. We found no locally published adult newspapers, incidentally. The most common are *California Swingers* which apparently is published in Denver, and the old standard *LA Express* from that big city up the coast. These tabloids are filled mostly with classified ads from frisky folks who want to meet other consenting adults, singly or in groups. "Hi, my name is Ferdie and I'm bi-curious." "I'm a full-figured blonde, 198 pounds..." "We're looking for a slave. He must be male and good looking. We expect him to have money and wait on us hand and foot."

In your dreams, ladies!

3 DIAL A DATE • *In the San Diego Yellow Pages, under "Escort service, personal."*

So listen, how about a date? The phone book contains eleven pages of ads and listings for "Escort service." Are these legitimate businesses that provide nothing more than a date for lonely guys? Many probably are and, being happily married, we've never called on them. However, we do wonder about some of their ads that suggest such things as leather fantasies, wet & wild moments and erotica exotica.

"Hi, Mom! I just met this wonderful woman through an escort service ad in the Yellow Pages. She's into S&M, velveteen couches and group fantasies. I know you just can't wait to meet her. By the way, is Dad home?"

4 GET RUBBED—POSSIBLY THE WRONG WAY— BY A MASSEUSE.

Back to those Yellow Pages, we found fourteen sheets of listings under "Massage." Of course, there are many legitimate massage parlors. You can tell by the tone of the ads that some masseuses perform *shiatsu* and others probably can't even pronounce it. When an ad offers "massage from blonde centerfold beauties in the privacy of your hotel room," you might be a little suspicious.

Funny thing. Many of the ladies with ads in the "Escort" section also show up under "Massages." They certainly must be versatile.

5 LET THEM ENTERTAIN YOU

A final visit to the San Diego telephone book reveals three pages of "Entertainers—adult." Many of the ads are for "fantastic foxes" and "California dream girls" who'll shed their wardrobe or stage a private lingerie show to liven up bachelor parties. Lest you think this is too macho, some of the ads tout big hunks and hard bodies for bachelorette gatherings. After all, this is the age of equality, so why should the future groom have all the fun?

6 CHECK OUT LES GIRLS • *3201 Hancock at Camino del Rio; (619) 295-1484. Weekdays noon to 2 a.m. and weekends 6 p.m. to 2 a.m. GETTING THERE: Take the Highway 209-Rosecrans exit from I-5 and head west toward Point Loma. Camino del Rio is a short link street just before Highway 209 becomes Rosecrans Street.*

This pink and white building offers plenty of pink inside, advertising live nude shows and "gala nude-ins." A sign proclaims this to be the "biggest nude show in California," although we weren't inclined to go inside and take a census. Flanking Les Girls is another nude dancing place called The Body Shop, and the Hi-Lite adult book store that we've listed below. Thus, this convergence of Camino del Rio and Hancock appears to be as close as San Diego gets to an adult district.

7 BROWSE THROUGH A VERY ADULT BOOK STORE • *Hi-Lite, 3203 Hancock St.; (619) 299-0601. Daily 9 a.m. to 2:30 a.m. Major credit cards. GETTING THERE: It's next to Les Girls; see above.*

This large adult store not only sells every conceivable type of porno book, magazine, video and "marital device," it offers free gift wrapping. ("Happy birthday, Sweetie, but wait until your folks leave before you open it...") The extensive book selection includes *Erotic Power: An Exploration of Dominance and Submission* and *The Illustrated Sexual Encyclopedia*. Looking quite tame in this environment are old copies of *Playboy*, presumably with the centerfolds intact. I noticed an item in the sexual aids department called the "Oriental Love Kit" but I decided I'd better pass on that one.

8 SEE A BIG SCREEN SKIN FLICK • *Kitty Kat Adult Theatre, 4652 University Ave., (619) 280-1879; and Pussycat Theatre, 930 National City Blvd., National City, (619) 477-4477. GETTING THERE: Kitty Kat is between 46th and 47th avenues in the City Heights District, northeast of downtown. Pussycat is in National City about four miles south of downtown; take the Main Street/National City Boulevard exit from I-5 and go south about nine blocks on the boulevard.*

Most adult book and video stores have peep shows for viewing their naughty films. However, these two places have full-sized movie screens. Kitty Kat features a wide screen and promises new movies several times a week. The Pussycat offers senior discounts, so get on over there, Grandpa!

9 SHED YOUR INHIBITIONS AND EVERYTHING ELSE AT A NUDE BEACH • *Black's Beach, Torrey Pines State Reserve. GETTING THERE: To reach Torrey Pines State Reserve, take the Genesee Avenue exit from I-5 and go west; Genesee blends into North Torrey Pine Road. Follow it south and downhill about two miles to the park entrance. The safest way to reach the beach is to walk about a mile south along the seacliffs at low tide.*

Nude sunbathing is illegal at this remote beach, so if you're caught in a raid and there's no place to put the ticket, don't blame us. Black's Beach at the foot of Torrey Pines' 300-foot seacliffs is a popular hangout for those who like to let it all hang out. On a warm summer day, hundreds of sunbathers—with and without suits—gather here. It's a very nice beach with soft sand and almost sheer cliffs rising above, although the surf is treacherous and swimming is not advised. Because of its wild waves, it's a popular surfing area. Incidentally, the beach has no facilities—not even restrooms. Trails lead to it from the cliffs above, but they can be unstable and dangerous, and we don't recommend using them. A safer approach—when the tide is low—is to leave your car at the parking lot just inside the reserve's entrance and walk south about a mile along the base of the seacliffs. You'll know when you've arrived at Black's Beach.

10 BUY HER A SEXY NIGGLE-JIGGLE: Victoria's Secret • *Mission Valley Center at 1640 Camino del Rio North, (619) 298-6360; Fashion Valley at 7007 Friars Rd., (619) 291-0323; Horton Plaza downtown, (619) 236-0816; and at 1111 Prospect, La Jolla, (858) 459-0688.*

Unmentionables are quite mentionable these days, and Victoria's Secret has brought new levels of exotic dignity to scanty and sexy underthings. The firm even advertised during the Superbowl a few years ago. Always with class and never in poor taste, these shops are the best places in town to buy something nice for your lady. The naughty comes later.

"What is the use of a book," thought Alice, *"without pictures?"*
— **Lewis Carroll,** from *Alice's Adventures in Wonderland*

Chapter ten

POINTS OF VIEW
WHERE TO STARE AND SHOOT

This city built on several hills and nearly surrounded by water has some first rate vista points. And it certainly lends itself to photography. San Diego is favored by frequent sunny days and those Kodachrome blends of blues and greens, where the sky meets the land that meets the water.

However, the best vista points don't always produce the best photos. Our eyes provide us with three-dimensional vision and a near 180-degree angle of sight. A camera, unless it's equipped with a fisheye lens, has a much narrower field of view and the resulting photos are two dimensional.

Thus, we provide separate lists. We begin with the Ten Best Viewpoints in and about San Diego, and then we follow with the Ten Best Picture Spots. In between, we offer a quick course in scenic photography, so you can take home some good photos of Sunshine City instead of just snapshots.

145

THE TEN BEST VIEWPOINTS

We begin by taking you to a place that takes in the entire San Diego area and considerably beyond:

1 *BEST OVERALL VIEW* ● *From Mount Soledad at the end of Mount Soledad Road in eastern La Jolla. Gates open from 8 a.m. to midnight. GETTING THERE: Two roads reach Mount Soledad. From La Jolla, turn inland onto Nautilus Street off La Jolla Boulevard, just over a mile south of the downtown area and drive uphill, following directional signs. Or follow I-5 north from San Diego and take the Grand/Garnet Avenue exit, which puts you on Mission Bay Drive. Continue north about half a mile on Mission Bay, go west (left) about a quarter of a mile on Garnet and turn right up Mount Soledad Road.*

No view of the greater San Diego area matches this vista from the top of 822-foot Mount Soledad, the highest point in the inland hills of La Jolla. The mountain is topped by a 43-foot cross, dedicated on Easter Sunday, 1954, to honor America's veterans. It's the site of annual Easter sunrise services. Walk a slow circle around a brick terrace at the base of the cross and take in the entire sweep—La Jolla peninsula with its red-roofed homes, the blue Pacific and distant Coronado Islands offshore, Mission Bay and Point Loma, San Diego Bay and the downtown highrises, the brushy inland areas of Mission Valley, Kearny Mesa and Clairemont Mesa, the thickly landscaped Golden Triangle with highrises sprouting through its vegetation, the campus of the University of California at San Diego and—finally completing your sweep—Torrey Pines and back to the Pacific. On a good day, you can see up the coast to Oceanside and quite possibly beyond, and down the coast to Tijuana.

2 *BEST BAY VIEW* ● *From Cabrillo National Monument at the tip of Point Loma. GETTING THERE: The easiest approach is to follow Rosecrans Street (State Route 209) southwest through Point Loma; you can pick it up near the junctions of I-5 and I-8.*

Although Mount Soledad has the best overall view of the greater San Diego area, the vista from Cabrillo National Monument is a close second. It occupies the tip of Point Loma, more than 400 feet above the bay and the ocean. Views of the bay side are best from the big-windowed visitor center, from the statue of Juan Cabrillo just below it, or from the Old Point Loma Lighthouse, which occupies the highest piece of land here. From any of these vantage points, you can see ships and pleasure boats sailing in and out of San Diego Bay, planes flitting about Coronado's North Island Naval Air Station and San Diego International Airport, the skyline of San Diego and the thickly vegetated and populated hills rising behind it. Do bring your binoculars! If you don't have a pair, you can borrow them at the visitor center.

3 BEST DOWNTOWN SKYLINE VIEWS • *From Harbor Island and from Ferry Landing Marketplace on Coronado. GETTING THERE: Harbor Island is off Harbor Drive, opposite San Diego International Airport. To reach Ferry Landing Marketplace, cross the Coronado Bridge, turn right onto Orange Avenue, then right again onto First Street. The landing is about two blocks down.*

San Diego's downtown skyline has become rather visually dramatic in recent years. Several curiously modern skyscrapers have risen along lower Broadway, and the waterfront is marked by the tall and slender 40-story Hyatt Regency and glittering twin glass towers of the Marriott hotel. The best vantage points for this contemporary architectural collection are from Harbor Island, since it sits in San Diego Bay and offers an unimpeded view; and from Marketplace Landing on the Coronado shore, directly opposite downtown.

4 BEST DOWNTOWN AERIAL VIEW • *The View Lounge at the Hyatt Regency San Diego, 1 Market Place. GETTING THERE: The Regency is adjacent to Seaport Village just off Harbor Drive. From downtown, follow Broadway to Harbor Drive and go left about four blocks.*

Cresting one of southern California's tallest buildings, the fortieth story Top of the Hyatt cocktail lounge provides an awesome view of San Diego Bay, the waterfront north and south, Point Loma and Coronado. You don't have to lean over a bar patron to enjoy this vista. An area called the View Lounge just off the elevator lobby outside the cocktail lounge offers the same vantage point.

5 BEST LA JOLLA COVE VIEW • *From The Coastwalk. GETTING THERE: This shopping and dining complex is in downtown La Jolla, opposite Ivanhoe Street and just above La Jolla Cove.*

The Coastwalk has appeared frequently in this book, since this shingle-sided complex is built above La Jolla Cove, which is the town's prettiest enclave. A couple of restaurants have splendid views down to the cove, with lounges where you can enjoy this vista for the price of a drink. If you're too cheap or just not thirsty, wander among The Coastwalk's corridors and you'll encounter this view between buildings and from shop windows. Another great vantage point is from the lower lobby of La Valencia Hotel, next door at 1132 Prospect Street.

6 BEST MISSION VALLEY VIEW • *Father Serra Museum tower, 2727 Presidio Drive above Old Town; (619) 297-3258. Tuesday-Saturday 10 to 4 and Sunday noon to 4 in summer; Friday-Sunday 10* to 4:30 the rest of the year. GETTING THERE: The museum sits atop Pre-sidio Hill. Drive north through Old Town, turn right onto Taylor Street then go right again onto Presidio Drive and follow signs.

The Father Serra Museum tower offers a nice panorama of the San Diego area through its four windows—from Mission Valley and Mission Bay west to the Pacific and south to the downtown area. You'll see a lot of asphalt from up here, since I-5 and I-8 converge below the museum at the base of Presidio Hill. Old photo and sketches beneath each window show how the area looked in earlier days. This area busy with freeways, homes and harbors essentially was a brushy desert when Father Serra arrived in 1769.

7 BEST MISSION BAY AND BEYOND VIEW • *The tower at San Diego Paradise Point Resort, 1404 W. Vacation Rd. GETTING THERE: The resort is on Vacation Isle in the middle of Mission Bay Park. To reach it, take Ingraham Street through Mission Bay and turn west onto Vacation Road.*

An 81-step tower rises above this extensive 44-acre tropical resort. From the top, you'll get a great view of the resort at your feet, the rest of Mission Bay, Mission Beach and the Pacific Ocean, the ridge of Point Loma, the downtown San Diego skyline and Coronado. It's a great place to watch the white triangles of sailboats at play on Mission Bay below you.

8 BEST SEACLIFF VIEW • *Torrey Pines State Reserve, North Torrey Pines Road (Old U.S. 101); (858) 755-2063. GETTING THERE: Take the Genesee Avenue exit from I-5 and go west; Genesee blends into North Torrey Pine Road. Follow it south and downhill about two miles to the park entrance near the beach.*

Take your pick of seacliff views at this state park, which preserves several hundred acres of ocean bluffs and beaches. From the entrance gate you can walk along the narrow beach, staring up at those impos-ing slopes. Don't try this walk during high tide or you could get stranded. (Walk far enough—about a mile—and you'll encounter Black's Beach, where some folks like to get an overall tan.) For aerial views, drive to one of the reserve's upper parking lots near the visitor center and follow trails to the bluffs. Or follow signs to the Torrey Pines Glider Port, where hang gliders launch themselves from those cliffs and sail out over the ocean. We cover Torrey Pines State Reserve in greater detail in Chapter Fourteen, page 196.

9 THE BEST COUNTYWIDE VIEW • *From Cowles Mountain in Mission Trails Regional Park. GETTING THERE: Drive about seven miles east on I-8 and take the College Avenue exit north (opposite the San Diego State University campus). Follow College Avenue a mile north,* *then go right on Navajo for two miles to Golfcrest Drive. Turn left on Golfcrest for a trailhead parking area.*

Mission Trails Regional Park covers 5,760 acres of arid, brushy hills northeast of San Diego, and the highest of these is 1,591-foot Cowles Mountain. On a clear day, the views from up here take in a great 360-degree panorama of southern San Diego County, from the Pacific Ocean, north toward Escondido, east toward the desert and south over Mission Valley into the city itself. A mile and a half trail leads from a parking area to the crest. Wear comfortable shoes and bring plenty of water, since it's a steep climb with more than a thousand foot elevation gain. Hopefully you will decide—panting and puffing at the top—that the view is worth the effort.

10 **THE BEST PLACE TO WATCH PLANES LAND** • *Corner of Pacific Highway and Laurel Street. GETTING THERE: Take the Laurel Street exit from I-5 and go west three blocks to Pacific Highway.*

Not all pilots love San Diego International Airport. It's on a mudflat just below the city, and the final approach is over hilly residential areas. From the intersection of Pacific Highway and Laurel Street, you can watch the jets skim over those neighborhoods, pass directly overhead and thump down on the runway a few hundred yards away.

PHOTO TIPS: SHOOTING SAN DIEGO

Because photographs are two-dimensional, good photographers apply several techniques to give them depth. You can suggest dimension in a scenic view by placing a tree limb or interesting street lamp in the foreground, and perhaps something in the middleground. On the other hand, if you're focusing on a single object, don't clutter your photo with framing; let the viewer see nothing but that subject.

Most outdoor photos are predominately blue, green and brown, the colors of the sky and the earth. With San Diego's abundance of water and sunny skies, you'll get plenty of blue in your photos. To brighten them, add colors from the warm side of the spectrum—reds, yellows and oranges. Dress Auntie Maude in a bright yellow dress or place a brilliant flower in the foreground of your photo, off to the side where it won't interfere with the main subject.

When you photograph people, don't force them to squint into the sun. Position them with the sun behind you but to the right or left so it strikes them at an angle, accenting their features. Also, have your subjects interact with the setting instead of just staring morosely at the camera or—worse—wearing a silly grin.

Light and shadow are key elements in photography, giving two-dimensional photos more a feeling of shape and contour. Early morning and late afternoon are the best times to shoot, when shadows are stronger, bringing out detail in your subject. This is particularly true for structural photos. At midday when the sun is shining straight down, objects appear flat, washed out and uninteresting. Further, in the late afternoon, the atmosphere attains a subtle golden quality, giving warm tones to your pictures. If clouds are drifting overhead, watch for the likelihood of a spectacular Pacific sunset.

Aiming your canon: the ten best picture spots

You can get good results at our suggested picture spots with an adjustable camera (we're partial to Canons) or a simple point and shoot. If you have an adjustable camera, a 28mm to 80mm zoom lens will greatly improve your photo opportunities.

1 *BEST SHOT OF DOWNTOWN SAN DIEGO • From the waterfront off Harbor Drive, near Laurel Street. GETTING THERE: Harbor Drive parallels I-5 and you can take the airport exit at Laurel Street.*

This photo, perhaps more than any other, captures the essence of this great waterfront city. A pedestrian and bike route extends along the San Diego bayfront paralleling Harbor Drive. Walk along the waterfront below the junction of Harbor Drive and Laurel Street and you can get several fine shots of downtown San Diego, with boats, masts and seagulls and possibly a flotilla of mudhens in the foreground. You can compress the views with a medium range telephoto or use a normal lens to widen your perspective. This can be either a horizontal or vertical shot. It's an afternoon-only picture since—from this vantage point—you're looking east and directly into the morning sun. If you have a tripod along, you can get some really nice sunset and early evening shots.

2 *THE BEST AERIAL SHOTS OF SAN DIEGO • From the View Lounge on the fortieth floor of the Hyatt Regency San Diego, 1 Market Place. GETTING THERE: The Regency is adjacent to Seaport Village just off Harbor Drive.*

This is the same vantage point we suggested for one of the city's ten best views above. Take your pick of panoramic shots through picture windows of the View Lounge, which is just outside the Top of the Hyatt cocktail lounge. A particularly nice angle from up here is down toward the much shorter dual towers of the Marriott and its large marina. Photos from this perch can be horizontal or vertical, employing a variety of lenses, depending on which subjects you choose. Watch the windows to make sure you don't get a light glare or the reflection of your own image. One way to avoid flare or reflection is to press the lens right against the glass.

3 *THE BEST SHOT OF BALBOA PARK'S CALIFORNIA BUILDING AND TOWER* • *Beside the Sculpture Garden, north side of El Prado. GETTING THERE: Follow Laurel Street east to Balboa Park, which becomes El Prado as it passes through the west entrance.*

Balboa Park's most recognized landmarks are its Moorish-Spanish buildings along El Prado, preserved from the 1915 Panama-California International Exposition. Perhaps the most photographed of these is the domed California Building housing the Museum of Man and the adjacent California Tower near the park's west entrance. For a nice angle, walk east away from the museum on El Prado for about a block until you're beside the Sculpture Garden. Turn and shoot the two Moorish domes, framed in foreground eucalyptus limbs and overhanging ferns. This shot is particularly nice in late afternoon when the sun casts strong shadows on the buildings. It's a vertical, using a medium range lens.

4 *BEST SHOT OF HOTEL DEL CORONADO* • *From the hotel beach. GETTING THERE: Cross the Coronado Bridge, turn left onto Orange Avenue and follow it a mile the hotel, which is on your right.*

Hotel del Coronado's signature—and one of the most photographed objects in southern California—is its curious conical tower with multiple turrets. Most photographers frame it in the landscaping near the front drive. However, we like a different angle—from the strand near one of the beach volleyball courts. Take a shot over an iceplant-covered sand dune (busy with blooms in spring and summer), and frame the grand old hotel tower between a couple of palm trees. The format is rather square, best taken with a medium range lens.

5 *BEST SHOT OF THE MARRIOTT TOWERS* • *From Embarcadero Marina Park, south end of the waterfront walk, alongside Harbor Drive. GETTING THERE: From downtown, take Broadway to the waterfront, turn left onto Harbor Drive, follow it about a mile south and then east, then go right on Kettner Boulevard for about a block. You'll see a parking area for the bayside park.*

The twin towers of the San Diego Marriott comprise one of the most dramatic structures in the city. The most impressive view is missed by most photographers, since it's between the hotel and the harbor, away from surrounding streets. Get to Embarcadero Marina Park and you can frame the two towers in gnarled trees in the foreground, with masts of boats in the marina as a middleground. We like to shoot to the right of the southernmost of the trees, placing an overhanging branch above the glass towers. This is a horizontal format and can be shot from noon to late afternoon. You're looking northeast so the sun is behind you most of the day.

6 **BEST SHOT OF MISSION SAN DIEGO** • *The* campanario *or bell wall, taken from gardens on either side. GETTING THERE: Follow I-8 about seven miles east from San Diego and take the Mission Gorge Road exit (near the I-15 interchange). Follow Mission Gorge north about half a mile, then go left on Twain Avenue for another half mile; the mission is on your right.*

The bell wall of Mission San Diego de Alcalá is one of the city's most photographed landmarks. To give capture the simplicity of this rustic structure, shoot it straight on, with a bit of landscaping in the foreground. There are garden areas on both sides of the bell wall. Because of the position of the sun, it's best shot from an interior garden in the morning and from the front of the church in the afternoon. If you want a silhouette, reverse your shooting times. This is a vertical, using a normal lens.

7 **THE BEST SHOT OF POINT LOMA LIGHTHOUSE** • *Cabrillo National Monument at the tip of Point Loma. GETTING THERE: Pick up State Route 209 (Rosecrans Street) near the junctions of I-5 and I-8 and follow signs through Point Loma to the national monument.*

Two lighthouses occupy the tip of Point Loma. The original, now a museum, sits on the area's highest bluff and this old white brick structure is a favorite of photographers. The newer one is lower down, still operational and closed to the public. If you walk a few hundred feet along the access road that leads to the new lighthouse, you'll see the old one nicely framed in pine trees. This shot is best in the late afternoon, when the sun's slanting rays cast shadows on the whitewashed building. It's a vertical shot, using a medium range lens.

8 **BEST SHOT OF OLD TOWN** • *Casa de Bandini, taken from the northeast corner of Old Town Plaza. GETTING THERE: Take the Old Town exit from I-5 or I-8 northwest of the city.*

One of the most handsome buildings in Old Town San Diego State Historic Park is Casa de Bandini adobe, now a popular restaurant. And the best place to photograph it is from the northeast corner of the Old Town Plaza, where you can use a large pine tree and gnarled eucalyptus as foreground foliage. Stand near the marker indicating the "End of the Kearny Trail." This is best as a horizontal shot, with a medium range lens.

9 **BEST SHOT OF A PLANE LANDING** • *Grape Street and Harbor Drive, from the bayfront promenade. GETTING THERE: Take the Laurel Street exit from I-5, go west past the edge of the airport and curve south onto Harbor Drive; follow it four blocks to Grape Street.*

In the Ten Best Viewpoints, we mentioned that planes must swoop low over San Diego on their final approach to the airport. For a particularly dramatic shot of one of the landings, position yourself on the bayfront walk parallel to Harbor Drive, near the intersection of Grape Street. As a plane makes its final approach, you can catch it with palm trees in the foreground and hillside residential areas behind. For further drama, use a slow shutter speed and practice "panning." By this technique, photographers track a moving object, following its trajectory as they squeeze the shutter. With luck, the object—a plane in this instance—will be in focus and the background will be blurred. Use a medium range telephoto for this shot to bring the plane in close.

10 BEST SANTA FE STATION SHOT • *Lower Broadway, from the train tracks.*

The restored 1915 Spanish colonial style Santa Fe train depot with its twin Moorish domes stands in sharp contrast to the sleek glass and steel highrises of lower Broadway. The old depot was dressed up recently with new landscaping. If you stand below the train tracks that cross Broadway between Kettner and the Pacific Highway and wait for a trolley to show up, you can get a great shot, with the muted colors of the depot, the bright red trolley and glistening glass towers behind. You'll have to shift around a bit to avoid light standards and other distractions in the foreground. This shot will require either lucky timing or patience; trolleys pass this way about every fifteen minutes.

An extravagance is anything you buy that is of no earthly use to your wife.
— Franklin P. Jones

Chapter eleven

CREDIT CARD CORRUPTION
SHOPPING UNTIL YOU'RE DROPPING

As the second largest city in California, San Diego provides ample opportunity for pushing the limits of your credit cards. It's large enough to have a tremendous variety of shops and stores, including all the major national and regional chains. Its proximity to Mexico adds an Hispanic flavor to its shopping venues.

THE TEN BEST MALLS, MERCADOS AND SHOPPING AREAS

Because of San Diego's balmy climate, all of its malls are open to the sky, or only semi-covered. Most are attractive places, with large courtyards, fountains and sunny dispositions not generally found in enclosed malls. Our list isn't limited to malls. We also focus on areas that have high concentrations of interesting shops, including that grand Mexican marketplace, Bazaar del Mundo in Old Town.

1 **HORTON PLAZA** • *Downtown area; (619) 238-1596. Most stores open weekdays 10 to 9, Saturday 10 to 7 and Sunday 11 to 6. GETTING THERE: The shopping complex is rimmed by First and Fourth avenues, Broadway and G Street.*

Horton Plaza is a large complex with more than 140 stores, specialty shops and cafés. It's our favorite San Diego shopping venue because of its convenience, its variety of stores, its cheerful multicolored Disneyesque look and its access to downtown. There's plenty of covered parking and three hours are free with any merchant's validation. Although the plaza was born of urban renewal by demolition, it has played a key role in stemming the flow of commerce to the suburbs. In addition to its shops, it has a multi-screen movie theater, a legitimate theater and seven restaurants. A 17-stall food court offers everything from sushi to gyros. Three department stores—Nordstrom, Macy's and Mervyn's—anchor this bright and cheery mall. It's built on split levels, which can lead to confusion when it's time to find the right passageway to the parking garage, although helpful mall employees can quickly set you on course.

2 **BAZAAR DEL MUNDO** • *2754 Calhoun St.; (619) 296-3161. Most shops open daily 10 to 9; various hours for restaurants. GETTING THERE: It's the western end of Old Town San Diego State Historic Park.*

For decades, Bazaar del Mundo has been the brightest spot in Old Town—a technicolor carnival of shops, restaurants, plazas, fountains and piped in music. Although the ambiance and accent are heavily Hispanic, the bazaar features an international brew of imports, from Russian folk art and Portuguese dinnerware to European crystal and Indonesian masks. One shop is devoted entirely to animals, from figurines to hand puppets. The quality of goods in the bazaar's dozen or so stores runs the gamut from rubber snakes and other tourist gimmicks to some really fine art and decorator items. If all of this shopping works up an appetite, you can chose from half a dozen nearby restaurants, including Casa de Pico, an outdoor restaurant surrounded by this rainbow-colored shopping center.

3 **COST PLUS WORLD MARKET** • *372 Fourth Ave.; (619) 236-1737. GETTING THERE: The market is in Gaslamp Quarter near the bayfront, at J and Fourth.*

This "world market" is so large that it can be regarded as a shopping complex, although it's under the single lofty roof of a cavernous waterfront warehouse. This is classic Cost Plus, with every conceivable kind of imported item. Selections include woven baskets, specialty coffees, teas, foods and candies, clothing, kitchenware and kitchen gadgets, rugs and furnishings, general curios and a large wine selection.

4 *FASHION VALLEY MALL* • *7007 Friars Rd.; (619) 688-9113. Most stores open Monday-Saturday 10 to 9 and Sunday 11 to 7. GETTING THERE: Follow Freeway 163 about a mile north from I-8 and take Friars Road west; the mall is on your left.*

San Diego County's largest shopping mall with more than 200 stores and restaurants, Fashion Valley is anchored by Macy's, Robinsons-May, Saks Fifth Avenue, Neiman Marcus, Nordstrom and JCPenny. Tucked in among them is a large assortment of specialty shops, restaurants and a multi-screen movie theater. A second level food court has more than a dozen takeouts, offering everything from sushi and designer coffees to *cous cous* and yogurt. If you're afoot in San Diego, you can take the trolley to the mall. The facility has a kind of California-Spanish look, although most of this is lost in an encirclement of rather austere parking structures.

5 *FERRY LANDING MARKETPLACE* • *In Coronado at the terminal. GETTING THERE: Cross the Coronado Bridge from San Diego, turn right onto Orange Avenue, then right again onto First Street for a couple of blocks.*

This shopping venue is quite appealing with its Cape Cod style blue and white gabled buildings. Its walkways are lined with tables and benches, and the views across the bay to the San Diego skyline are just great. Further, if you're afoot in town, you can take the ferry across from the San Diego waterfront, since the Coronado terminal is adjacent to this shopping area.

Although Ferry Landing Marketplace is attractive, it appears that planners couldn't decide whether to make it a serious shopping venue or a tacky tourist place, so they've done both. You'll find art galleries next to Hebrew National hot dog stands and jewelry stores adjacent to trinket shops. And now matter how you shape it, a Burger King done up in Martha's Vineyard style architecture is still a Burger King.

6 *GROSSMONT CENTER* • *5500 Grossmont Center Dr., La Mesa; (619) 465-2900. Most stores open weekdays 10 to 9, Saturday 10 to 6 and Sunday 11 to 6. GETTING THERE: Go east to La Mesa on I-8, take the La Mesa Boulevard/Grossmont Center Drive exit, go left under the freeway and turn left into the center, at the third stoplight.*

Grossmont is a nicely landscaped, single level, open air center with more than 100 shops and restaurants. We like its simple "X" layout, which is easy to navigate. All shops are one story except the anchors of Macy's and Montgomery Ward.

7 *LA JOLLA DOWNTOWN* • *Prospect Avenue between Drury Lane and Cave Street.*

Downtown La Jolla is the Carmel of Southern California—a tidy and compact gathering of trendy shops, boutiques and cafés. Many of the shops are right above the beach, and some stores even have views of La Jolla Cove below. The above-the-beach shopping area begins with 1250 Prospect Place, housing George's at the Cove restaurant and several shops. Moving north, you'll encounter more shops and then the handsome shingle-sided Coastwalk with the Crabcatcher and Trattoria Acqua view restaurants and several shops and boutiques. These downtown La Jolla shops offer the kinds of goods one expects in this environment, with the prices that you'd expect—paintings, art prints, sculptures, Italian leather goods, fine sportswear, designer shoes and jewelry.

8 *MISSION VALLEY CENTER* • *1640 Camino del Rio North; (619) 296-6375. Most stores open Monday-Saturday 10 to 9 and Sunday 11 to 6. GETTING THERE: Go east about four miles on I-8 from the I-5 interchange and take the Mission Center Road/Auto Circle exit. Go north over the freeway, then east onto Camino del Rio and turn north into the mall.*

Multi-colored support posts holding up bright canvas sails and tarps give this mall a kind of cheery world's fair look. One of the area's larger shopping centers, it has more than a hundred stores and restaurants, with Robinsons-May, Macy's Home & Furniture, Nordstrom's Rack and Wards as its anchor stores. It's an open-air mall, with most of the shops on one level.

9 *SEAPORT VILLAGE* • *849 W. Harbor Dr.; (619) 235-4014. Shops open 10 to 10 in summer and 10 to 9 the rest of the year. GETTING THERE: From downtown, follow Broadway toward the bay, turn left on the Pacific Highway and follow it to the end. From the bayfront, follow Harbor Drive or Pacific Highway south.*

This appealing Spanish California style shopping area is low level and low key, rambling leisurely over several acres of lawns, fountain courtyards and the bayfront. A central attraction here is the Broadway Flying Horses carousel, with animals carved by the legendary carousel creator Charles I.D. Looff. It was built in Coney Island, New York, in the 1890s. Seaport Village has about seventy-five stores, boutiques, cafés and food take-outs. Its large and inviting central plaza is the scene of frequent entertainments. Like the carousel, the entertainment is mostly from a gentler era, such as accordion concerts, mimes and kazoo shows.

10 *UNIVERSITY TOWNE CENTRE ● La Jolla Village Drive at Genesee Avenue in the Golden Triangle; (858) 546-8858. Most stores open weekdays 10 to 9, Saturday 10 to 7 and Sunday 11 to 6. GETTING THERE: Go north about nine miles on I-5 from the I-8 interchange, take the La Jolla Village Drive exit east and follow it about a mile to Genesee; the center is on your right.*

Anchored by Macy's, Robinsons-May, Sears and Nordstrom, this large, modern facility has more than 150 shops and restaurants, and even an indoor ice rink. It's an appealing open air shopping complex rimmed by eucalyptus trees and built around a large palm tree plaza. Particularly appealing, west of the plaza, is a series of fountains with spouting bronze dolphins and other sea creatures. University Towne Centre's Marketplace is one of the largest foods court in the area, with indoor and outdoor tables; see below.

The TEN BEST SPECIALTY PLACES

There is no Number One in this list since it's a rather unrelated selection of some of the more interesting places to browse, barter, buy and eat.

1 *THE BEST FOOD MARKET: Trader Joe's ● 1092 University Avenue in the Hillcrest District, (619) 296-3122; and in La Jolla Village Square at 8657 Villa La Jolla Drive, (858) 546-8629. Daily 9 to 9; MC/VISA. GETTING THERE: Despite the address, the Hillcrest Trader Joe's is about two blocks north of University Avenue. Either turn onto Tenth Avenue and curve through a Ralphs supermarket parking lot, or turn north onto Vermont Street. For the La Jolla market, drive north about eight miles from San Diego on I-5, take the Nobel Drive exit, go west over the freeway and turn left into the La Jolla Village Square shopping center.*

Trader Joe's is our kind of market—a health conscious store that has essential food items, kosher, organic and preservative-free products and a good wine selection. The focus here is on imported and specialty foods, although you also can get your basic milk, meats and fresh veggies. We enjoy browsing through the store without a shopping list, just to see what we might encounter—pasta from Italy, maple pecan crunch cereal, canned Thai curry soup, blue corn chips, dried papaya spears, imported candies, aloe vera juice or Holland mini-toasts. Need picnic fare? Go to the prepared foods cooler for a turkey pita sandwich with *cous cous* salad, or a complete sushi setup. The wine section has a good imported and domestic mix and you often can find some great buys. In fact, prices in general are competitive with those in conventional markets.

2 *THE BEST FARMERS' MARKET: Farmers Bazaar* • *At the corner of Seventh Avenue and K Street. GETTING THERE: The market is just outside Gaslamp Quarter; follow Sixth Avenue south, then go right on K Street.*

Although you'll find weekly farmers markets scattered about San Diego County, this is the only one that's permanently anchored and open daily. Actually, it's more of a large produce and grocery mart, housed in an old brick warehouse just up from the waterfront. It has a strong Mexican accent and you can buy such essentials as cactus pads, Mexican squash, fresh tortillas and other Hispanic culinary essentials. The large building also contains several other shops that sell flowers, Mexican curios and bakery goods. If you need a bite to eat, you'll find Mexican, Chinese and Italian takeouts.

3 *THE BEST PLACE TO BUY FINE FOLK ART: Mingei International Museum* • *In Balboa Park at 1439 El Prado; (619) 239-0003. Tuesday-Sunday 10 to 4; closed Monday;* **$$**. *GETTING THERE: Mingei is on the House of Charm on the southwest corner of Plaza de Panama.*

The gift shop at this fine museum offers an outstanding selection of international folk art and artifacts. Choices range from whimsical carved walking sticks from Indonesia and expensive antique lacquer ware from China to inexpensive and brilliantly colored wood and *papier mache* folk art from Mexico. The shop also has good selection of books on folk art and collectibles.

4 *THE BEST PLACE TO FIND CHEERFUL DECORATOR ITEMS: Design Center Accessories* • *Bazaar del Mundo; (619) 296-3161. Daily 10 to 9. Major credit cards. GETTING THERE: The Design Center occupies several shop fronts in the bazaar on the western end of Old Town San Diego State Historic Park.*

Does your house need cheering up? You'll find hundreds of vividly colored decorator items and accessories for your kitchen and other rooms in this string of Bazaar del Mundo shops. Choices range from gaudy Mexican lacquer ware and Guatemalan wood carvings to Portuguese dishware and locally crafted terra cotta. Looking for a spoon-rest in the shape of a flattened Tabasco bottle? This is your place.

5 *THE BEST PLACE TO SHOP FOR THE PERSON WHO HAS EVERYTHING: Uforia* • *In Horton Plaza; fourth level; (619) 238-1596. Weekdays 10 to 9, Saturday 10 to 7 and Sunday 11 to 6. GETTING THERE: Horton Plaza is downtown, rimmed by First and Fourth avenues, Broadway and G Street.*

Can't find the right gift for that special person in your life? How about a T-shirt with a portrait of Jesse "The Body" Ventura, or a life-size standup cutout of Marilyn Monroe or James Dean, a Betty Boops beach towel or perhaps a rather naughty greeting card? This shop has an intriguing clutter of logo items, smartass gifts and offbeat trinkets. That's where I found my Tweetie throw-pillow.

6 THE BEST PLACE TO SHOP FOR CARS YOU PROBABLY CAN'T AFFORD: **Symbolic Motor Car Company** • *7440 La Jolla Blvd., La Jolla; (858) 454-1800. Daily 9 to 6. GETTING THERE: It's at the intersection of Pearl Street, a few blocks from downtown La Jolla.*

This crowded automobile showroom displays more classic cars that some auto museums. It sells both new and "previously driven" models of some of the finest cars in the world. It is said that if you have to ask the price of a Bentley, you can't afford it. We can't, so we'll tell you that the price tag on a 1996 model was $279,000. A new Rolls Royce Silver Spur was marked at $216,000. The most expensive item we saw was a 1998 Bentley for $319,000. The company also sells classic Porsches, Lotuses, Lamborginis and Ferraris. Some were tagged at even less than $100,000. Sell the house, Betty; I've always wanted a Ferrari.

7 THE BEST PLACE TO BREAK BREAD: **Bread & Cie Bakery & Café** • *350 University Ave.; (619) 683-9322. Monday-Saturday 7 a.m. to early evening, Sunday from 8. GETTING THERE: It's in the Hillcrest District, between Third and Fourth avenues.*

This cavernous place is a serious bakery and more. It's a favorite breakfast stop for the people of Hillcrest, who come by for their fresh baked goods and designer coffees. Lunch offerings include roast turkey breast, black forest ham and tuna salad, or a foccaccia pizza. Mostly, however, this is a venue for baked goods, and you can sample whatever is fresh from the ovens. Among its regular bread selections are anise and fig, black olive, jalapeño and cheese, and sourdough baguettes. Daily specials include such curious breads as goat cheese and garlic, pumpkin seed, roasted corn and red pepper, and walnut and scallion.

8 THE BEST PLACE TO BUY SAN DIEGO SOUVENIRS: **The San Diego City Store** • *Horton Plaza, third level; (619) 238-1596. Weekdays 10 to 9, Saturday 10 to 7 and Sunday 11 to 6. GETTING THERE: Horton Plaza is downtown, bounded by Broadway, G Street, First and Fourth avenues.*

There's no shortage of souvenir shops in Old Town, Sea World and other obvious tourist places. However, for mementos that really say San Diego, this the place. You can buy replicas of local street signs, "I Love San Diego" bumper stickers, personalized license plates, city logo hats and T-shirts, and San Diego Monopoly games and jigsaw puzzles. We even saw replicas of a sign citing a local ordinance: "Swimsuits optional beyond this point." And we thought old San Diego was rather conservative.

9 *THE BEST MALL FOOD COURT: University Towne Centre* • *La Jolla Village Drive at Genesee Avenue in the Golden Triangle; (858) 546-8858. GETTING THERE: Go north about nine miles on I-5 from the I-8 interchange, take the La Jolla Village Drive exit east and follow it about a mile to Genesee. The center is on your right and the food court is south of the central plaza.*

University Towne Centre's Marketplace surely will capture a fast food freak's fancy. Under a single roof is Arby's roast beef sandwiches, Sbarro pizzas, Taco Bell, A&W, the Great Gyros Greek food, Humphrey's yogurt, a large salad bar called California Crisp, Teriyaki House Japanese food, Sub King submarine sandwiches, Waz Wan Indian food, Cinnabuns, Panda Express Chinese takeout, Lucita's Mexican Café and Hot Dog on a Stick. Just around the corner is Starbuck's. You can dine indoors, on the edge of the shopping center's Ice Chalet skating rink or outdoors on a large plaza. If you've got kids in tow, turn them loose in an adjacent video game parlor called Yellow Brick Road.

10 *THE BEST PLACE TO FIND ANTIQUES: Unicorn Antique Mall* • *704 J St.; (619) 232-1696. Most dealers accept major credit cards. GETTING THERE: The mall is on the southeastern edge of Gaslamp Quarter at J Street and Seventh Avenue.*

Looking for a Panama-California International Exposition souvenir plate to hang above the mantel? How about an antique phone stand or a Wendell Wilkie campaign button? Unicorn is one of the largest antique and collectible malls in the country. Eighty dealers occupy three floors of an old Gaslamp building, covering 30,000 square feet.

True enjoyment comes from activity of the mind and exercise of the body; the two are ever united. —**Humboldt**

Chapter twelve

GETTING PHYSICAL
THE BEST PLACES TO WORK OFF
CHAPTERS THREE & FOUR

Don't get too comfortable at poolside in San Diego. You'll need some exercise to shed all those enchilada calories! Fortunately, Sunshine City lends itself to physical fitness. Its many parks and miles of shoreline provide dozens of inviting places to take a hike or pedal a bike. And all that sunny weather practically begs visitors and residents to get out and do something. The distances indicated for all of our walks, hikes and bike routes are for round trips or loop trips, since we assume you'll want to get back to where you left your car.

THE TEN BEST WALKS AND HIKES
Most of these routes involve walking more than hiking, since many of the city's more scenic pedestrian paths are along the waterfront, in Mission Bay Park and on the beach.

A helpful guide for strolling about the city is *San Diego on Foot* by Carol Mendel. This little book suggests about twenty walks in San Diego, in neighboring La Jolla and at Torrey Pines State Reserve. You'll find it at local book stores, or contact the author-publisher: Carol Mendel, P.O. Box 6022, San Diego, CA 92116.

1 BALBOA PARK GARDEN WALK • *In Balboa Park. About two miles; easy to moderate. GETTING THERE: The walk starts at the Japanese Friendship Garden, south of El Prado and west of Park Boulevard.*

With its lush gardens, historic Spanish-Moorish buildings along El Prado, hidden enclaves and great expanses of grass and eucalyptus groves, Balboa Park is the best walking venue in the city. And a great way to see the best of the park is to follow a route linking its main gardens. We don't need to describe this outing in detail because it's all explained in a free brochure called *Self-Guided Walk: The Gardens of Balboa Park.* It's available at the Visitor Center in the northwest corner of the House of Hospitality, just off Plaza de Panama. You'll also find it at racks in the park's various museums and other attractions. The brochure even tells you what's blooming in the gardens at various times of the year, so you can look for azalea and camellia blossoms in January, Bougainvillea in May and Chinese flame trees in the fall.

In case you can't lay your hands on a brochure, you can follow a regular park map. The walk begins at the Japanese Friendship Garden, dips down into Palm Canyon, takes you to the formal hedgerows of Alcazar Garden and to the most attractive horticultural venue in the park—the Botanical Building. From there, you'll trek to the Desert Garden and Rose Garden on the park's eastern edge, skim past the Zoo Garden and wind up near your starting point, at Casa del Ray Moro Garden, adjacent to the House of Hospitality.

2 DOWNTOWN SAN DIEGO • *Two or more miles, depending on how much you wander through Horton Plaza and Gaslamp Quarter. It's a moderately easy stroll with only one modest upgrade. GETTING THERE: Begin at First Avenue and G Street, at the northwest corner of Horton Plaza.*

This route will take you past the most interesting elements of downtown—some of its historic buildings, gleaming new skyscrapers and the old Victorian and brickfront structures of Gaslamp Quarter. Our starting point is in Gaslamp at the corner of First and G Street, since it's near several parking lots.

To begin, walk a block north on First Avenue alongside the Horton Plaza shopping complex, then turn left onto F in front of the block-long rose granite Federal Building and U.S. Courthouse. Two blocks below, at Union and F, note an odd looking windowless highrise. That's San Diego's city jail, the Metropolitan Correction Center, and we suppose it's windowless because the bad guys don't deserve nice views.

Turn right onto Union here and walk past the large patio of the Federal Building; note the two huge black granite trapezoidal triangles that presumably represent modern art.

Turn left and march down the south side of Broadway, passing several of the city's glittering new highrises. You'll encounter the Koll Center at Broadway and India, with a great glass barrel arched foyer. Step inside to admire its lofty heights and towering potted palm trees. A block below at Kettner Boulevard, cross Broadway to explore the imposing Spanish colonial style 1915 Santa Fe Station with its twin Moorish domes. The San Diego Museum of Contemporary Art is on the east side of Kettner, near a San Diego Trolley station.

Now, walk up Broadway's north sidewalk, passing the tapered glass box of One America Plaza, which suggests a giant frozen stalagmite, then—in sharp contrast—the 1924 square-shouldered Spanish colonial style Army-Navy YMCA. It offers inexpensive lodgings; see Chapter Five, page 98. From budget we go to upscale, crossing in front of the stunning hexagonal glass towers of the Wyndham Emerald Plaza Hotel. Check out its lofty and dramatically modern atrium lobby. Next you'll pass the Hall of Justice with its vaguely art deco façade of fluted columns. Turn left up Union Street between the Hall of Justice and the San Diego County Courthouse, then turn right onto C Street, which is a rail corridor for the San Diego Trolley. It's also a pedestrian way with a few shops and cafés along the route.

Follow this corridor to Second Avenue and turn right toward Broadway, pausing to step inside the ornate lobby of the Westgate Hotel, fashioned after a reception room of France's Palace of Versailles. Turn left onto Broadway and peek into the old fashioned dark wood paneled lobby of the U.S. Grant Hotel between Third and Fourth avenues. Now, cross Broadway to Horton Plaza Park, a landscaped patch of green in front of the entrance to Horton Plaza.

After exploring this cheerfully decorated and multi-tiered shopping complex—where you'll undoubtedly get lost—find an exit on the east or south side, which puts you into Gaslamp Quarter. We won't suggest a specific route through this area of fine old brick buildings; just wander at will to explore its many shops and perhaps pause for lunch. Most of its restaurants have sidewalk tables. The sixteen-block Gaslamp Quarter is roughly bounded by Broadway, Fourth and Fifth avenues and Market Street. You might finish your exploration by walking down Fifth to L Street. This takes you past the Quarter's main restaurant row and virtually all of the cafés here have outdoor tables. We prefer these places on lower Fifth because they're away from the heavier traffic that rumbles through the heart of Gaslamp.

If you cross L, you can load up on material about greater San Diego and next-door Mexico at the International Information Center. It's on a plaza with a sidewalk-level "dancing fountain." On a hot day, kids love to scamper through it, not knowing when little jets of water will shoot up and douse them. From this plaza, you'll get a nice view of some of

San Diego's most interesting buildings, including its really strange convention center with giant concrete triangles, the highrise Marriott and Hyatt hotels and the skyscrapers of lower Broadway.

For an interesting route back to your starting point, follow Harbor Drive northwest past the Marriott and Hyatt; both are worth exploring. Swing left toward the harbor and walk through the imposing, lushly landscaped twelve-story atrium lobby of Embassy Suites-San Diego. It's at the juncture of Harbor Drive, Pacific Highway and Market. And as long as you're here, you might as well poke about Seaport Village, at the site of the old Coronado Ferry landing. From here, you can follow Market back to your starting point at First Avenue. If you're interested, the Children's Museum of San Diego is a block below Market, at 200 Island Avenue, corner of Front Street.

3 **BAYSIDE TRAIL** • *Cabrillo National Monument at the tip of Point Loma. About three miles; moderate with a 300-foot elevation change. GETTING THERE: Follow Rosecrans Street (State Route 209) southwest to Point Loma; you can pick it up near the junctions of I-5 and I-8. The trail starts just below the path to Old Point Loma Lighthouse.*

This isn't an awesome route, and a comment in the national monument's brochure that it passes through "coastal sage scrub" doesn't sound terribly inviting. However, it's a nice hike along the coastal bluff of Point Loma, with views down to the ship traffic of the San Diego Bay entrance. And it gets you away from the crowds visiting the national monument.

The route begins as an asphalt road leading toward a forest of communications antennae, then it peels off as a gravel path and winds gently downward along the bayside bluff of Point Loma, following the route of a former access road. Signs along the way describe the flora and fauna of this area and you'll learn that "coastal sage scrub" offers a surprising botanical variety. The trail ends at the national monument fence line; take a deep breath and start back up. It isn't too steep and the views are fine.

4 **CORONADO BEACH WALK** • *Along Ocean Boulevard at the southern edge of Coronado. The walk is about three miles round trip, or it's a 3.5-mile loop trip if you detour through downtown Coronado on the way back. GETTING THERE: Cross the Coronado Bridge from San Diego, which puts you on Third Street. Follow Third about twelve blocks until it T-bones into Alameda Boulevard. Turn left and take Alameda south several blocks to Ocean Boulevard at the beachfront, then go right and follow Ocean until it ends at Sunset Park near the North Island Naval Air Station fence line.*

Beginning at Sunset Park, you can either walk along the beach or on the Ocean Boulevard sidewalk. However, for the first half mile or so, your view from the sidewalk will be blocked by a stone breakwater—unless you're tall enough to see over. There are benches along here where you can take a break and contemplate the open sea and seagulls. At Hotel del Coronado, about a mile from the starting point, you can explore the lushly landscaped grounds or stay to the beach.

Below the "Del," you'll cross in front of a row of highrise condos called Coronado Shores. Again, you have a choice between a concrete promenade and the open beach. The concrete path curves away from the beach at the U.S. Naval Amphibious Base and hits State Highway 75, which travels south along Silver Strand. If you want to make this a loop trip, turn left at the highway, which becomes Orange Avenue and passes through the cute shopping district of downtown Coronado. After strolling through the area, go left onto Eighth Street. Walk about five blocks to G Avenue, go left again and you'll eventually wind up back on Ocean Boulevard, not far from Sunset Park.

5 *COWLES MOUNTAIN TRAIL* • *Mission Trails Regional Park. Three-mile round trip; a tough uphill climb. TO GET THERE: Go about seven miles inland on I-8 and take the College Avenue exit north (opposite the San Diego State University campus). Follow College Avenue a mile north, then go right on Navajo for two miles to Golfcrest Drive. Turn left on Golfcrest for a trailhead parking area.*

After those easy strolls, are you ready for a *real* hike? This steep climb takes you a mile and a half—with several hundred feet elevation gain—to the top of 1,591-foot Cowles Mountain. The views from here are quite impressive—from the Pacific to San Diego to inland wilderness mountains. Mission Trails Regional Park encompasses several dry, brushy hills on the outer edge of a newly developing suburb called San Carlos. The dividing line between carefully manicured subdivisions and the brushy wilds is quite striking, particularly from above.

Although the terrain is wild, this isn't a wilderness hike. It's very popular on weekends, with long lines of hikers plodding up the trail. You might prefer to go on a weekday. You'll find potties and a fountain at the parking area, where you can fill your water bottles. If it's a warm day, you'll need plenty of water.

6 *FATHER JUNÍPERO SERRA TRAIL* • *In Mission Trails Regional Park. Easy round trip of less than four miles. GETTING THERE: Take I-8 about seven miles east to the Mission Gorge Road turnoff, follow it just over four miles northeast and turn left into Mission Trails Regional Park Visitor & Interpretive Center. The trail starts just below the center. (See Chapter Two, page 42 for details on the visitor center.)*

A former two-lane paved road through historic Mission Gorge has been fashioned into a combined walking/biking and driving route, with a divider strip separating the walkers and cyclists from the cars. Don't worry about traffic whooshing by; the speed limit is 15 mph and speed bumps every few hundred feet ensure that motorists comply.

What's historic about this canyon? The first irrigation project on the Pacific Coast was started here in 1811 when Indians from the mission built a stone dam to divert San Diego River water to agricultural fields. This walk will end at a picnic area, where another trail will take you to the site of the dam, which has been partially restored.

To begin this easy stroll, park at the visitor center, then walk down to a gate where the trail begins. As you stroll through rock-ribbed Mission Gorge, interpretive signs along the way will tell you about the flora, fauna, geology and history of this region. From the picnic area at the end of the Father Serra Trail, follow a path alongside the riparian woodland of the creek-sized San Diego River to the dam site. Several interpretive signs here discuss its historic significance.

NAVIGATIONAL AND PARKING ADVISORY • Although hikers and bikers can go both ways, this is a one-way trip for vehicles. To get back to San Diego, continue on the driving route until it merges with Mission Gorge Road. Follow it about four miles to the town of Santee, then go south on Freeway 67 to I-8.

Gates on both ends of the Father Serra Trail are closed from 7 p.m. until 8 a.m. April through October and from 5 to 8 the rest of the year. If you park there after closing time, you'll get locked in. (If you've left your car at the visitor center parking lot, that gate also closes, so if you're making a late start on your walk, park outside.)

7 **HARBOR ISLAND** • *In San Diego Bay, opposite the international airport. Easy three-mile round trip. GETTING THERE: Turn south onto Harbor Island off Harbor Drive opposite the airport, then go right to the island's western tip.*

This is one of San Diego's many pleasant bayside strolls. It takes you along a concrete promenade on the northern edge of Harbor Island, with lawns and benches on one side and bay waters on the other. Views are pleasing as you stroll—south toward Coronado and North Island Naval Air Station and southeast to the San Diego skyline. The walkway is limited to pedestrians only, so you won't have to contend with wheeled objects. The route is simple. Park near a restaurant called Tom's Lighthouse on the island's western end, and stroll along the bayside until you reach a pretend paddlewheeler housing Charlie Brown's and Jared's restaurants. You can follow the other side of the island on the return trip, although marinas, resorts and cross streets will disrupt your walking pattern.

8 **LA JOLLA BEACHFRONT** • *Downtown La Jolla. Easy walk, less than three miles loop trip. GETTING THERE: The walk starts on the northern side of downtown, above La Jolla Cove.*

This easy stroll takes you along the pretty wave-sculpted bluffs of La Jolla Cove and beyond. To begin, find a place to park near the point where Coast Boulevard forks toward La Jolla Cove from Prospect Street. Public parking is available at a shingle-sided shopping complex called The Coastwalk. Once afoot, you might want to explore The Coastwalk's shops, then drop down to the sidewalk of Coast Boulevard. Head beachward and stroll through the grassy parkland above La Jolla Cove, called Ellen Browning Scripps Park. Continue through the cove and beyond, past a lifeguard station and swimming beach. You'll eventually re-join the Coast Boulevard sidewalk. After a little more than a mile, elegant coastside homes will deprive you of your view. Coast Boulevard peels away from the beach, curving back up to Prospect. To make this a loop trip, you can follow Prospect past the trendy boutiques and cafés of downtown La Jolla.

9 SHELTER ISLAND • *On San Diego Bay, off Rosecrans Street. Easy two-mile round-trip stroll. GETTING THERE: To reach Shelter Island, head toward Point Loma on Rosecrans (State Route 209) and turn left onto Shelter Island Drive. Follow it a few blocks to a traffic circle, then go either left or right to the end of the island.*

Like the Harbor Island walk, this stroll is obvious. Simply drive to either end of this manmade island—which is shaped like a putting iron—then walk to the other end and back. A landscaped sidewalk follows the island's bay side, providing nice views of the distant city skyline, Coronado and the curving Coronado bridge. Like the Harbor Island promenade, this concrete path is limited to walkers and joggers. Since this is an "old" island, dredged up from the bottom of the bay in the 1950s, landscaping along the park strip between the road and the bayfront is mature and inviting. You'll encounter picnic tables and shade ramadas along the way. Particularly appealing, about mid-point in this stroll, is the Shelter Island Fishing Pier. You can get refreshments at a small bait shop and deli. It's a nice place to lean against a railing and watch the parade of watercraft playing on the bay or heading out to sea.

10 THE LOWER WATERFRONT • *Between Broadway Pier and Embarcadero Marina Park. Easy walk; about 3.5 miles round trip. GETTING THERE: Drive to the foot of Broadway from downtown.*

This walk along San Diego's Embarcadero duplicates the end of our favorite bike route below. That one is eight miles long, so this shorter version is probably more practical for walkers. Of course, this route can be followed by a bike or roller blades or skates, since it's an all-purpose recreational path.

Begin on the Embarcadero near Broadway Pier, opposite the San Diego Harbor Excursion and Hornblower Cruises berth. Or you can start at the San Diego Maritime Museum just to the north, adding about half a mile to your round trip. Broadway Pier, once an important freight dock, is now a recreational pier and you can walk out to the end for nice views back at the city skyline. (You can park on the pier, although you'll need to stuff quarters into meters. They'll take two hours' worth.) This pier has benches and a small landscaped area. It's a favored hangout for derelicts, who've shifted down here from nearby Gaslamp Quarter because that area apparently has become too gentrified for them.

From Broadway Pier, stroll south past Navy Pier, where thousands of servicemen set sail for the Pacific during World War II. It's now used by the U.S. Naval Reserve. Just beyond is a narrow park strip with a monument honoring the Navy's aircraft carriers, and a touching bronze statue of a sailor embracing his wife and son before going off to sea. This park strip blends into Tuna Fleet Park, named in honor of the great tuna trawlers that once operated out of San Diego. Two seafood restaurants sit over the water here—the Fish Market and Top of the Market, which we reviewed in Chapter Three, page 60. On the right side of this landscaped peninsula is a monument to Navy ships that have won Presidential Unit Citations for actions in combat. Walk to the left of the two restaurants and you'll pass G Street Pier, where a commercial fishing fleet is parked.

Pressing southward from Tuna Fleet Park, you'll next encounter a facility called Harbor Seafood Mart, once a complex of cafés and shops but now mostly unoccupied. At the Chesapeake Fish Company, you can peek through large windows and watch flippers being filleted. Just below here is Seaport Village, where you may want to pause and browse among its seventy or more shops and restaurants. Continuing south from the village, the shoreside promenade ends at Embarcadero Marina Park. From here, you'll enjoy fine views across the marina to three rather imposing structures—the forty-story Hyatt hotel, the dramatic glass towers of the Marriott and the strange looking San Diego Convention Center with its bold concrete triangles and white circus tent roof. Embarcadero Marina Park is your turnaround point, unless you want to swim across the marina's entrance.

THE TEN BEST BIKE ROUTES

San Diego County is a popular biking area and several community governments have formed an organization called RideLink. It produces the *San Diego Region Bike Map*, showing dozens of miles of separate bicycle routes and marked bike lanes. It's available at visitor centers or call RideLink at (619) 231-BIKE. Other useful sources for cyclists are the City of San Diego Bike Coordinator at (619) 533-3110 and the San Diego County Bike Coordinator at (619) 694-2811. Cyclists can take their bikes on the San Diego Trolley during off-peak hours with a permit, and on the Coaster commuter train that runs between San Diego and Oceanside. Also, bike racks are available on several Municipal Transit bus routes. Call (619) 233-3044 for information.

Our favorite bike route provides the complete panorama of San Diego's waterfront. The next three are along the oceanfront and in Mission Bay Park, since those areas have several miles of concrete pathways open to cyclists, rollerskaters, rollerbladers and walkers.

1 SAN DIEGO WATERFRONT ● *From Spanish Landing to Harbor Village. Level and easy, about eight miles round trip. GETTING THERE: Follow Harbor Drive west from downtown or east from Point Loma and you'll encounter Spanish Landing opposite the airport.*

This is the ultimate San Diego bike route, offering a fine panorama of the city's waterfront. Virtually all of it is separated from traffic and it's a also great walking route, if you're up to striding for eight miles. It travels along the bayfront from Spanish Landing to Embarcadero Marina Park. The views take in much of the San Diego scene—the busy bay on one side and hillside residential areas and glittering highrises on the other. You'll encounter a few public potties and bike racks, and occasional interpretive displays about San Diego and its waterfront.

Spanish Landing, the starting point, is a long, skinny and nicely landscaped waterside park. Just beyond is the U.S. Coast Guard Station with its appealing California mission style buildings. You'll then pass—to use the old cliché—forests of masts, since the waterfront area is busy with marinas. The route takes you past the San Diego Maritime Museum with its three historic ships; see Chapter Two, page 29. You'll then encounter the triplicate of Anthony's seafood restaurants—the Star of the Sea Room, Fish Grotto and an outdoor takeout called the Fishette. This is a good place for a lunch break.

Beyond Anthony's are berths for Hornblower Yacht Cruises and San Diego Harbor Excursions, and the terminal of the Coronado Ferry. Next door is the San Diego Cruise Ship Terminal and one of those huge ocean-going resorts might in port. A sign out front lists upcoming arrivals and departures. Beyond the terminal, you'll encounter Tuna Fleet Park (see walking tour number ten above) and a commercial fishing pier where several boats are moored. Most of the seagoing tuna trawlers that once sailed out of San Diego are gone, put out of business by environmental regulations and shortage of fish. Just beyond the park, Harbor Drive—which you've been paralleling—curves around and bumps into the Pacific Highway. However, the biking and walking route continues alongside the waterfront.

Pressing southward and now duplicating walk number ten, you'll encounter Seaport Village, and beyond that, Embarcadero Marina Park. Across the way, with the marina in the foreground, are the imposing forty-story Hyatt hotel, the dramatic glass-towered Marriott and the odd looking San Diego Convention Center. This is your turn-around, since the bayfront promenade ends at the marina's harbor entrance.

2 OCEAN FRONT WALK • *Between Mission Beach and Pacific Beach. Five mile round trip; level and easy. GETTING THERE: Drive through Mission Bay Park on West Mission Bay Drive, turn left (south) onto Mission Boulevard and follow it to the end. Swerve to the right into a parking lot on North Jetty Road. Park, unload your bike and start riding northward along the beachfront.*

The promenade along the ocean side of Mission Beach and Pacific Beach is popularly called the "Boardwalk," although it's concrete, with not a board in sight. There was a boardwalk in this area several decades ago, but the proper name today, says the City of San Diego, is Ocean Front Walk. It begins just inland at North Jetty Road near a volleyball area then swerves beachward and stays beside the strand for the next two and a half miles. It passes through the communities of Mission Beach with its classic Belmont Park fun zone and Pacific Beach. You'll find plenty of public potties and a few bike racks along the way.

The route passes long strings of beachfront homes, with occasional commercial enclaves where you can pause for a snack and a cooling drink. Less than a mile into your ride, you'll pass Belmont Park. A short street called Ventura Place is busy with fast food joints, pubs, bikini shops and even a tattoo parlor. If it's a hot day, cool off with a cone of shaved ice; two places here serve this chilly delicacy.

Continuing northward, you'll pass more than a mile of beachfront homes as the "Boardwalk" blends from Mission Beach into Pacific Beach. Near the upper end, a little walkup with patio tables called Mission Coffee House serves quite tasty lattés and other specialty coffees. The promenade ends less than half a mile beyond at Crystal Pier, a small commercial area with several cafés and curio shops. The pier is privately owned and lined with cute little white and blue rental cottages. Bikes aren't permitted, but you can tie up to a bike rack and walk to the pier's end for nice views up and down the beach. The beachfront route ends a couple of blocks above Crystal Pier, so reverse your route and return to your starting point.

3 MISSION BAY'S WEST SIDE • *Mission Bay Park. Nine-mile round trip; level and easy. GETTING THERE: To reach your starting point, use the same approach as for number two above, in the Mission Point parking lot. Then pedal along the east side, on the edge of Mission Bay instead of following the western side toward the oceanfront. A Mission Bay Park map will be useful for this and the next route. To get one, stop by park headquarters at 2581 Quivira Court; (619) 221-8900. As you pass through the park on West Mission Bay Drive, turn onto Quivira Way near the Hyatt Islandia, head away from the Hyatt and follow the road to its end.*

This route follows the contours of the many inner bays of Mission Bay Park's western reaches. The sidewalk rimming the Mission Point parking lot becomes your bike route. It curves around the point, first following the Mission Bay breakwater, then passing several beachside homes lining Mariner's Basin, a small inlet. Pressing northward, you'll roughly parallel Mission Boulevard (although it's well out of sight) and then do a right turn across the top of Bonita Cove Park. You'll next swing left (north), pass beneath West Mission Bay Drive and pedal for a couple of miles north, keeping close to Mission Bay's many coves.

A long loop around Sail Bay will take you east, south and then north again as you cross Ingraham Street near Fisherman's Channel. This long bayside ride terminates at the northern end of Crown Point Shores, just below an undeveloped wildlife preserve. You'll know you've finished because the biking/walking route suddenly spills into a parking lot. Assuming you haven't arranged for a shuttle, do a U-turn and retrace your route.

4 **MISSION BAY'S EAST SIDE** ● *Mission Bay Park. Five-mile round trip; level and easy. GETTING THERE: From Interstate 5, enter Mission Bay Park on East Mission Bay Drive and follow it north to De Anza Cove Park.*

This is a nice route because it stays well away from civilization and traffic, with no beachfront homes along the way. You'll encounter only water and beaches on one side and green lawns on the other. It's generally more lightly used than the two routes above. To begin, park in De Anza Cove and pedal east and then south along Mission Bay's eastern shoreline—which has fewer bays and is less convoluted than the western side. You'll pass the San Diego Hilton Beach & Tennis Resort and then Tecolote Shores Park, a swimming and picnicking area.

Just below Tecolote Shores, a road leads to the right onto Fiesta Island, which is a large peninsula extending into Mission Bay. Despite its name, it's undeveloped and there's nothing festive about it. If you want to add a few miles to your route, you can follow a one-way road that travels Fiesta Island's perimeter. You'll have to share it with vehicles, although this uninteresting piece of dirt isn't heavily traveled.

About half a mile below the island turnoff, you'll pass under Sea World Drive and hit a trail junction at the San Diego River flood control channel. Paths lead both ways from here, although they're even less interesting than Fiesta Island, so this is a good turn-around point.

5 **POINT LOMA TO CABRILLO NATIONAL MONUMENT** ●
*Point Loma Peninsula. A thirteen mile loop trip; mostly easy with one tough climb over the Point Loma ridge. GETTING THERE: Follow I-8 to its western terminus, blend onto Sunset Cliffs Boulevard and follow this about eighteen blocks to Point Loma Avenue. **NOTE:** The road into Cabrillo National Monument closes at 5 p.m.*

After being spoiled by the previous three traffic-free bike routes, you'll have to mingle with motor vehicles on this one. The first part of the run isn't a designated bike route, although traffic isn't heavy. The final section into Fort Rosecrans Military Reservation has marked bike lanes on the shoulder of the road.

Once you've parked near Point Loma Avenue and unleashed your bike, continue south on Sunset Cliffs Drive. Within a block or two, you'll emerge onto a headland, with the open sea far below and the homes of Point Loma above. Although it doesn't have a marked bike lane, Sunset Cliffs Drive isn't heavily traveled and it's fairly wide—except in areas where chunks of the cliff have fallen into the sea.

After a bit over a mile along the ocean bluff, Sunset Cliffs Drive comes to an abrupt end. Swing hard to the left and uphill, following first Ladera and then Cornish Drive, effectively doubling back on your route, which is now below you. Within less than half a mile, turn right at a stop sign and make a steep uphill climb over the ridge of Point Loma. After this tough grunt, you'll be rewarded with an impressive panorama of the entrance of San Diego Bay, with North Island Naval Air Station below and the skyline of downtown San Diego beyond.

Coast down the other side, hit another stop and turn right onto Catalina Boulevard. This takes you through more residential areas, headed for the tip of Point Loma and Cabrillo National Monument. Catalina is a rather busy route, although you can drop down to a frontage road to get away from traffic. After less than a mile, as you blend back onto the main road, it becomes Cabrillo Memorial Drive, and it's marked with a bike lane. You'll pedal into Fort Rosecrans Military Reservation, passing the neat and sad ranks of white crosses of Fort Rosecrans National Cemetery. Soon you'll hit an entry gate to Cabrillo National Monument, where you pay your hiker/biker entry fee and continue to the visitor center.

Coming back out, instead of repeating that tough Hill Street crossing over Point Loma's hump, stay with Catalina Boulevard for a few more blocks, then go left on Point Loma Avenue, which will deliver you to your starting point.

6 *CORONADO TO IMPERIAL BEACH* • *Coronado peninsula. About twenty miles round trip; level and flat all the way and mostly traffic-free. GETTING THERE: Drive across the Coronado Bridge from San Diego, veer to the right onto Glorietta Boulevard immediately beyond the bridge and park at Tidelands Park, near the bridge anchorage.*

This is a good route if you don't mind the constant hum of nearby traffic and just want to crank off several miles. Start at Tidelands Park and pedal south on Glorietta Boulevard alongside Coronado Golf Course. Most of Glorietta has marked bike lanes and you'll pick up a separate paved bike path as Glorietta approaches the town's business district, near Orange Avenue. The route then travels down the Silver

Strand, following alongside busy Highway 75. However, the bike route is isolated from the highway traffic.

You'll pass through the U.S. Naval Amphibious Base, then enter Silver Strand State Beach, where you can pause and take a break either on the San Diego Bay side or on the open sea. Just below is the turnoff to Loews Coronado Bay Resort, should you want to pedal in for a lunch break, or simply to admire this handsome retreat. Below Loews, you'll cruise past an upscale waterfront development called Coronado Keys, then you'll enter Imperial Beach. The dedicated bike route ends just beyond Miles Bowler Park, and this is a good turnaround spot.

7 *MOUNT SOLEDAD CLIMB • This can be ridden from two directions—either from La Jolla on Nautilus Street (four-mile round trip) or from inland Pacific Beach on Mount Soledad Road (six-mile round trip). Either way, it's a tough climb. GETTING THERE: From La Jolla, start pedaling at the corner of La Jolla Boulevard and Nautilus Street. For the Pacific Beach approach, drive I-5 north from San Diego and take the Grand/Garnet Avenue exit. Continue north, then go west about a quarter of a mile on Garnet and turn right onto Mount Soledad Road to start the bike route.*

This is the toughest of our cycling routes, climbing to the best vista point in the San Diego area, Mount Soledad. If you're really an iron person, you can ride from either starting point to the top, go down the other side and then repeat the process. However, that's a rough day's work. There are marked bike lanes most of the way on both of these routes, although they aren't separated from vehicle traffic.

If you approach from La Jolla Boulevard, Nautilus is a slender city street for the first couple of blocks. Then it widens to four lanes with bike lanes on either side. You'll pass through some of La Jolla's nicest neighborhoods as you climb upward toward Mount Soledad Park. Near the crest of your climb, you'll hit Mount Soledad Road at a traffic signal; go left a couple of blocks and then right for the final climb to the top. (There's no bike lane for these last few blocks.)

The other approach is more straightforward, although longer. Starting from Garnet Avenue, you simply pedal persistently up Mount Soledad Road for nearly three miles until you've reached your goal. It's a four-lane road with a marked bike route.

Your goal is a low hill topped by a cross, and it provides a grand panorama of southern San Diego County. For details, see Chapter One, page 17 and Chapter Nine, page 134.

8 *TORREY PINES ROUTE • From Torrey Pines State Reserve to La Jolla. Moderately strenuous with one long upgrade and several shorter ones, followed by breezy downhill runs; about fifteen miles round trip. Bike lanes are marked on the shoulder most the way, although they are not separated from vehicles. Traffic is often heavy along this route* and the speed limit in some areas is 55 mph, so don't try this unless you're a fairly alert and confident rider. *GETTING THERE: Drive to Torrey Pines State Reserve north of La Jolla and park in the lot at the entrance gate.*

This is one of the most scenic—and most challenging—of our Ten Best bike routes. Begin at Torrey Pines State Reserve (Chapter Fourteen, page 196), and start a long uphill climb on North Torrey Pines Road. Longtime residents will remember this as old U.S. 101 before the arrival of Interstate 5. Although it will seem longer, the climb to the top of the grade is just over a mile and a half. The rearward view of the ocean and of Los Penasquitos Lagoon and its inland valley are spectacular, but save them for the return trip. This is a busy highway!

Once at the top of the grade, you'll pedal past Torrey Pines Golf Course, home of the annual Buick Invitational. Then North Torrey Points Road swings to the right as it passes the junction of Genesee Avenue. (This is the terminus of bike route number nine below.) For the next couple of miles, you'll travel through the lushly landscaped campus of the University of California at San Diego. You may be tempted to shed North Torrey Pines Road occasionally and pedal through portions of the campus. It lends itself to cycling since it's only slightly hilly and several areas are traffic-free. If you haven't yet visited the Birch Aquarium at Scripps Institute of Oceanography (Chapter Two, page 25), you can cruise down Expedition Way at the southern edge of the campus.

Just beyond the aquarium turnoff, Torrey Pines Road (no longer "North") swings right, skims more of the UCSD campus, then begins a fast downhill drop toward downtown La Jolla. This area also is often thick with traffic, so stay alert. The bike lane ends as you approach the "Y" intersection of Torrey Pines Road and Ardath Road. To make this a loop trip, you can swing right onto La Jolla Shores Drive just below that junction and enjoy Pacific vistas as you pedal through some of La Jolla's more opulent neighborhoods. There are some breaks in the route so just keep working toward the beach to stay your course. La Jolla Shores blends into North Torrey Pines Road just north of the aquarium turnoff. However, none of this route is a marked bike lane.

9 *GENESEE TO THE GOLDEN TRIANGLE • North on Genesee Avenue to the Torrey Pines area above La Jolla. Moderately strenuous with several upgrades; about eighteen miles round trip. GETTING THERE: Head north on Freeway 163, take the Genesee off-ramp and drive about half a mile west to Linda Vista Road. Start your bike route here.*

The Golden Triangle is an area of dramatic new development in the Torrey Pines highlands north of San Diego and this route approaches it through an attractive shallow wooded canyon. You'll follow a marked bike lane on the shoulder of a rather busy boulevard, so it isn't recommended for those intimidated by traffic. It's particularly busy during commute hours.

Begin by heading north on Genesee from Linda Vista Road; the marked bike lane starts within a couple of blocks on Linda Vista. It's a pretty route through a mix of brushy hillsides and upscale homes. You'll encounter a long, relatively gradual upgrade, which levels out after about 2.5 miles as you cross Balboa Avenue. You'll dip into another shallow valley, then pedal uphill to Clairemont Mesa through a rather modest neighborhood. The sleek glass, steel and concrete towers of the Golden Triangle will begin appearing on the green clad horizon ahead.

After crossing under Freeway 52, you'll enter this triangle of commerce and attractive homes and condos. If you want to stop and shop or grab lunch, the large University Towne Centre shopping complex is at the corner of Genesee and La Jolla Village Drive. Its Market Place food court has more than a dozen food stalls, with tables beside an indoor ice skating rink and outside on an attractive plaza. North of La Jolla Village Drive, Genesee swings west, crosses over Interstate 5 and skirts the campus of the University of California at San Diego. It then blends into North Torrey Pines Road, which is the end of our route.

10 LINDA VISTA ROUTE • *Northeast on Linda Vista Road.*
Moderate with a few mild upgrades; nine mile round trip. GETTING THERE: Take the Morena Boulevard off-ramp from I-8, near the I-5 interchange, then fork to the northeast onto Linda Vista Road.

This route through the middle class neighborhood of Linda Vista isn't scenic. It will appeal mostly to cyclists who just want to crank off several miles while facing the challenge of a few modest hills. Most of our designated portions of Linda Vista Road have marked bike lanes, although they're not separated from traffic.

Start at the corner of Linda Vista and Napa Street and begin pedaling northeast. You'll be on a gradual uphill grade and pass the Spanish style campus of the University of San Diego on your left. You might want to pause and pedal around the campus, although it's a bit hilly. To do so, turn left onto a street marked "USD Main Drive." Beyond the university, the route begins to level out as it enters a mixed commercial and residential area. There are several Vietnamese and other Asian businesses here; small cafés might tempt you with a lunch stop.

After four and a half miles, as you cross the complicated I-805 and Freeway 163 overpass, the bike lane ends and Linda Vista becomes Convoy Road. An "Asian restaurant row" begins just north of here on Convoy, with Vietnamese, Thai, Japanese, Chinese and Korean restaurants, and most of them do lunch. (See Chapter Thirteen, page 182.) As you pedal back toward your starting point on Linda Vista, at a high point near Tait Street, you'll be able to see the faraway Pacific on a clear day.

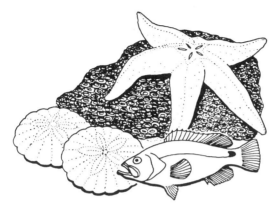

Chapter thirteen

ASSORTED LISTS
...THAT DON'T FIT INTO OTHER LISTS

San Diego is a cornucopia of attractions, flavors, sights and sounds. This chapter is intended to gather up all those loose ends that just don't seem to fit anywhere else.

ODD ENDS: A MISCELLANEOUS TEN BEST
Where's the city's best "wilderness park," it's most interesting neighborhood and its best ethnic restaurant rows? You'll find out in this eclectic list, beginning with the best way to see San Diego's sights.

1 THE BEST AUTO TOUR: *Fifty-nine Mile Scenic Drive* •
San Diego through La Jolla and back. GETTING THERE: Start at the foot of Broadway at Harbor Drive.

For as long as we can remember—and that's a few decades—visitors have been able to follow the Fifty-Nine Mile Scenic Drive that covers the best of San Diego and La Jolla. It's marked by square blue and yellow signs with white seagulls. Most of the drive is rather obvious and you've already seen many of its highlights if you've been dutifully pursuing the attractions and tours we've suggested in this book. However, the "official" drive is worth following since it provides a good sampler of scenic San Diego.

The last time we checked, the Convention and Visitors Bureau no longer issued a map outlining this route, although you can buy a commercially produced *San Diego Visitor's Map* at most visitor centers and souvenir stores. This color map covers most of San Diego County, with special markings for the tour route. If you can't find a copy, read the following guidelines and trace them with a felt pen onto a San Diego-La Jolla map. The Automobile Club of Southern California's *San Diego Area* map is a good one to use. As you travel, look for the seagull signs. The last time we ran this route, most of them were still in place.

NOTE: We've simplified the drive in some areas where we feel the original route is too complicated, or street patterns have changed.

Following the gulls

Start at the foot of Broadway and go north and west on Harbor Drive, dipping into **Harbor Island** as you go. Toward the western end of Harbor Drive, turn left onto Scott Street, take it to Shelter Island Drive, turn left and circle **Shelter Island**. Pop back out, continue briefly west on Scott, go right onto Talbot Street and then left on Catalina Boulevard (State Route 209) to **Cabrillo National Monument**. Departing the monument, follow Catalina north, turn left on Hill Street to cross over the spine of **Point Loma**. Go right on Sunset Cliffs Boulevard, which gives you some nice views of the Pacific Ocean.

Follow Sunset Cliffs into **Mission Bay Park**, where the seagull will direct you onto West Mission Bay Drive. (Stay alert for off-ramps and on-ramps.) Take this to **Mission Beach** and **Belmont Park**, where you'll veer right onto Mission Boulevard. Follow the boulevard through **Pacific Beach** then, at a rather complex intersection, jog briefly left onto La Jolla Boulevard and then immediately right onto La Jolla Mesa Drive. Take this uphill and go right onto **La Jolla Scenic Drive** for some nice aerial views of that upscale community. You'll pass a few multi-million-dollar mansions en route. Then, turn left at a traffic signal onto Nautilus Street and follow it downhill to La Jolla Boulevard.

Go right (north) for several blocks to the junction of Pearl Street and Coast Boulevard, then go left onto Coast, which takes you down to **La Jolla Cove**. You'll soon hit a "do not enter" sign, so retrace your route and turn left from Coast onto Prospect Street and drive through **downtown La Jolla**. Just to the north, turn left onto Torrey Pines Road and then fork left onto La Jolla Shores Road. Take this through another posh residential area just above the beach. Go left on Vallecitos, then right on Camino Del Oro, which takes you past pretty little

La Jolla Shores beach and park. Keep pressing northward along the coast and you'll eventually rejoin La Jolla Shores Drive.

Follow this uphill above the ocean it until it merges with North Torrey Pines Road at the landscaped campus of the **University of California**. Go right and you'll soon pass Expedition Way that leads down to **Birch Aquarium** at Scripps Institution of Oceanography. At a traffic signal just beyond this turnoff, go right to stay with Torrey Pines Road and follow its sweeping course downhill. Continue on Torrey Pines through the edge of downtown La Jolla until it makes a half-left onto Girard. Go one block to Pearl Street, turn right and then left onto Fay Avenue. Take Fay three long block to Nautilus Street and go uphill, following signs to **Mount Soledad**. This is the highest point in La Jolla, offering a grand panorama of the greater San Diego area.

Go south from here to Soledad Mountain Road and start downhill. After about a mile, fork to the right onto Soledad Road. It becomes Lamont Street, which ends at Ingraham Street, back in **Mission Bay Park**. Take Ingraham through the park and follow signs to Sports Arena Drive at Mission Bay's lower end. Go east briefly on Sports Arena, turn left onto Rosecrans Street and follow it under Interstate 5. It becomes Taylor Street and takes you to **Old Town San Diego State Historic Park**.

From Taylor, hop briefly onto southbound I-5, get off at Laurel Street and go uphill to **Balboa Park**. (Laurel becomes El Prado as it enters the park.) After you've investigated this grand patch of greenery and museums, retreat back down Laurel, turn left (downhill) onto Sixth or Fourth avenues, go right onto Broadway in downtown San Diego and return to your starting point.

2 *THE BEST URBAN AREA: Gaslamp Quarter* • *A sixteen-block section bounded by Broadway, Fourth and Sixth avenues and the waterfront.*

This area of downtown San Diego has come full circle. The urban city began here in 1867 when Alonzo Erastus Horton bought nearly a thousand acres of "sagebrush and mudflats" at about twenty-seven cents an acre. He laid out a town by the waterfront, shifting it away from the Presidio Hill area. A century later, the town had moved farther west and back uphill, and "Horton's Addition" became an urban slum called Stingaree. Then in the 1970s and 1980s, it was urbanly and gentrified into Gaslamp Quarter. It's now a national historic district, with dozens of fine old brick and masonry buildings housing boutiques, restaurants and clubs. From downtown San Diego's most decrepit area, it has become its most vibrant. You can spend hours strolling these sixteen blocks, ducking into shops and enjoying a glass of wine or lunch at any a score of sidewalk cafés. If you're a history buff, you can study plaques that label the various buildings and discuss their prior uses.

Adjacent to Gaslamp Quarter, the result of urban renewal by bull-dozer, is Horton Plaza, named in honor of old Alonzo. Bounded by Broadway, First and Fourth avenues and G street, this outdoor mall contains more than a hundred shops and cafés on several levels, plus a multi-screen theater and an outdoor food court. With dozens of out-door tables and chairs, Horton Plaza is a great place to people-watch.

3 THE BEST NEIGHBORHOOD: Hillcrest District ● *Extend-ing several blocks from the intersection of University and Fifth avenues, northwest of downtown.*

Take a bit of Berkeley's Telegraph Avenue, salt it with a little of San Francisco's Haight-Ashbury and Castro districts and stir in a measure of Seattle's "U-District" and you've got San Diego's Hillcrest. This is the city's ethnic restaurant row, its gay district (although not as overtly so as San Francisco's) and its most eclectic shopping area. You'll find everything from organic markets, design studios and used book stores to galleries and safe sex shops. A slowly reviving older neighborhood, Hillcrest is immediately northwest of Balboa Park.

4 THE BEST COMMUNITY: Coronado ● *The town occupies the eastern end of Coronado peninsula. GETTING THERE: Take the San Diego-Coronado Bay Bridge, and turn left onto Orange Avenue to reach the downtown area.*

If travel writers made more money, we'd cash in our chips and buy a home on Coronado. Isolated from the booming swirl of San Diego, it is a charming and charmed village still living in a more genteel era. Even the traffic seems to slow down once it spills off the Coronado Bridge. (We liked Coronado better when it was served only by ferry-boats.) The Spanish-Roman style downtown area, built around a traf-fic circle, offers appealing boutiques and outdoor cafés and it's rimmed by white stucco, red tile roofed homes that speak of old California. Coronado has all that a visitor or resident might desire—ample shop-ping from trendy boutiques to a single supermarket, miles of beaches, biking and walking paths and regal resorts, including that most grand hideaway of all, Hotel del Coronado.

If there is a flaw in this otherwise carefully composed picture, it's the Ferry Landing Marketplace across the peninsula from the down-town area. Although it's attractively landscaped, some of the shops are a bit tacky and it has too many fast food places. If you're basking in the Coronado sun, scuffing along the beach or cycling idly along palm-lined streets, why do you need fast food? Another irony is that two-thirds of this tadpole-shaped peninsula—many people call it Coronado Island, knowing full well that it isn't one—is occupied by North Island Naval Air Station. Fortunately, most of the air traffic patterns point away from the community.

5 *THE BEST PLACE TO ENJOY WILDERNESS NEAR THE CITY:* **Mission Trails Regional Park** • *Eight miles northeast of downtown. The visitor and interpretive center is at 1 Father Junípero Serra Trail; (619) 668-3275. Open daily 9 to 5; free. GETTING THERE: Take I-8 about seven miles east to the Mission Gorge Road turnoff, follow it just over four miles northeast and turn left into the interpretive center.*

Overlooked by most other guidebooks and thus missed by most visitors, Mission Trails Regional Park is one of the largest urban parks in America, covering 5,760 acres. Hiking trails lead alongside the creek-sized San Diego River, to the tops of mountains and into wilderness areas that have changed little since Juan Rodríguez Cabrillo dropped anchor in San Diego Bay in 1542. In addition to trails and general boondocks, the park has several specific attractions. Among them are Mission Trails Golf Course, (619) 460-5400; Lake Murray reservoir, rimmed with a walking/biking trail and stocked with fish, (619) 465-FISH; the Old Mission Dam, where early padres funneled water to their fields; and the excellent Mission Trails Regional Park Visitor and Interpretive Center, (619) 668-3275. The dam site and interpretive center are discussed in more detail in Chapter Two, page 42; and Chapter Twelve, page 181.

6 *THE BEST DOWNTOWN RESTAURANT ROW* • *Fifth Avenue in Gaslamp Quarter. GETTING THERE: Turn south from Broadway onto one-way Fourth or Sixth Avenues; from Harbor Drive on the waterfront just beyond the San Diego Convention Center, turn up Fifth Avenue.*

Most of downtown San Diego's restaurants are in Gaslamp Quarter, and most of these are along Fifth Avenue, extending between Broadway and L Street, just off Harbor Drive. There are more than a dozen diners along this route, embracing every food persuasion from contemporary American to French to Mexican to Spanish to Asian. If you like dining *al fresco,* most have sidewalk tables or dining patios. Among those we've reviewed elsewhere in this book are Croce's and Croce's West, contemporary American, 802 Fifth, Chapter Three, page 55; Dakota Grill and Spirits, Southwest, 901 Fifth, Chapter Three, page 55; Blue Point Coastal Cuisine, seafood, 565 Fifth, Chapter Three, page 59; The King and I, Thai, 620 Fifth, Chapter Four, page 82, La Strada, Italian-American, 702 Fifth, Chapter Four, page 82; and Hang Ten Brewing Company, brewpub, 310 Fifth, Chapter Eight, page 126.

7 *THE BEST NEIGHBORHOOD RESTAURANT ROW* • *The northwest end of India Street. GETTING THERE: Take any of several off-ramps from parallel I-5 or follow one-way India Street from downtown. NOTE: Because it's one way, to return you'll have to take India to Wash-*

ington, left under the freeway and come back on Kettner. There are several I-5 on-ramps along the way.

Rarely visited by tourists, this "India Street Restaurant Row" contains an interesting mix of cafés, and most have outdoor dining areas. This area, called Middletown, was almost swallowed up when Interstate 5 was cut through here several years ago. Despite the rumble of traffic, its string of more than half a dozen small cafés survives. Most serve remarkably cheap food.

The row's residents include Gelato, serving light Italian food; Saffron, a Thai take-out specializing in grilled chicken, which we reviewed in Chapter Five, page 96, (619) 574-0177; Candora's sandwich shop; Shakespeare Pub & Grille, serving British fare, reviewed in Chapter Four, page 74, (619) 299-0230; El Indio Mexican restaurant, reviewed in Chapter Four, page 64, (619) 299-0385; and Banzai Cantina, reviewed in Chapter Three, page 54, (619) 298-6388.

8 **THE BEST ASIAN RESTAURANT ROW** ● *Convoy Street, between Clairemont Mesa Boulevard and Othello Avenue. GETTING THERE: Follow Freeway 163 about seven miles north of downtown and go east on Balboa Street (State Route 274) about half a mile to Convoy. The restaurants extend in both directions, north to Clairemont Mesa Boulevard and south to Othello Avenue.*

Normally, you picture Asian communities as urban enclaves, perhaps with dragon-entwined lamp posts and turned up eaves on buildings to prevent evil spirits from entering. Not in San Diego. Its Asian community—an ethnic brew of Chinese, Japanese, Thai, Korean and Vietnamese—is in the suburbs. It shares a vee-shaped plot on Kearny Mesa between freeways 163 and 805 with, hardware stores, bridal shops and billiard parlors. This also is one of the San Diego area's largest automobile rows.

Folks familiar with San Francisco's Chinatown may be surprised that most cafés in this "Asian Triangle" are in small strip malls. What the area lacks in ethnic character, it more than makes up for in ethnic variety. You'll find Japanese sushi parlors, Chinese cafés and take-outs, Korean markets, Thai and Vietnamese restaurants.

Most of the restaurants are quite inexpensive. Here are some of our favorites: Thai House Cuisine, 4225 Convoy in Convoy Center, (619) 278-1800; Katzra Japanese sushi, 4233 Convoy, also in Convoy Center, (619) 279-3430; Phuöng Trang Vietnamese and Chinese restaurant at 4170 Convoy in Convoy Plaza, (619) 565-6750; Imperial Mandarin Restaurant at 3904 Convoy in an unnamed plaza just below and across from Home Depot, (619) 292-1222; and Dumpling Inn, 4619 Convoy Street in First Korean Market center; it's reviewed in Chapter Five, page 95. Dumpling Inn is just north of Balboa; all the others are south.

9 *THE STRANGEST DOWNTOWN BUILDING* • *Metropolitan Correction Center, 808 Union at F Street.*

That odd looking windowless highrise structure near the waterfront is San Diego's city jail. Why would a prime piece of real estate worth millions of dollars be used for a lock-up? Only some unidentified bureaucrat would know the answer to that. We can guess why it's windowless. Bad guys don't deserve nice harbor and city views.

10 *THE UGLIEST DOWNTOWN BUILDING* • *San Diego Convention Center on Harbor Drive, opposite the Marriott.*

Who designed that thing, anyway? It contains enough harsh angles and circles to send the ghost of Frank Lloyd Wright into hysterical fits of laughter. This ungainly creature consists of a concrete structure with a peaked circus tent roof, and with façades of sixteen tilted concrete triangles that suggest giant capital "A's." Within them are blue and red circles. The structure is supposed to be a surrealistic ship. The white tarp roof represents sails and the blue circles are waves lapping at the bow. What do the red circles represent? We wonder if any serious architect might be tempted to use them as targets.

THE TEN BEST PLACES TO SIT AND DO NOTHING

What this list really contains is the Ten Best Places to slow down, relax and watch the rest of the world pass by. These are pleasant and appealing areas where you can practice the fine art of people watching. People-watching is like being a couch potato in public, without the distraction of a TV set.

1 *EMBASSY SUITES LOBBY* • *601 Pacific Hwy.; (619) 239-2400. GETTING THERE: The Embassy Suites-San Diego Bay is just below downtown, at the corner of Pacific Highway and Market Street.*

This is one of the finest interior spaces in town—a twelve-story courtyard atrium with a lush tropical garden, fountains and lagoon. Glass elevators scoot up the walls to rooms lining interior balconies. Walkways through this indoor jungle are lined with small tables and chairs, inviting one to sit and watch the leisurely passage of people. This would be a great place for a lobby bar, a potential easy winner in that Chapter Seven category. However, the hotel doesn't exactly have one. A service bar here is used for morning continental breakfast and evening happy hour for hotel guests, so it's not a regular bar. Pity. Stop by this lush lobby on Monday, Wednesday and Friday evenings at 6 to watch bright orange koi being fed in the lagoon.

2 BOTANICAL BUILDING • *In Balboa Park at 1550 El Prado; (619) 235-1110. Daily except Thursday 10 to 4. GETTING THERE: It's on the north side of El Prado, just east of the San Diego Museum of Art.*

This is one of our favorite places for sitting and doing nothing. This domed horticultural building, created for the 1915 international exposition, is the only one of its kind in the world, constructed entirely of redwood laths. Never crowded, its a grand place for relaxing and admiring the more than 500 tropical and semi-tropical plants that surround you. In this almost surrealistic environment with its lush landscaping and trickling fountains, you can forget the tourist crowds moving up and down busy El Prado, just outside the lath-house door.

3 ALCAZAR GARDEN • *In Balboa Park, just inside the west entrance. GETTING THERE: Drive or walk east past the Museum of Man and the garden is on your right.*

Alcazar is the most formal of Balboa Park's many gardens, with plantings and pathways set off by neatly trimmed hedges. We like to perch on one of the Spanish tile benches at a hedgerow crossroad and watch the people admiring the blossoms.

4 BELMONT PARK • *3146 Mission Blvd. (at Mission Bay Drive); (619) 491-2988. Rides start at 11; grounds open all the time. GETTING THERE: Take I-8 west to Mission Bay Park and follow West Mission Bay Drive through the park to Mission Beach; it blends into Ventura Place and ends at the amusement center's parking lot.*

So maybe you think you're too old to ride the Giant Dipper or the Tilt-A-Whirl at this classic beachside amusement park. No matter. Belmont Park is a great people-watching place. Pick up a snack or soft drink at Shaw's Belmont Grill, sit at one of the many green wrought iron tables and watch the others play. When you hear those kids scream on the roller coaster, you may be glad you're still on the ground.

5 CASA DE BANDINI'S PORCH • *2660 Calhoun; (619) 297-8211. GETTING THERE: It's just northeast of the Plaza in Old Town San Diego State Historic Park.*

Once the home of a wealthy Peruvian family, Casa de Bandini is now a popular restaurant. The old two-story adobe is rimmed by a porch and its owners have installed a long counter and stools along one side of this veranda and small cocktail tables on the other. These are great places to sit—frosty margarita in hand—and watch the activities of Old Town San Diego.

6 **HORTON PLAZA** • *Downtown area. GETTING THERE: The shopping complex is rimmed by First and Fourth avenues, Broadway and G Street.*

The fourth and fifth levels of this shopping complex have dozens of outside tables and benches where you can sit and watch other people shop. Or you can take a break from your own shopping and grab a quick bite the fourth level food court. Seventeen food stalls offer such quickie fare as chicken, sushi, pizza, hot dogs, Chinese takeout, frozen yogurt and hamburgers. For something more substantial, try the adjacent California Café, which also has outdoor tables.

7 **OCEAN FRONT WALK, NEAR CRYSTAL PIER** • *In Pacific Beach at Mission Boulevard and Garnet Avenue. GETTING THERE: Take the Grand/Garnet Avenue exit from I-5, go several blocks north then turn left onto Garnet Avenue and follow it about two miles to the beach.*

Several concrete benches on either side of Pacific Beach's Crystal Pier are fine places for admiring the incoming surf or the tanned bodies cruising up and down the beach promenade. The pier itself is an interesting place—privately own owned and lined with little cottages that you can rent; see Chapter Nine, page 135.

8 **FERRY LANDING MARKETPLACE** • *In Coronado at the Coronado ferry terminal. GETTING THERE: Cross the Coronado Bridge, turn right onto Orange Avenue, follow it to its end and go right for two blocks on First Street.*

This Cape Cod style shopping complex is ideal for those seeking to sit in the sun. Its walkways are lined with tables and chairs and many offer views of the San Diego skyline across the bay. If you'd like to commune with feathered friends, several tables are alongside a pond that's busy with resident ducks. This shopping complex is easy to reach if you're afoot in San Diego. As the name states, it's at the ferry landing, so you can catch a boat across from the city's waterfront.

9 **THE LIBRARY OF HOTEL DEL CORONADO** • *1500 Orange Ave., Coronado. GETTING THERE: Cross the Coronado Bridge from San Diego, turn left onto Orange Avenue and follow it about a mile.*

Hotel lobbies are great places for people watching. However, if you really want to just sit and do nothing—or perhaps sit and read a book—retreat to the Hotel Del Coronado's library, a quite enclave just off the lobby. It's a functioning library; if you didn't bring a book, you can pull one down from the shelves. And if you require a libation with your reading, a lobby bar is adjacent.

10 THE MARKETPLACE AT UNIVERSITY TOWNE CENTRE

TRE • La Jolla Village Drive at Genesee Avenue in the Golden Triangle; (858) 546-8858. GETTING THERE: Go north about nine miles on I-5 from the I-8 interchange, take the La Jolla Village Drive exit east and follow it about a mile to Genesee. The center is on your right.

This is a really cool place to sit, relax and people-watch. The Marketplace is a huge indoor food court with a dozen takeouts, and many of its tables are terraced above the shopping center's Ice Chalet skating rink. Nibble your gyro or hot dog-on-a-stick while watching skaters cut figure-eights below. Or you can adjourn to a large outdoor plaza in the center of this attractive 150-store shopping mall.

THE TEN BEST FESTIVALS

San Diego knows how to celebrate. Its festivals range from the summer-long aquatic celebration known as Bayfair to the air show at Marine Corps Air Station Miramar and the Holiday Bowl football classic. With its large Hispanic population, *Cinco de Mayo* is a major celebration, particularly in and about Old Town.

If you want a detailed list of San Diego city and county annual event, send a check for $15 to: International Visitor Information Center, 11 Horton Plaza, San Diego, CA 92101. For dates of a specific event, you can call the San Diego Visitors and Convention Bureau at (619) 232-3101.

We begin with the city's largest annual festival, then follow with the next nine best celebrations chronologically.

1 SAN DIEGO BAYFAIR • *Early August through mid-October; (619) 268-1250.*

Bayfair is many celebrations wrapped into a summer-to-autumn fiesta. Activities include a film festival, the Navy's Fleet Week (see below), tennis and volleyball tournaments, walking and running races, hydroplane races and art shows.

2 SAN DIEGO BOAT SHOW • *San Diego Convention Center and marina in early January; (619) 274-9924.*

Want to select your dream boat, or perhaps just look at it with envy? Hundreds of watercraft are displayed indoors and on the water.

3 BUICK INVITATIONAL • *Torrey Pines Golf Course in mid-February; (800) 888-BUICK or (858) 281-4653.*

Watch the world's top golfers and celebrity amateurs play in this major tournament.

4 CINCO DE MAYO • *The week including May 5 or the weekend nearest May 5, at Old Town San Diego and other places; (619) 296-3161 or (619) 220-5422.*

Old Town gets all dressed up for Mexico's most important holiday with food booths, dances, lots of mariachis and other entertainment. Most other San Diego County communities observe this holiday as well. For a really ethnic celebration, attend *Cinco de Mayo* in the border town of Calexico in Crummett Park, just north of Mexicali; (760) 357-1166.

In case you never wondered, *Cinco de Mayo* does not celebrate the fact that a guy named José Cinco invented mayonnaise. It marks the Battle of Puebla on May 5, 1862, when a greatly outnumbered Mexican force defeated the invading armies of Napoleon III.

5 LESBIAN AND GAY PRIDE FESTIVAL • *In Balboa Park at Sixth and Juniper, in late July; (619) 297-7683.*

San Diego's gay community, focused mostly in the Hillcrest District, celebrates its pride with a wonderfully outlandish parade, rally and other festive events.

6 FLEET WEEK • *Second week of August; (619) 236-1212.*

This salute to and from the Navy and Marine Corps includes a military ship parade, the sailing of the Star of India, close-order aerial maneuvers by the Blue Angels, fireworks and more.

7 RED SANDS VOLLEYBALL TOURNAMENT • *At Ocean Beach in mid-August; (619) 222-2826.*

This AA-sanctioned tournament sponsored by the California Beach Volleyball Association features some of the state's best men and women competitors. We hope the "red sands" reference isn't suggestive of the ferocity of the competition.

8 SAN DIEGO STREET SCENE • *Gaslamp Quarter in mid-September; (619) 557-0505.*

The sixteen-square-block Gaslamp Quarter becomes an urban fair of food, music and dance during this festival.

9 TORREY PINES CONCOURS d'ELEGANCE • *The Lodge at Torrey Pines State Reserve in mid-October; (858) 642-7469.*

Classic cars of the 1920s through 1940s are displayed beneath the pines; it's one of the area's largest vintage auto shows.

10 CHRISTMAS IN SAN DIEGO • *Late November through the holidays. At various places around the city.*

San Diego dresses splendidly for the holiday season. Activities include the Festival of Lights at Old Town's Bazaar del Mundo; holiday decorations, foods, crafts and carolers along El Prado in Balboa Park; La Jolla Christmas Parade and Holiday Festival, Coronado Holiday Lights Walk and the San Diego Bay lighted boat parade.

THE TEN DUMBEST THINGS YOU CAN DO IN OR NEAR SAN DIEGO

Most of the dumb things you can do involve your car—rental or otherwise. It's easy to get into trouble on strange, crowded streets, particularly in a city where drivers like to pretend that it never rains. Also, there are some special driving conditions in next-door Mexico that, if ignored, can get you into really big trouble.

1 DRIVE IN RUSH HOUR TRAFFIC IN THE RAIN

You have to realize that, despite its location on the ocean, San Diego has a desert climate, with about ten inches of rainfall a year. In fact, fairweather San Diegans are reluctant to admit that it rains at all. It is such an infrequent event that, between rainfalls, commuters forget that wet pavement greatly reduces stopping distances. They drive at normal speeds, tailgate and collide with one another, creating monumental rush hour traffic jams. If it's raining, or if it rained the previous night, stay off the freeways and main highways from 7 to 9 a.m. and 3 to 6 p.m.

2 DRIVE FAST THROUGH AN INTERSECTION

Another result of San Diego's infrequent rainstorms is that many of the streets were designed with surface storm drains. These are shallow channels that cross through many intersections, particularly in residential areas. Hitting these at high speed is like hitting a reverse speed bump; you and your car will get quite a jolt. These dips can be very treacherous at night because they're hard to see. And of course when it does rain—and it occasionally rains its brains out—these intersections frequently flood, and that's an even worse time to drive through them in a hurry.

3 WEAR A DODGER'S CAP AT A PADRE'S GAME.

San Diego Padre fans are pretty nice folks, so you'll undoubtedly emerge unscathed if you wear the colors their arch National League rivals when you catch a game at Qualcomm Stadium. You might get a bit of heckling, however, and don't let the San Diego Chicken see you in Dodger blue.

4 GO MUSEUM-HOPPING ON A MONDAY

If you want to learn the San Diego meaning of "blue Monday," plan a cultural outing on that day. Most of the museums in Balboa Park and elsewhere take Monday off. Among archives that will lock you out on Mondays are the Mingei International Museum, Museum of San Diego History, San Diego Model Railroad Museum, San Diego Museum of Art and Timken Museum, all in Balboa Park; Junípero Serra Museum above Old Town; Children's Museum of San Diego downtown; Firehouse Museum on Columbia Street near downtown; and the Museum of Contemporary Art in downtown San Diego and in La Jolla.

5 TRY TO PARK IN DOWNTOWN LA JOLLA ON A SUMMER WEEKEND

Charming La Jolla is the darling of summer visitors, with its boutiques, shops and restaurants and a beachfront with wind-and-wave sculpted cliffs. To use the old cliché, tourists love La Jolla to death in summer, and then the nearby locals join the throngs on weekends. If you plan to visit La Jolla on a summer weekend, get an early-morning start and secure your parking place before the crowds arrive.

6 CLIMB THE CLIFFS OF TORREY PINES STATE RESERVE • *North Torrey Pines Road (Old U.S. 101) just north of La Jolla; (858) 755-2063. GETTING THERE: Take the Genesee Avenue exit from I-5 and go west; Genesee blends into North Torrey Pine Road. Follow it south and downhill about two miles to the park entrance.*

Torrey Pines State Reserve shelters several hundred acres of rare pine trees on a bluff 300 feet above the ocean. From these high cliffs, remote beaches far below look mighty tempting, particularly—for some—Black's Beach, where sunbathers are working on overall tans. Some "goat trails" lead down to the beach, although the cliffs are very unstable and hikers have been injured and killed on these steep descents. A better approach to the beaches is use the large parking lot just inside the main gate and walk along the base of the bluffs. Be careful that you don't get stranded during a high tide.

South of the border trouble

The next dumb things involve visiting our neighbors to the south. Our Mexican friends are great people and we love hanging out in Tijuana. However, some of Mexico's laws and conditions differ from ours. Here are some ways you can run into trouble when you make a run for the border:

7 EAT A STREETSIDE TACO

The spirit of Montezuma takes out his revenge on tourists who are careless about what and how they eat in Mexico. A nasty bug often found in drinking water can give you a nastier case of diarrhea. Mexicans' tummies have gotten use to this microbe, but ours haven't. The bug can be killed by heat, so eat only hot food while it's still hot. That would seem to cover those good-smelling streetside taco stands, where meat is peeled off a roasting shank of beef and installed in a fresh tortilla. However, salsa and guacamole also are added, and these possibly can be contaminated by the hands of the vendor. Even worse, contamination can result in hepatitis, a really serious illness.

8 DRIVE INTO MEXICO WITHOUT MEXICAN AUTO INSURANCE

You face two problems when you drive a vehicle across the border. First, Mexico does not recognize nor accept American auto insurance. Second, Mexico functions under Napoleonic law, which says that you're guilty until proven innocent. Thus, if you're involved in a traffic accident, your vehicle and possibly your body may be impounded until fault and liability are established. Further, if your auto is stolen while you're in Mexico, all you'll have left is car payments, because your American insurance carrier won't cover the loss.

The solution is simple. Before entering Mexico, buy Mexican auto insurance. You can get it at the border, or look under in the "Insurance" section of the San Diego Yellow Pages. It's not expensive and rates don't vary from one firm to the next, since they're set by the Mexican government. Generally, they're comparable—prorated to a daily basis—as American auto insurance.

9 DRIVING A RENTAL CAR INTO MEXICO WITHOUT PERMISSION

Generally, the insurance you carry on your vehicle at home also covers a rental car (but check your policy to make sure). However, since this insurance probably isn't valid in Mexico, it won't cover a rental car there. If you plan to drive a rental car into Mexico, *make sure* that you tell the rental agent, so arrangements can be made for Mexican auto insurance.

10 DRIVE INTO MEXICO AND BACK ON A WEEKEND, EVEN WITH PROPER INSURANCE

Except for refusing to recognize American car insurance, the folks south of the border are pretty easy-going. Officials usually will wave you right through, with little more than a nod and a friendly smile.

However, American customs and immigrations people are a bit more fussy, particularly because of the problem with illegal immigrants coming into California. They're much more thorough in checking vehicles and their occupants. Which leads us to our problem:

Thousands of people pass between San Ysidro and Tijuana each day, and that number increases greatly on weekends. In fact, it's the world's busiest border crossing. If you make a run for the border on a weekend, you'll probably pass through Mexican customs effortlessly, but on your way back, you're likely to get stuck in a long traffic jam that extends—it will seem—halfway to Ensenada. The solution is simple: Instead of driving, walk into Tijuana, particularly on a weekend. If you just want to do a bit of shopping and maybe slam back a *cervesa* or two, you'll find plenty of places immediately across the border. The main shopping area, Avenida Revolución, is just a mile away. There are plenty of parking lots on the American side. Even better, take the "Tijuana trolley," the San Diego light rail train that stops right beside the border.

NOTE • For more on visiting Mexico, see Chapter One, page 17, and Chapter Fifteen, page 216.

THE TEN BEST SPECIALTY GUIDES TO THE SAN DIEGO AREA

Now that you've purchased this guidebook—assuming you're not still standing in the book store taking a free read—we can recommend several others that may prove useful. These are specialty guides, generally available only in the San Diego area. We've listed address of the publishers, so you can order copies before you start out. However, don't just send them a check; there'll be shipping charges and prices may have changed, so drop a note and inquire first.

1 PHOTOSECRETS: SAN DIEGO, THE BEST SIGHTS AND HOW TO PHOTOGRAPH THEM • *By Andrew Hudson. Photo-Secrets, P.O. Box 13554, La Jolla, CA 92039-3554; 336 pages; $18.95.*

This book is quite attractive, illustrated in color by its photographer author. It even lists the ten best places to photograph San Diego, providing considerably more detail than our suggested photo angles in Chapter Ten.

2 AFOOT AND AFIELD IN SAN DIEGO COUNTY • *By Jerry Schad. Wilderness Press, 2440 Bancroft Way, Berkeley, CA 94704; 336 pages; $15.95.*

This book lists several interesting hiking and walking trails in the county, with specific directions on routing.

3 **BACKCOUNTRY ROADS AND TRAILS, SAN DIEGO COUNTY** • *By Jerry Schad. Centra Publications, P.O. Box 191029, San Diego, CA 92159; 96 pages; $8.95.*

The title spells it out; this small book details interesting driving routes in San Diego County, followed by descriptions of hiking trails once you get there. Maps help keep you on course.

4 **THE ECLECTIC GOURMET GUIDE TO SAN DIEGO** • *By Steve Silverman. Menasha Ridge Press, Inc., P.O. Box 43059, Birmingham, AL 35243; 202 pages; $11.95.*

The author provides detailed reviews of more than 150 restaurants, with specifics on hours, price ranges, menu items and such. He writes dining reviews for the city's KPBS Radio and a local magazine called *San Diego Home/Garden.*

5 **HIDDEN CYCLING ROUTES OF SAN DIEGO** • *By Derek Emge; 104 pages; $12.95.*

This long, skinny book outlines thirty-one cycling routes throughout the county, with attendant maps. The title page doesn't list a publisher's address so you'll have to check local book stores when you get here.

6 **RELOCATE IN SAN DIEGO COUNTY** • *By William Carroll. Coda Publications, P.O. Box 711, San Marcos, CA 92079-0711; 174 pages; $16.95.*

If you like the area so much that you can't stand to leave, this book will give you all the necessary details about making San Diego County your new home.

7 **SAN DIEGO'S $DEALS & STEALS** • *By Sally Gary. Pacifica Books, etc., 2726 Shelter Island Dr., Suite 94, San Diego, CA 92106; 360 pages; $16.95.*

While not fancily done, this book is a bargain-hunters delight, advising its readers how to get the best prices on everything from fabric and furniture to food and lodging.

8 **SAN DIEGO ON FOOT** • *By Carol Mendel, P.O. Box 6022, San Diego, CA 92166; 96 pages; $6.95.*

The author takes you on nineteen walks in and near San Diego. Each route includes interesting historical background about the area, and the book is nicely illustrated with sketches.

9 *A SHORT HISTORY OF SAN DIEGO* • *Michael McKeever. Lexicos Press, San Francisco; 142 pages; $12.95.*

This highly readable book tells the city's story from the earliest native people the present. It's busy with historic photos and interesting vignettes. The author, a Chula Vista resident, wrote and helped produce a San Diego TV show for Public Television for several years.

10 *ZAGAT SURVEY: SAN DIEGO RESTAURANTS* • *Edited by Maureen Clancy and Judith Adams. Zagat Survey, Inc., 4 Columbus Circle, New York, NY 10019.*

Zagat came to town in 1997 to do its first readers' survey of local restaurants, and it issues periodic revisions. The Zagat guides are noted for their brief reviews and pithy commentary.

EASY LISTENING: THE TEN BEST RADIO STATIONS

What turns you on? Mellow sounds, light rock, classics or Garth Brooks? Our choices, while quite varied, reveal that we don't like hard rock or rap and that we tilt toward mellow sounds.

1 *KJQY—FM 94.1* • This is our favorite San Diego radio station. For easy listening that ranges from pops classics to contemporary vocalists, spin your dial to "K-joy."

2 *KPBS—FM 89.5* • This is the local Public Broadcast Station, offering the usual good music, international news and cultural fare.

3 *KSON—FM 97.3* • Misplaced your Merle Haggard tape? This is your dial spot if you're into country music.

4 *KIFM—FM 98.1* • Into Jazz? "The Breeze" plays lots of smooth jazz instrumentals and vocals, from contemporary to old standards.

5 *KKBH—FM 102.9* • Calling itself "The Beach," this easy listening station plays light rock and popular vocals.

6 *KPLN—FM 103.7* • This rather hip station plays classic rock from the Sixties through the Eighties, with no rap or acid rock.

7 *KYXY—FM 96.5* • If you like strictly smooth sounds of the present and the recent past, dial up "Kixi." Some describe this kind of music as "adult contemporary."

8 *KOGO—AM 600* • "Kogo" is the city's all-purpose news, talk and sports station, with news, weather and traffic every half hour.

9 *KPOP—AM 1360* • Does Doris Day still make your day? This station plays pops classics of yesteryear and it features news and traffic on the hour.

10 *"X-BACH"—AM 540* • Need a Bach or Beethoven fix? This commercial station plays classical music and offers ongoing coverage of the San Diego cultural scene. It's an English language station although it's transmitted from Tijuana.

San Diego County, as seen by nine-tenths of those who have heretofore visited it, is anything but inviting to the settler or tourist.
— **T.S. Van Dyke in *The History of San Bernardino and San Diego Counties*, 1883**

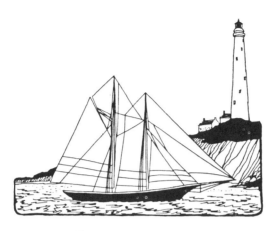

Chapter fourteen

THE COUNTY SCENE
BEST REASONS FOR GETTING OUT OF TOWN

San Diego County has changed dramatically since a historian wrote the negative commentary in 1883 that's quoted at the top of this chapter. Early travelers coming down the coast by steamer saw only rocky hills with "dreary black brush" and "bristling with cactus." What they failed to see was the great topographical variety of the county farther inland, busy with tree-clad mountains, hidden green valleys and dramatic stretches of desert. They could not foresee that those "stony slopes scarred with gullies and washes" above the coast would become lushly landscaped, upscale beach communities such as Del Mar, Solana Beach and Encinitas.

The county is the sixth largest in America, more than seventy miles wide and nearly sixty miles deep. It features an interesting mix of attractions, from the string of beach towns along Historic Highway 101 to citrus groves, historic missions and national forests. Outback San Diego County is home to one of the world's largest telescopes, America's largest state park and—perhaps surprisingly for southern California—an old mining town.

THE TEN BEST COUNTY ATTRACTIONS

Our favorite county attractions are a mixed lot, from interesting towns to historic missions to a famous wild animal park. Since county exploration obviously requires an automobile, we've listed the our top lures in more or less geographical order, as they would appear on a driving trip from San Diego. Thus, you can string them together and fashion this into a tour of one or more days. (If you plan to include Anza-Borrego Desert State Park, you'll definitely need more than one day.)

We begin our county exploration with Torrey Pines State Reserve on the northern edge of La Jolla. We'll then head north to the next attraction—an historic highway that passes through the county's "golden coast." This beach area rivals San Diego itself in surfside popularity.

1 *TORREY PINES STATE RESERVE* • *North Torrey Pines Road (Old U.S. 101); (858) 755-2063. GETTING THERE: Take the Genesee Avenue exit from I-5 and go west; Genesee blends into North Torrey Pine Road. Follow it south and downhill about two miles to the park entrance near the beach.*

This 1,750-acre facility preserves several thousand torrey pine trees growing on high coastal bluffs, along with a nice stretch of beach at the base of those bluffs. The rare *pinus torryana* grows only on these bluffs and in a couple of other places in southern California. It has no distinctive features other than a tendency to be twisted into pleasing bonsai shapes by the wind. The pines add a nice mantle of green to this otherwise sandy, brushy promontory. Several hiking trails lead through the foliage to the bluffs, providing nice views of the beach far below, Los Penasquitos Lagoon and the brushy hills of the University of California. A small visitor center housed in an old pueblo style resort built in 1923 has exhibits on the flora, fauna and geology of the region.

A popular pastime is watching hang gliders soar from the 300-foot bluffs of Torrey Pines. When the wind's right, men and women with nylon wings of eagles launch from the Torrey Pines Glider Port, often spending hours seeking updrafts and drifting over the sea. Those who catch the right wave of air can ride the currents right back to the cliff tops. Others spiral lazily down to the strand, occasionally—to the giggling delight of spectators—landing among the skinny dippers at Black's Beach, the local nudie spot.

Speaking of beaches, the state park includes about three miles of strand, starting with easily-accessible areas near the entrance station and extending south. Many of the more appealing and isolated beaches at the base of the bluffs—including Black's Beach—can be reached by hiking south from the main parking area. However, take care during high tides to avoid getting trapped. Also, climbing up or down the bluffs is definitely not advised, for they are both fragile and dangerous. Hikers have been injured and even killed in falls from these steep slopes.

2 THE BEACH ROUTE: OLD PACIFIC HIGHWAY • *Torrey Pines to Oceanside. About twenty-one miles. GETTING THERE: This route starts near the entrance to Torrey Pines State Reserve and heads north along old U.S. 101. Incidentally, don't try this drive on any fair weather weekend; the highway and its adjacent beaches become very congested.*

Old timers will remember this route as the main highway between Oceanside and San Diego until Interstate 5 took most of the traffic inland. Now regarded as "Historic Highway 101," it links together a string of coastal communities as it passes within a stone's throw of many of the county's best beaches. This route begins at Torrey Pines and heads north along the coastal edge of Los Penasquitos Lagoon to the upscale beach city of **Del Mar**. An attractive community with Tudor style architecture downtown, it's home to the San Diego County Fairgrounds and **Del Mar Racetrack**. You can reach this complex by branching right onto Jimmy Durante Drive and following it under the nearby I-5 freeway. However, unless the ponies are running or it's fair time—late June to early July—there's not much to see there, so bear left onto Camino del Mar to stay close to the coast.

Next in this chain of run-together seacoast towns is **Solana Beach**, a bit less upscale than Del Mar. You'll encounter a small beach in a lagoon between Del Mar and Solana Beach that offers the choice of sticking your toes into the surf or the calm lagoon waters. A bit farther along, you can follow Plaza Street left to **Fletcher Cove**, another small beach.

Just north of here, you'll pass through a trio of communities under the wing of incorporated Encinitas—first **Cardiff-by-the-Sea**, then central **Encinitas** and finally **Leucadia**. They all occupy coastal bluffs, with strings of homes between the highway and the seacliffs. If you're still in a beachin' mood, stay alert for access signs; there are several city and state beaches below these bluffs. The best is **Encinitas City Beach**, reached by turning left onto B, going a block to the right then left again on C Street; see below on page 208. If you want to visit the luxurious **La Costa Resort and Spa**, turn inland from Leucadia onto La Costa Avenue. The lushly landscaped grounds and elegant buildings are worth a look.

Beyond Leucadia, the highway finally sheds this string of beach communities and drops down to the shoreline as it passes between two coastal lagoons, Agua Hedionda and Batiquitos. **South Carlsbad** and **Carlsbad state beaches** occupy slices of sand in this marshy lowland. Climbing out of the lagoon, you'll enter **Carlsbad**, once a sleepy coastal hamlet and now a rather trendy shopping and resort center. After brushing the edge of Carlsbad State Beach, the highway swings inland through the downtown area to become Carlsbad Boulevard. It then skims the beach again, passing through Buena Vista Lagoon. It next enters **Oceanside** which, like neighbor Carlsbad, has become rather a boomtown of late. With a population approaching 150,000, it's passing Chula Vista to become the second largest city in the county. Both cities follow on our Best County Attractions list.

3 *CARLSBAD AND AULT KARLSBAD* • *For more information, contact the Carlsbad Convention & Visitors Bureau, P.O. Box 1246, Carlsbad, CA 92018-1246, (760) 434-6093; or San Diego North Convention & Visitors Bureau, 720 N. Broadway, Escondido, CA 92025-1899, (800) 848-3336 or (760) 745-4741.*

Many years ago when I worked for Oceanside's small daily newspaper, Carlsbad was a quiet little beach community where not much happened. In the past few decades, quite a bit has happened. Old Carlsbad has become a major destination, with resorts, upscale shopping centers and—just to the south—the famous La Costa Resort. Three public beaches—Carlsbad and South Carlsbad state beaches and Robert C. Frazee city beach—lure swimmers, sunbathers and surfers. A promenade connects the city beach with Carlsbad State Beach.

Most of what's interesting about Carlsbad is accessible from Historic U.S. 101, here called Carlsbad Boulevard. Approaching from the south, you can easily reach the three beaches from the highway. Once in the heart of town at Grand Avenue, note the wonderfully complex Victorian style structure on the east side of the street, once called Twin Inns and now housing Neiman's Restaurant. It's nearly surrounded by a large Spanish style shopping complex called Carlsbad Village.

Just north of Grand Avenue, you'll encounter a bit of Carlsbad history. The town was established in 1882 when one Captain John A. Frazee discovered mineral water here, which he claimed was similar to the water of a famous spa in Karlsbad, Bohemia. He built a fancy hotel that thrived well into this century, then it burned to the ground. About forty years ago, local realtor Chris Christiansen built a fancy witch's hat shelter over the original well and began constructing a cluster of half-timbered buildings he called *Ault Karlsbad.* Only one remains, now Carlsbad Mineral Water Spa, which is open by appointment only; (760) 434-1887. A statue of Frazee stands nearby and an adjacent street has been named in Christiansen's honor.

4 *OCEANSIDE* • *For information, contact Oceanside Chamber of Commerce, 928 N. Coast Hwy., Oceanside, CA 92054, (760) 722-1534; or San Diego North Convention & Visitors Bureau, 720 N. Broadway, Escondido, CA 92025-1899, (800) 848-3336 or (760) 745-4741.*

Although it doesn't have the historic and cutesy appeal of smaller neighbor Carlsbad, Oceanside is the fastest growing and perhaps most visited city in the north county. Particularly inviting is its old fashioned three-mile-long public beach that runs the length of the city. At its midpoint is the longest public pear on the west coast. It also has a small craft harbor, and the city is next door to a huge Marine base that's open to visitors.

Continuing north from Carlsbad, you can explore the best of Oceanside by following the highway into the southern edge of town. Turn left from onto Cassidy Street, go about three blocks toward the beach and take a right onto Pacific Street. This skirts the oceanfront for about two miles, passing through a residential area on a bluff just above the beach. A lower, parallel street called the Strand is right alongside the sand, although it's interrupted at several points by barriers and one-way zones, so Pacific is a better route. You'll soon see the long Oceanside Pier, worth a stroll for its views back to the beach and the palm-lined city skyline. Perched on the far end is—not a seafood restaurant—but a franchise back-to-the-Fifties style café called Ruby's. While it isn't gourmet, it's a handy place for lunch with a view. Oceanside's beach offers all the usual sun-surf-and-sand amenities; see the "Ten Best Beaches" listing below, on page 206.

Continuing north along Pacific Street, you'll cross a small lagoon and encounter Oceanside Harbor; (760) 966-4570. Despite its southern California location, its structures have a kind of Nantucket look. You can dine at a couple of seafood parlors, rent boats or fishing gear, charter an offshore fishing trip or just prowl among the shops. Beyond the harbor, the road takes you to Interstate 5 with easy access heading north or south.

If you'd like to tour the world's largest amphibious base, continue straight ahead from the harbor on Vandegrift Boulevard into Camp Joseph H. Pendleton. Once a Spanish land grant, this 125,000-acre Marine Corps base covers seventeen miles of shoreline and stretches far inland. At the main gate, you can pick up a pass and a self-guiding tour map. A valid driver's license and proof of vehicle insurance are needed for entry.

5 NORTH COUNTY MISSIONS: SAN LUIS REY and PALA

• *San Luis Rey de Francia, 4050 Mission Ave., Oceanside, (760) 757-3651; daily 9 to 4:30. San Antonio de Pala in Pala, (760) 742-1600; Tuesday-Sunday 10 to 4 from April through October and 10 to 3 the rest of the year. GETTING THERE: San Luis Rey is four miles east of Oceanside off State Route 76. Pala is about fifteen miles farther east on Highway 76.*

San Luis Rey de Francia was established in 1798 as one of California's twenty-one original missions. Then in 1816, an *asistencia* or extension mission was started a day's ride east. Several such satellites were founded during California's mission era, to bring more native people into the flock and to seek additional agricultural lands.

San Luis Rey de Francia was named for Saint Louis, the king of France, and indeed it is a kingly mission—one of the most handsome in California. Restored far beyond its original crude adobe appearance, it is a dazzling white structure with a gracefully curving Spanish colonial façade and an octagonal bell tower. The church is equally imposing inside, with thirty-foot ceilings held up by massive carved beams. The altar is busy with saintly niches and the walls are brightened by painted borders and scroll work. Ranks of votive candles flicker from two side altars, creating an almost surreal scene. Several rooms in a wing of the complex have nicely done museum exhibits; one sees the work of a professional curator here. Displayed behind glass cases are vestments, church icons, native peoples' artifacts and typical implements of the mission period, such as kitchen utensils, carpentry tools, candle molds and a crude loom and spinning wheel. Other exhibits trace the history of the mission movement.

Fifteen miles east, Mission San Antonio de Pala is equally appealing, although in quite a different manner. It's more rustic, with rough textured whitewashed adobe walls brightened by hand-painted decorations. Instead of a bell tower, it has a *campanario* or bell wall, similar to the one at Mission San Diego and more typical of the early California missions. The simple chapel has a rough log beam ceiling and a tile floor worn smooth by the sandals of nearly two centuries of worshipers. A small museum and gift shop are adjacent to the chapel. This *asistencia* carries a special distinction. Located on the Pala Indian Reservation, it is the only California mission still ministering to native people.

6 **SAN DIEGO WILD ANIMAL PARK** • *15500 San Pasqual Valley Rd., Escondido; (760) 747-8702 or (760) 480-0100. Open daily at 9, various closing times. Major credit cards; admission charge plus a parking fee. Combination tickets available with the San Diego Zoo.*

GETTING THERE: If you're hitting county attractions as we've listed them and you've just finished with Pala Mission, return to I-15 and head south through Escondido. Just below that city, take the Felicita Park exit and go east for six miles, following directional signs.

At the risk of ruffling a few feathers, we've come to like the San Diego Wild Animal Park even better than its parent attraction, the San Diego Zoo. Although very popular (don't go near it on a summer weekend or any holiday weekend), the animal park is not quite as crowded as the zoo. In the decades since it was established, it has expanded considerably, with several open air animal enclosures accessible by foot, in addition to its famous tram ride through hundreds of acres of critter pastures.

Large expanses of the hilly, rocky terrain have been fashioned into realistic wild animal habitats, representing various sections of Africa, Asia and Australia. Animals that would live together in the wild are able to roam free over these expanses, so visitors can watch them do their own thing—and that often includes mating. The Wild Animal Park has had great success in breeding endangered species and even reintroducing some of them to the wild. Only carnivores and an occasional cranky zebra or hippo are separated from the free-roaming groups.

When you get to the park, make a bee-line for the tram ride, since the waiting lines build up quickly, particularly on weekends and most summer days. And take your binoculars, or you can rent them at an outlet near the entrance. After doing the tram, you can roam through several acres of animal exhibits, which through the years since the park's creation have grown lush and jungle-like. (Officials say there are more than a million plants in the park, although we wonder who took time to count.) A stroll of nearly two miles takes visitors past open air habitats along the Kilimanjaro Safari Walk and through the new Heart of Africa exhibit. Some of the walkways are elevated, putting you eye-to-eye with tree-dwelling critters. Perhaps the most interesting exhibit is the gorilla enclosure, where the beasts sit on their haunches like great black Buddhas while their offspring frolic about. We also like the Hidden Jungle, a thickly landscaped swatch that shelters brightly colored butterflies, hummingbirds and flowering plants.

7 **PALOMAR OBSERVATORY** • *Atop Palomar Mountain; (760) 742-2119. Museum open daily 9 to 4; gift shop open daily in summer and weekends only the rest of the year. Picnic area nearby.*

GETTING THERE: If you've just come from San Diego Wild Animal Park, go northwest on State Route 78 toward Escondido, then turn north onto County Road S-6. It will wind for more than fifteen miles through hilly, unpopulated back country, passing lakes Dixon and Wolford. It eventually merges with State Route 76 just south of Pauma Valley. This is rather a pretty basin, adorned with dark green citrus groves that begin at roadside and extend high into the flanking mountains. Go east for five miles on Highway 76 then branch to the left, staying with S-6 as it makes a twisting, scenic climb up Palomar Mountain. Views back down to Pauma Valley are quite splendid.

Sitting high atop its namesake mountain, Palomar Observatory houses the world's most honored starfinder. The 200-inch Hale telescope unveiled in 1948 is no longer the world's largest, having been eclipsed by a 236-inch Russian lens. However that instrument has never worked quite right and the Hale is still regarded as the globe's best gatherer of starlight.

Astronomers at Palomar don't sit within the telescope's giant framework and squint into the eyepiece as they once did. Although more than half a century old, the Palomar complex has been constantly upgraded to keep it state of the art. Stellar images are now videotaped in a modern control center that looks capable of launching a space shuttle. Linked to computers and spectrographs, the great Hale telescope continues to make significant discoveries.

You can watch a video in the visitor center about the telescope's development, peer at sky photos and be dazzled by the usual astounding astronomical figures. You may or may not want to know, for instance, that a light year is six trillion miles. Our nearest galaxy, Andromeda, is two million light years away and—well, you get the idea. From the museum, a short walk takes you into the Hale telescope's dome, where a couple of nicely done graphics describe how it works.

8 *JULIAN and SANTA YSABEL* • *For information, contact the Julian Chamber of Commerce at 2129 Main St. (P.O. Box 1866), Julian, CA 92306; (760)765-1857.*

GETTING THERE: Julian is at the junction of state highways 78 and 79. To get here from Palomar Mountain, descend from the observatory, turn right at Palomar Junction onto County Road S-7 and follow it about eleven miles to State Route 76. Continue southeast as the highway blends into Route 79, passing first through San Ysabel.

Julian may come as a surprise to folks who think of Southern California as mostly beaches and desert. This town sitting on an oak-thatched ridge 4,220 feet above sea level was founded as a gold mining center in the late 1880s, and it still has that properly rustic frontier look. The gold soon ran out and Julian was on the verge of dying. Then folks realized that the high altitude was ideal for apple production and the town got its second lease on life. Next came the tourists, and they're still coming—particularly coastal San Diegans needing a breath of cool mountain air. You might want to avoid Julian on summer and fall weekends. (The town celebrates the autumn apple harvest with festivities that draw major crowds; see the "Ten Best County Celebrations" below on page 211.)

If you're approaching Julian from Mount Palomar, you'll pass some interesting lures on the way. A few miles after Highway 76 merges with Route 79, watch on your left for the tiny and charming **Santa Ysabel Mission,** founded in 1818. Weathered yet tidy, the complex includes a whitewashed chapel built in 1924, a small museum and picnic tables beneath gnarled oaks. This exceedingly pleasant retreat is open daily 8 to 5:30 in summer and 8 to 4 the rest of the year.

Just below is the tiny old town of **Santa Ysabel.** Most of its structures are occupied by shops and galleries, a spillover from nearby Julian. On your right as you enter town are the Julian Pie Company and adjacent Julian Pie Company Restaurant. The bakery, in a cheery red building, sells exceptionally tasty pies, plus other baked goods, specialty coffees and ice cream. The apple pies are worth writing to Mom about. Also savory are "apple memories," small, feather-light cookies made of cinnamon-dusted pie crust.

From here, follow Highway 79 into thickly wooded hills past apple orchards and roadside fruit stands. The largest and oldest—dating from 1916—is Farmers Fruit Stand and Bakery. It has a large selection of apples and apple pies, plus specialty foods, breads, bakery goods and apple cider. Next door is the Codarossa Winery "tasting saloon" in a tiny false front store.

As you enter **Julian** from this direction, the first thing of interest you'll see is the Julian Pioneer Museum at Washington and Fourth. It's nicely done, with pioneer artifacts and photos displayed on wood panel walls. Other exhibits include an entire surrey, saddles and a horse-drawn sleigh. The museum is open daily 10 to 4 April through November, and weekends only the rest of the year; (760) 765-0227.

From the museum, head uphill on Main Street to prowl the shops and boutiques of this old town. Although most buildings are original, no tourist lure has been left unturned. The former town hall is a venue for weekend melodramas; the Julian Drugstore is a working pharmacy and a pharmaceutical museum; the next-door Miners Diner has red checkered tablecloths, an old fashioned soda fountain and fare to match. There's another Julian Pie Company outlet just below the heart of downtown at 2225 Main, in an old cottage with a shaded patio out front.

Note the 1897 Julian Gold Rush Hotel at 2032 Main St.; (800) 734-5854 or (760) 765-0201. Now a bed & breakfast inn, it has been restored and dressed in early American finery, including print wallpaper, scalloped drapes and old fashioned bedsteads with country style spreads. The sitting room is particularly comfy, with overstuffed furniture and a cast iron stove. The hotel was built by freed Missouri slaves Albert and Margaret Robinson. A sign outside suggests that only guests may enter the hotel parlor, although if you feign interest in staying, you'll probably be admitted. And it certainly is a pleasant place to spend the night, offering several comfortable rooms.

9 CUYAMACA RANCHO STATE PARK • 12551 Highway 79, Descanso, CA 91916; (760) 765-0755. GETTING THERE: The state park is immediately below Julian; head south on State Route 79.

This former Spanish ranch (pronounced *kwey-uh-MAK-uh*) contains 25,000 acres of oak, chaparral and pine woodlands, more than a hundred miles of hiking trails and several campgrounds. About three miles from Julian, before you enter the park, watch on your left for a vista point. It provides an impressive panorama of the **Anza-Borrego Desert**, which we've scheduled for your next visit. A bit farther along is small **Lake Cuyamaca** with a store, café, tackle shop, boat rentals and RV hookups.

As you enter Cuyamaca State Park's lush woodland, look to your left for 5,730-foot Stonewall Peak, a green clad conical mountain with a bald knob. A few miles below, turn left at the park headquarters sign and drive about a quarter of a mile to an attractive three-story stone structure. One of the original ranch buildings, it now houses a visitor center and museum open weekdays 8:30 to 4:30 and weekends 10 to 4. The museum has exhibits about the native Kumeya'ay people, plus the flora, fauna and geology of the park, and historic photos of the ranch. This complex also has a small store open 10 to 4, daily in summer and weekends only the rest of the year. Several hiking trails begin at the visitor center area.

If you intend to return to Julian and head for our final San Diego outback attraction, you can enjoy a change of scenery by making this a loop trip. Continue through Cuyamaca Rancho State Park to **Descanso** and go about seven miles east to Pine Valley just above I-8. Pick up County Road S-1 and follow its winding course through the oak and chaparral woodlands of Cleveland National Forest's Laguna Mountains. Traveling along the eastern slope, this road is appropriately called the Sunrise Highway. Of course, you also can use I-8 to get back to San Diego in a hurry.

10 *ANZA-BORREGO DESERT STATE PARK* • *P.O. Box 299, Borrego Springs, CA 92004-0299; (760) 767-4684. Modest day use fee is collected at park headquarters in Borrego Springs. For more information on the town surrounded by the park, contact Borrego Springs Chamber of Commerce, 622 Palm Canyon Drive, Borrego Springs, CA 92004; (760) 767-5555.*

GETTING THERE: If you're coming from Julian, you'll spiral quickly downhill on State Route 78, through a vee-shaped valley cradled by green-clad hills. The route levels off briefly in a high basin, then it loses more altitude until it reaches a beige desert, where it enters America's largest state reserve.

Anza-Borrego Desert State Park is interesting although not awesome. The same can be said for Borrego Springs, the town that it surrounds. Although the adjacent mountains are imposing, particularly in late light, there are much more dramatic desert settings and more attractive desert towns in California. Mostly, Anza-Borrego is *big*, covering 600,000 acres—nearly half of the county. Much of the park is in the Colorado Desert that extends westward from the Colorado River. It's generally under a thousand feet above sea level, so it doesn't have the rich cactus gardens of some of California's higher desert areas.

However, Anza-Borrego does have its moments. Some areas have impressive spring wildflower blooms from mid-February to early April; see the "Ten Best County Celebrations" below on page 210. The park has one of the largest native palm groves in California and it has several dramatic land formations such as the Borrego Badlands and Split Mountain. This is a serious hikers' park, with more than thirty trails and nature walks. Incidentally, the double-jointed name honors a trek through here in 1776 by Juan Bautista de Anza, bound for San José to establish California's first city, and for the desert's elusive bighorn sheep. *Borrego* is Spanish for a yearling sheep or lamb. (You'll recall from this book's introduction that San Diego claims California's first mission, although the first civil settlement was San José.)

We'll detail a driving trip that you can accomplish in one or more days, basing it on an approach from Julian. Several miles after you've entered the park on Highway 78, turn left onto County Road S-3 toward Borrego Springs. You'll shortly pass **Tamarisk Grove Campground**. Across the highway, the short Cactus Loop Trail will provide an introduction to local plant life; pamphlets are available at the trailhead. Beyond Tamarisk Grove, the highway climbs a low, rocky ridge and then descends into a broad desert basin. In the middle is **Borrego Springs**, the only town in California completely surrounded by a state park. Road S-3 forks to the right at the edge of town and carries you into the heart of this scattered, low-rise community of about 3,000 residents. However, you might want to pause first at the junction to admire La Casa del Zorro, a strikingly elegant resort; (800) 824-1884 or (760) 767-5323. It's one of the most appealing of all California desert retreats, with comfortable accommodations in rooms and casitas.

Continuing toward town, you'll encounter a landscaped traffic disc called Christmas Circle. Do a three-quarter turn and spin off onto Palm Canyon Drive to pass through the heart of Borrego Springs. Don't expect a Palm Springs; this is a rather simple little community. On your right about midtown is the Borrego Springs Chamber of Commerce, open weekdays 9 to 5. Across the street is the town's main shopping area, simply called The Mall. Incidentally, nearly all of the streets and roads in and around Borrego Springs have bike lanes, so this is a nice area for peddling off a few calories. You can get a bike route map at the chamber or the state park visitor center.

Continue toward the rocky face of the San Ysidro Mountains and you'll soon reach the **state park visitor center**. It's a rather striking affair, bunkered into a slope and fronted with a fieldstone wall. Its earthen roof serves as an observation platform, where you can admire the surrounding sweep of desert. The center is open 9 to 5, daily October through May, then weekends and holidays only the rest of the year.

Just north of the visitor center is Borrego Palm Canyon Campground. A popular park hike, the **Borrego Palm Canyon Trail**, leads from the campground into a spectacular rocky ravine, ending at one of California's largest native fan palm groves. This three-mile round trip isn't strenuous, although it does involve a little rock-hopping. At trail's end, you'll find just what you'd expect in a desert canyon oasis—a cool, shady palm grove, but with no nubile maidens bathing in a sylvan pool. In fact, there's no sylvan pool; the hundreds of palms in this canyon get their water from underground springs. The trail goes into the grove only a few dozen yards; the palms are so thick that further progress would be difficult.

You can see the park's other major attractions by following County Route S-22 toward the Salton Sea, then dropping south on Highway 86 and returning on State Route 76. Heading out of town on S-22, you'll see a dirt road on your right that leads four miles to **Fonts Point**, an overlook of the eroded **Borrego Badlands**. The road can be rough and sandy in spots, depending on what recent storms have done. Check at the visitor center before attempting it. Back on S-22, now called the Borrego Salton Seaway, you'll hit a low crest offering a view of that giant pale blue oval. Just beyond, the highway passes through another badlands area, then it leaves the state park and San Diego County and enters Imperial County. The road soon ends at State Route 86 near the edge of the **Salton Sea**. This pale pond was created accidentally in 1905 when a levee on a diversion canal near Yuma broke and water flowed unabated into a low desert basin for several months. Now cut off from outside water sources, it's slowly dying and it doesn't smell very nice.

Go south to the Highway 86/78 junction and head west, back into San Diego County and the state park. At the hamlet of **Ocotillo Wells**, go south on Split Mountain Road for two natural attractions. **Elephant Tree Nature Trail** takes you past a rare collection of curiously twisted low trees with chubby, fleshy trunks. They're common in Mexico and rare in the United States. At the end of the road you'll hit **Split Mountain**, a steep-walled ravine with a flat, sandy bottom. Unless the weather's bad, you can drive your car right up to the canyon mouth, and then take a hike past its eroded formations.

To avoid winding back through all of those mountains around Julian and Cuyamaca Rancho State Park, you can return to State Route 86 and follow it southeast through Brawley, then pick up I-8 just east of El Centro. This is a longer but faster way to get back to San Diego.

THE TEN BEST COUNTY BEACHES

This a countywide look at surf and strand, including beaches both in the San Diego city limits and beyond. We brushed past many of these in the Historic Highway 101 tour above.

1 *OCEANSIDE BEACH* • *It stretches for nearly three miles along the city's waterfront. GETTING THERE: From Oceanside's main drag, drop down three blocks to Pacific Street which travels just above the beach for about two miles. You'll encounter parking and beach access areas at several points along Pacific.*

This is our favorite San Diego County beach—an uninterrupted strip of sand along Oceanside's entire oceanfront. It's busy with picnic tables, volleyball nets, play equipment for the kids and endless acres of soft sand. You can climb a ramp up to one of the longest public piers on the Pacific Coast to stare down at the scalloped surf and admire the view back to the palm-lined beach. A Fifties style diners called Ruby's perches at pier's end—a handy place for lunch. If you want to spend several days here, a beachfront drive called the Strand is lined with old fashioned beach cottage rentals and some modern condos. Contact the Oceanside Chamber of Commerce for details on the town and its beach; see the address above, on page 198.

2 CARLSBAD and SOUTH CARLSBAD STATE BEACHES
● *Off Old Highway 101 between Batiquitos and Agua Hedionda lagoons. RV and trailer camping available. Parking free at Carlsbad; modest parking fee at South Carlsbad. GETTING THERE: Both beaches are right beside the highway. Go coastward on La Costa Avenue for South Carlsbad and take Poinsettia Lane in the city of Carlsbad for the upper beach.*

Cradled between a pair of lagoons, this state beach comes in two pieces. More than three miles of empty sand stretches between them, appealing for those who like to jog or just stroll along and scuff at shells and seaweed. However, you'll have to shift to the highway to cross the opening of Agua Hedionda Lagoon. This stretch of beach was badly eroded during the *El Niño* year of 1998, although time and tides are bringing back the sand.

3 CRYSTAL PIER BEACH ● *In Pacific Beach, north of San Diego's Mission Bay Park. GETTING THERE: Follow either Mission Boulevard north from Mission Bay Park or Garnet Avenue west from I-5 to Pacific Beach.*

We like the convenience and comfort of this beach, which extends both directions from Crystal Pier. It's at the base of a low bluff providing shelter from incoming breezes, and there are public facilities nearby, plus a couple of small cafés near Crystal Pier. The pier itself, privately owned and lined with little rental cottages, is a nice place for a stroll when you want to scuff the sand off your feet.

4 ENCINITAS CITY BEACH ● *At the base of seacliffs below central Encinitas. GETTING THERE: Take old U.S. 101 to Encinitas. If you're coming from the south, go left onto D Street, take the next right, then go left on C Street to the Beach. If you're approaching from the south, go right on B Street.*

This is one of our favorite beaches in the string of communities between La Jolla and Carlsbad. It has free parking areas (although they fill up quickly in summer), several picnic tables in a little enclave off the sand, beach showers and volleyball nets. The beach sits at the base of a coastal bluff and when the tide's not too high, you can walk for miles in either direction.

5 *HOTEL DEL CORONADO BEACH* • *The hotel is at 1500 Orange Avenue in Coronado. GETTING THERE: Cross the Coronado Bridge from San Diego, turn left onto Orange Avenue and follow it about a mile.*

The legendary Hotel del Coronado sits practically on the beach, although the strand itself is open to the public. You can gain access by strolling through the grounds and looking for one of several corridors between buildings. There are even a couple of outdoor beach showers for rinsing away the sand. However, you'll probably want to park off the property, since there's an hourly parking charge for non-guests. The beach stretches for more than a mile in either direction, giving you plenty of room to roam. There's a concrete promenade in case you want to walk off a few calories. Or you may prefer to simply lie in the sand, alternating your gaze between the blue Pacific and those striking red-orange roofs that are the "Del's" signature.

6 *LA JOLLA SHORES BEACH* • *Between downtown La Jolla and Scripps Institution of Oceanography. GETTING THERE: The easiest way is to take the La Jolla Village Drive exit from I-5, go about a mile west then turn briefly north as it blends into North Torrey Pines Road. After about half a mile, take a hard left onto La Jolla Shores Drive and follow it south through coastal residential areas to the beach.*

Although locals know this beach and keep it busy in summer, most visitors miss it because of its rather isolated location, surrounded by thick La Jolla residential areas. It's an inviting little spot, with the usual strip of sand, backed up by a park strip of lawns, benches and picnic tables. The surf is usually rather calm here since it's on the outer edge of La Jolla Bay. From the beach and park strip, you'll enjoy nice views south to the La Jolla peninsula and the red-roofed homes on the hillsides above. The little beach's only visual flaw is that it has too many refuse containers; these ugly cans seem to be an obsession of park and beach planners.

7 *SAN ONOFRE STATE BEACH* • *About seventeen miles north of Oceanside; (949) 361-2531. GETTING THERE: Follow Interstate 5 north through the Camp Pendleton Marine Base, take the San Onofre/Basilone Road exit, cross over the freeway and follow a frontage road south. Camping available; modest parking fee.*

San Onofre is surrounded by undeveloped terrain of Camp Pendleton, so there are no services for miles, other than potties at the beach. Thus, this is your place if you want to get away from the urban coastal crowds lower down the county, or if you simply want to surf. There are two elements to San Onofre, which occupies a narrow band two hundred feet below coastal bluffs. The northern end, not far from a nuclear power generating plant, is primarily a surfing beach. If you follow a frontage road farther south past the nuclear plant, you'll encounter a swimming beach and campground.

8 **SILVER STRAND STATE BEACH** • *Along State Route 75 on the Silver Strand landspit between Coronado and Imperial Beach; (619) 435-5184. RV and trailer camping available. GETTING THERE: Take the San Diego-Coronado Bridge to Coronado, turn left onto Orange Avenue and follow it through the downtown area. It becomes State Route 75 and leads you down Silver Strand.*

The special appeal of this beach is that it offers you choices—the livelier water of the Pacific Ocean, or the calmer San Diego Bay. Further, you can stroll into nearby Lowes Coronado Bay Resort for a lunch or just for a look about. A beachside promenade passes through the park, so you can bike or rollerblade as well as splash in the surf.

9 **TORREY PINES STATE RESERVE** • *North Torrey Pines Road (Old U.S. 101). GETTING THERE: Take the Genesee Avenue exit from I-5 and go west; Genesee blends into North Torrey Pine Road. Follow it south and downhill about two miles to the park entrance.*

Torrey Pines is noted mostly for its woodland bluffs where it shelters its namesake *pinus torreyana*. It also has a nice stretch of strand below those bluffs. The beach extends more than two miles south along the bluffs and north across the mouth of Los Penasquitos Lagoon. You can park in lots at the entrance to the reserve or on the north side of the lagoon, or try your luck along the shoulder of old U.S. Highway 101. To reach the southern beaches, hike below the bluffs, taking care not to become isolated by high tides. "Goat trails" leading down to these beaches from the bluffs above are very dangerous and should not be attempted.

10 **WINDANDSEA BEACH PARK** • *Southern La Jolla coast. GETTING THERE: The easiest approach is from the south (via Mission Beach and Pacific Beach) on La Jolla Boulevard, then turn beachward onto Nautilus Street.*

Expect this attractive beach below La Jolla's beautiful homes to be crowded in summer, since it has benefited from an odd kind of publicity. It was the locale for *The Pumphouse Gang*, a Thomas Wolfe satire about surfers who hung out at a sewer plant pumphouse and try to discourage "outsiders" from using their beach. We can't blame them; this is one of the best surfing beaches on the California coast. It's also quite pleasant, with sandy coves tucked among limestone ridges and grand views of coastal La Jolla. This is a very popular place for watching the sunset.

THE TEN BEST COUNTY CELEBRATIONS

The City of San Diego doesn't have all the fun. County communities offer a rich variety of annual celebrations. The list below is only a sampler. For a complete listing of San Diego city and county events, send a check for $15 to: International Visitor Information Center, 11 Horton Plaza, San Diego, CA 92101.

1 DESERT WILDFLOWER BLOOM • *Anza-Borrego Desert State Park from February through April; (760) 767-4684 or 767-4205.*

This annual event is set by Mother Nature. Cactus and other plant life of the Anza-Borrego Desert put on a color show every spring, generally from February through early April. If it has been a wet winter, spring floral display can be really spectacular.

2 DEL MAR NATIONAL HORSE SHOW • *San Diego County Fairgrounds at Del Mar in April; (868) 792-4288 or (868) 755-1161.*

One of America's major equestrian affairs, this annual meeting attracts top riders and their horses for hunter-jumper events, draft horse competitions and other riding activities.

3 RAMONA PAGEANT • *April and early May weekends in the community of Ramona; (800) 645-4456.*

The heroine Ramona, a Spanish beauty who dared fall in love with a native American, existed only in the mind of novelist Helen Hunt Jackson. However, this town that has taken Ramona's name dramatizes the book in a brightly costumed outdoor pageant. Ms. Jackson did visit this area in the 1800s and her novel may have been based on some actual events.

4 FALLBROOK AVOCADO FESTIVAL • *Main Street in Fallbrook in mid-April; (760) 728-5845.*

Holy guacamole! Although it's being crowded by spreading north county suburbs, Fallbrook remains one of America's major avocado producing regions. This festival salutes everybody's favorite dip with games, entertainment and avocado-based foods.

5 DEL MAR FAIR • *San Diego County Fairgrounds in Del Mar in June; (858) 755-1161; 24-hour events hotline (858) 793-5555.*

The San Diego County Fair is one of the largest in the nation, with the usual produce and jam exhibits, foods, carnival midway, horse racing and art displays.

6 *THRESHING BEE & ANTIQUE ENGINE SHOW* • *At the Antique Gas & Steam Museum in Vista, last two weekends of July; (800) 5-TRACTOR or (760) 941-1791.*

Participants fire up old steam threshing machines and other antique farm equipment at this rural festival. Other activities include blacksmithing demonstrations, log sawing and craft exhibits.

7 *THOROUGHBRED RACING* • *At the San Diego County Fairgrounds in Del Mar from late July through early September; (858) 755-1141 or (858) 792-4242.*

The ponies pound around the oval at one of America's best-known racetracks. Racing is daily except Tuesday with post time at 2 p.m.

8 *MISSION SAN LUIS REY FESTIVAL* • *Four miles east of Oceanside off State Route 76; first weekend of August; (760) 757-3651.*

Old California comes alive with this festival at the "King of Missions," featuring music, food and historic displays.

9 *JULIAN WEED SHOW* • *In the town of Julian, late August to early September; (760) 765-1857.*

Weeds finally get their respect in this show, in which participants make creative arrangements from the abused plant. Art exhibits also are part of the festival. On weekends from September through November, Julian celebrates its annual Fall Apple Harvest Festival, with apple-oriented foods, entertainment and exhibits.

10 *BATTLE OF SAN PASQUAL REENACTMENT* • *San Pascual Battlefield State Park in early December; (760) 489-0076. The park is just east of the San Diego Wild Animal Park.*

Americans and Mexicans clashed in one of the bloodiest California battles of the Mexican War at this site in 1846. Wanna-be soldiers dress up, create a military encampment, eat period grub and engage in mock black powder battles.

Twice a year the vaqueros gathered to ride across their golden hills. There...was time for fiestas and fandangos that might last a week or more.
— Michael McKeever in *A Short History of San Diego*, commenting on the area's Mexican period

Chapter fifteen

BEYOND THE BORDER
VISITING TIJUANA AND THE BAJA BEYOND

There was a time, just over a century and a half ago, when no border separated San Diego and Baja California; they were part of the same country. As author/historian Michael McKeever noted in his book, *A Short History of San Diego* (Lexicos, San Francisco, © 1985), these were good times, when great *rancheros* covered the tawny hills surrounding the city. "The *Californios* danced, and held cockfights and riding exhibitions," he wrote. "Food and drink were plentiful."

Mexicans are still very much a part of the social and commercial fabric of San Diego; Hispanics are the city's second largest ethnic group, after the Gringos. And many Gringo visitors to San Diego also want to explore that nation to the south—particularly Baja California, for this is where one finds San Diego's true roots. It was from Baja that the padres and soldiers came in 1769 to establish California's first mission and presidio.

Although no specific records are kept, Baja California—particularly Tijuana—may be the second most visited area after San Diego itself.

Entering Mexico is a relatively simple matter, particularly if you intend going only to Tijuana. Mexican border officials usually will wave you through with a friendly grin. U.S. officials require a photo I.D. such as a driver's license for re-entry; a passport isn't needed by American citizens. Mexican regulations state that proof of birth is required for entry into the country, such as a birth certificate with a photo ID or a passport, although these are rarely requested at the border.

Incidentally, if you are a foreign national entering Mexico from the United States, you may need a passport. Check with your own government to see what documents are required for entering Mexico and for reentry into the U.S.

Getting there and back

TOURIST CARDS • If you plan to stay longer and/or go deeper into Mexico than Ensenada, you'll need a Mexican Tourist Card, which can be obtained at the border. You must have proof of citizenship to get one; a driver's license won't work. You also should carry a current registration slip for your vehicle, or a rental car contract. If you're driving someone else's car, you may not permitted to enter Mexico. (Officials periodically demand proof of vehicle ownership or rental because of problems with stolen vehicles crossing the border from California.)

AUTO INSURANCE • Don't drive anywhere in Mexico without Mexican auto insurance. Although insurance isn't mandated by law, your vehicle might be impounded if you're involved in an accident. Few American insurance policies extend coverage to Mexico and even if they do, Mexican officials won't recognize them. If you have a rental car, make sure your rental agreement permits driving into Mexico, and get proper insurance coverage.

Mexican auto insurance is available on both sides of the border. Or look in the San Diego Yellow Pages under "Insurance" and you'll find several companies that sell short-term coverage for Mexico. Rates are comparable with American premiums and don't bother shopping for the best prices because they're set by the government.

CAR RENTALS • When you rent from any firm, make sure that you're permitted to take the vehicle into Mexico, and that it's covered by Mexican auto insurance. One San Diego outfit that specializes in south-of-the-border vehicle rentals is California Baja, offering cars, vans, motorhomes and four-wheel-drives; (619) 470-7368.

TOURS • Several companies sell guided tours from San Diego into Mexico, including Baja California Tours, (619) 454-7166; and Discover Baja Travel Club, (800) 727-2252 or (619) 275-4225.

BUS SERVICE • Greyhound runs between San Diego and Tijuana several times daily, departing from its depot at 120 W. Broadway; (800) 231-2222 or (619) 239-8082. Croc Cab offers taxi runs between

San Diego and downtown Tijuana and the airport; (619) 421-7234. Tijuana Airport Transfers has similar service; (619) 278-9441.

SHOPPING ● American money is widely accepted in border towns, so don't bother with currency exchanges. Expect to haggle over prices in curio shops. The rule of thumb is to counter with a third of what they ask, then meet somewhere in the middle. Don't embarrass the poor shopkeeper and take all the fun out of bargaining by paying full price. Because of lower labor costs and a favorable exchange rate, you'll find good buys. Booze is cheap because of the lack of tax, and Mexican-made liquor such as tequila and brandy are less than half the price that they are in the States. However, there are limits on what you can bring back; see below.

"SE HABLA INGLES?" ● You won't have to resort to your high school Spanish in Tijuana; English is spoken at virtually every shop, motel and restaurant.

HEALTH MEASURES ● We've traveled extensively in Mexico without getting anything worse that diarrhea, but that's awfully unpleasant, so take precautions. Even in the finest restaurants, we routinely avoid drinking unbottled water or eating fresh vegetables that may have been washed in tap water. Those nasty little bugs that commit Montezuma's revenge can be killed by heat, so eat only hot food while it's still hot. There's a simple solution to avoiding contaminated water. When in doubt, remember that Mexico makes great beer!

DRIVING THE INTERIOR ● It's generally as safe as driving around California, although there's a major difference. Once you get away from the border, service facilities are scarce and car parts even scarcer. For an extended trip into Mexico, take spare parts such as fan belts, water pumps and such—things that might likely conk out. And don't forget the tools needed to install them. Also, take plenty of bottled water in case you're stranded for a while. Paved Mexican roads are usually narrower than ours and sometimes in need of repair. Watch out for potholes, tractors and cows who seem oblivious to the risk of colliding with a car. Because of open ranges in the Baja, we never drive after dark. In the more remote towns, you may want to filter gasoline through a fine sieve or cloth, particularly if you have a fuel-injected vehicle.

RETURNING TO CALIFORNIA ● You can bring back $400 worth of duty-free goods per family member, plus one liter of liquor per adult. Mexico enjoys favored nation status with the U.S., and certain handicrafts can be imported in excess of the $400 limit. Check with a U.S. Customs office to see what's currently on the list. Bear in mind that some items can't be brought into the U.S. no matter where their origin, including ivory and certain animal skins and sea turtle oil. Also, there's a limit on the amount of American-brand perfume that you can bring in from Mexico.

Doing Tijuana

When I was a young Marine and went through boot camp in San Diego, we called Tijuana "T-town," and we regarded it mostly as a place to go raise a little hell, flirt with the señoritas and drink. Tijuana bartenders weren't much concerned about how old we were.

Tijuana has grown up considerably through the years, and while it still has no shortage of cantinas, pretty señoritas and strip joints, it is now more respected as a tourist destination. (A sign in front of the Mexicoach bus depot states: "Welcome to Tijuana. You can be arrested for immoral conduct.") The downtown area has been spruced up; trees have been planted and the sidewalks are kept swept clean. Tijuana has several first class hotels and some fine restaurants, in addition to countless cantinas and smaller cafés.

Some things to bear in mind if you plan a Tijuana visit. First, the city is *huge*—nearly twice the size of San Diego. With about two million people, it's the fourth largest city in Mexico. It is by far the largest Mexican border town, and it boasts of being "the most visited border town in the world." San Ysidro-Tijuana is the world's busiest border crossing, with thousands of tourists pouring into town and thousands of green card "guest workers" pouring out, headed for day jobs in California. Because it's a border town, it isn't a typical Mexican city, nor is San Ysidro a typical American city. Each is influenced by the other; both have become Gringo-Hispanic ethnic blends.

Don't be intimidated by Tijuana's size, however. Most things of visitor interest are within a rather compact downtown area. The main shopping district is along Avenida Revolución, within walking distance of the border.

If you plan a brief visit to Tijuana, we recommend leaving your car on the American side and walking in. There are plenty of parking lots at the border with modest fees. Another option is to take the "Tijuana Trolley" from San Diego. That's the Blue Line of the city's light rail system, which makes the forty-minute run every fifteen minutes from 5 a.m. until 9 p.m., then every half hour until 1 a.m. You can catch it at any San Diego Trolley station (although some will require a train transfer) and the fares are cheap; $2 the last time we rode. A good place to catch the train is at the transit center in Old Town San Diego State Historic Park. It's a direct run and if you get there early enough, you'll find plenty of free parking nearby; one lot is just across the street. For specifics on trolley service, call (619) 233-3004 or (619) 685-4900 for automated touch-tone phone information.

The train stops literally within a few feet of the border. Simply hop off and catch a bus into town for a dollar. You'll find one parked next to the trolley station. Cabs cost about $5. Or use a green pedestrian ramp directly across the street, if you don't mind a short walk. A one-mile stroll will take you through Mexican customs. You'll pass through

216 — CHAPTER FIFTEEN

a plaza where hawkers display there wares, cross a pedestrian bridge over the concrete-lined bed of the Tijuana River and an adjacent freeway, and then you'll pass through another curio shop area. From here, follow the crowds up a narrow street called Calle Commercio which, of course, is lined with souvenir shops and stalls. You'll soon hit the lower end of Avenida Revolución. A tourist information bureau is just across the street in a bright yellow cottage. You can pick up a map of the downtown area and brochures for lodging, dining and assorted amusements. The center is open Monday-Saturday 9 to 7 and Sunday 10 to 5, and the nice folks in there speak English as well as you.

Turismo: THE TEN BEST TIJUANA ATTRACTIONS

Tijuana doesn't have a lot of "typical" tourist attractions. You'll encounter a fine cultural center, a wax museum that we chose to ignore, a family amusement center and not much else. Of course, there's the *jai alai* palace, Caliente racetrack and two bull rings, which have been here for decades. Mostly, people go to Tijuana to shop, since the downtown area is one large, cacophonic, multi-colored shopping mall. These are the things we like best about this big, bustling border town:

1 THE BEST TOURIST AREA: *Avenida Revolución* • Between Calle Segunda and Calle Decima.

Avenida Revolución is a pulsing parade of curio shops, restaurants, bars, discount liquor stores, *farmacias* (Mexico isn't fussy about medical prescriptions), some small hotels and a few topless joints and discos that blast away day and night. You'll also find an abundance of fast food joints and if you're looking for a quick snack, we recommend these over streetside taco stands.

Although Plaza Río Tijuana (below) is a more upscale shopping area, we prefer browsing along Avenida Revolución. Here, you can find virtually everything you never wanted—leather backpacks, silly sombreros that a real *vaquero* wouldn't be caught dead beneath, steers horns real and *faux*, serapes, gaudy pottery and leaded glass wall hangings of howling coyotes.

As you stroll Avenida Revolución, shopkeepers and topless bar hustlers will try to steer you into their establishments, street vendors will proffer their trinkets or seek to shine your shoes, and photographers will offer to snap your photo aboard sad little burros that have been stained with zebra stripes. (You're expected to wear a silly sombrero and bright *serape*.) It's a circus of commerce that needs to be taken with humor. These are for the most part gentle folk just trying to make a living like the rest of us. If you're put off by their friendly persistence, perhaps Avenida Revolución isn't your kind of place.

2 THE BEST TOURIST ATTRACTION: Centro Cultural Tijuana ● *Paseo de Los Héroes and Avenida Independencia; phone 01152 (66) 84-11-11. Daily 9 to 5; free.*

Extensively remodeled in 1999, the Tijuana Cultural Center is a large complex with folk and history museums, sculpture garden, cafés and galleries, and an Omnimax wide screen theater. It's just off a traffic circle at the convergence of Paseo de Los Héroes and Avenida Independencia. The first thing that will catch your eyes is the theater structure, which looks like a monstrous stone yolk emerging from a broken eggshell. The cultural center is to the right; enter through a large courtyard. The Museum of the Californias here focuses on the history and lifestyles of the two Californias—Baja and Alta. Other displays include Mexican folk crafts and art. Many exhibits in this modern complex are displayed along a gently inclined, spiraling ramp. An outdoor sculpture garden has assorted shapes ranging from Mayan to modern. The complex also has a large restaurant and a good sized bookstore although—oddly—we found few books in English, despite the abundance of American visitors.

3 THE BEST SHOPPING COMPLEX: Plaza Río Tijuana ● *Across from the Tijuana Cultural Center at Paseo de Los Héroes and Avenida Independencia*

Rivaling some of the malls of San Diego, Plaza Río is Tijuana's largest shopping center, anchored by a familiar Sears store and a couple of big Mexican department stores. Tucked in between are more than a hundred smaller shops and stalls, selling everything from curios to clothing to cutlery. Río Tijuana also has a movie complex, restaurants and bakeries. The plaza is attractively landscape and a central courtyard often is used for local celebrations. And there's more. Adjacent to *El Río* are a mall with shops selling boots and shoe stores, and a huge food court called Plaza Fiesta. Walkways link Plaza Río Tijuana to the cultural center across Paseo de Héroes.

4 THE BEST FOLK CRAFT CENTER: Bazar de Mexico ● *Avenida Revolución at Calle Galena.*

Taking a cue from American merchandising gimmicks, a sign at this extensive crafts complex under a canvas roof proclaims "Forty Factory Artisan Shops." It has the best selection of Mexican folk craft—authentic and otherwise—that you'll find along Avenida Revolución, and you may see painters and potters at work. There's no pressure to buy; one can browse through this center relatively unmolested. Offerings include carved masks, paintings, pottery, fabric, pewter ware and assorted other arts and crafts.

5 **THE BEST PLACE FOR SHOPPING BARGAINS:** Calle
Commercio • *Between upper Avenida Revolución and the border.*

Commercio, indeed! Part of the fun of walking into Tijuana is passing through a one-mile stretch of stalls, shops, vendors and shopping
plazas. You won't top quality art goods or giftwares here. What you
will find is thousands of curios, souvenirs, cheap clothing, leather
goods and minor works of art. This avenue of commerce is definitely
out of the high rent district and bartering is expected.

6 **THE BEST PLACE FOR A BEER BREAK:** Buckets •
*Corner of Avenida Revolución and Calle Segunda (also signed as Calle
Benito Jaurez.)*

This lively cantina and restaurant occupies a second-story balcony
open to the street. It's a good place to take a break, enjoy a beer and
watch the harmless chaos along Avenida Revolución below. It's cleverly decorated with galvanized buckets of all sizes. Dozens hang from
the ceilings; large cut-off bucket bottoms serve as tables and your bot-
tle of Tecate or Corona comes in a little tin bucket filled with ice. And
you can't beat the prices. We got two bottles of beer—most days are
two-for-one days—and a basket of tortilla chips with a spicy salsa for
$4. The friendly bartender threw in a shot of tequila for nothing. (If
you're really cool, you take a bit of salt and a squeeze of lime, then
slam back a shot of tequila, followed by a sip of beer. And if you spend
too much time in Buckets, you'll be glad you followed our advice and
took the trolley from San Diego.)

7 **THE BEST PLACE TO TAKE THE KIDS:** Mundo Diver-
tido • *El Paseo de los Héroes at Calle Velasco. Weekdays noon to 9 and
weekends 11 to 10. Free admission; modest cost for rides, golf and video
games. GETTING THERE: It's about a mile southeast of the Tijuana Culture Center and Plaza Río Tijuana.*

Known mostly for its shopping, jai alai, nightspots and bullfights,
Tijuana isn't really much of a place for kids. If they do come along,
take them to Mundo Divertido. This family amusement park has mini-
ature golf, a video game parlor, batting cages and a roller coaster.

8 **THE BEST SPORTING ATTRACTION:** Jai Alai • *El Palacio Frontón, Avenida Revolución between Calle Septima and Calle Oc-
tava. If it's operating, day games start at noon on Monday and Friday;
night games are at 8 Tuesday-Saturday. Phone 01152 (66) 85-25-24 locally or (619) 231-1919 in San Diego; modest admission charge.*

You may or may not be able to catch this fast-paced game during
your Tijuana visit. At press time, the great old El Palacio Frontón was

closed, although it may have reopened by the time you arrive. *Jai alai* is a Basque game in which players hurl little balls furiously back and forth with wicker scoops attached to their wrists. It's one of the fastest games played by man; those tiny balls flash back and fourth in a blur. It has been played in the elaborate Spanish-Moorish style Palacio Frontón for generations, and visitors bet on individual players as one might bet on the ponies. Open or closed, the palace is worth a look with its elaborate colored tile and *bas relief* façade and the large figure of a *jai alai* player standing atop a ceramic tile globe.

9 *THE MOST GRUESOME SPORTING ATTRACTION: Bull fighting* • *El Toreo de Tijuana, Avenida Agua Caliente, phone 01152 (66) 85-22-10; and Plaza de Toros Monumental, near the beach on the road to Ensenada, phone 01152 (66) 85-22-10. Sunday afternoons at 4, May to October. Package tours to the bullfights are available from Mexicoach, (619) 232-5049; and Five Star Tours, (619) 232-5049.*

We attended a bullfight many years ago and the memory of death in the afternoon has kept us from going to another. Although the ritual was fascinating, the first encounter ended in a very bad kill and we didn't stay for the second. However, if you're interested, Tijuana has two bull rings and the crowds are of sufficient size that they draw some of the top bullfighters from Mexico and Spain. Bullfights alternate between the two arenas.

10 *BEST PLACE TO GO TO THE DOGS: Hipódromo de Agua Caliente* • *Boulevard Agua Caliente at Boulevard Salinas; (619) 231-12919 in San Diego or 01152 (66) 81-78-11 in Tijuana. Races nightly at 7:45, plus weekends at 2. GETTING THERE: It's several miles southeast of downtown, so it's best to take a cab.*

You can bet on the ponies at the Caliente racetrack, although they'll be running somewhere else. Horse racing ended here in 1993; patrons watch the races and other sporting events on TV monitors and place their bets as they would at a Las Vegas sports book. Greyhounds now do the running at Caliente, chasing mechanical rabbits around a track that once felt the thundering feet of thoroughbreds.

DOING THE BAJA PENINSULA

To discover the true fascination of Baja California, one needs to shed Tijuana and travel down the long, slender peninsula. This remote 800-mile-long appendage is home to fantastic desert gardens, wildly eroded mountains and peaceful blue lagoons where the great California Gray whales spend the winter. Rimmed by the restless Pacific on one side and the calm, wildlife-rich Gulf of California on the other, it has two thousand miles of beaches.

Many Americans may think of "Baja California" as a single geographic unit, although it's two political entities—the states of Baja California (the northern half) and Baja California Sur. They're divided at the 28th parallel, approximately in the peninsula's midpoint.

Until 1973, the only way to explore either Baja was by boat, airplane or a four-wheel drive over primitive roads and desert gullies (which often were the same thing). Late that year, the thousand-mile-long Transpeninsular Highway (Mexico Highway 1) was completed, linking Tijuana/Ensenada with Cabo San Lucas on the very tip of the peninsula. Traveling through this uncrowded land, you will encounter occasional swatches of civilization—towns and cities that are not overwhelmed by border tourism. Many have become tourist centers, for Baja is catching the visitor wave, while others are still quiet villages.

THE BAJA'S TEN BEST TOURIST SPOTS

We have visited this slender landspit several times and have compiled below a list of our ten favorite places. We don't expect you to drive from one to the other in any geographic order, since these involve great distances. People coming to San Diego for a vacation usually aren't prepared to travel a thousand miles to the tip of Baja California. Most of these places can be reached by plane and some by package tours, in case you do want to add a side trip to your San Diego vacation. Or you can simply file away our recommendations for future reference.

Incidentally, one of the best guidebooks to this area is the Automobile Club of Southern California's *Baja California: The Complete Travel Guide.* You don't have to be an AAA member to get one; it's sold to the public and you often can find it in San Diego book stores.

1 **CABO SAN LUCAS** ● *At the tip of the Baja California Sur, 1,059 miles from Tijuana.*

Our favorite place on the Baja Peninsula is not rustic village. It's a modern tourist community with nice resorts, lively nightlife and great beaches. Cabo San Lucas is one of the world's finest sportfishing venues. Fisherfolk have a choice between the open ocean and the Gulf of California, which is so rich in sealife that it's described as a "fish funnel." Cape San Lucas also has great places to dive, snorkel, swim and just toast your bones on clean beige sand. Although it's a city of 28,000, it's not difficult to find uncrowded beaches. It offers lodging and dining in every price range, from modest motels to luxury resorts, from mom and pop seafood cafés to fancy restaurants. Some of its elegant hideaways rival those in Cancun and Acapulco. Cabo also is a popular port of call for cruise ships and you can expect to see an occasional million dollar yacht in its marinas.

2 **BAHÍA DE LOS ANGELES** • *On the Gulf of California in the southern part of the state of Baja California, forty-two miles east of Highway 1.*

This is one of the peninsula's more charming hideaway villages, not yet caught in the growing wave of tourism. It's in an imposing setting, backdropped by raw, rough-hewn mountains and tucked deep into a peaceful bay. The large offshore Isla Angel de la Guarda (Island of the Guardian Angel) protects it from incoming surf, so its beaches are quite calm. Like Cabo San Lucas, this region is noted for its sportfishing. Bahía de Los Angeles is a modest, pleasantly scruffy little community, with a few stores and shops built around a plaza. Lodgings are humble as well—a handful of motels and RV parks.

3 **GUERRO NEGRO** • *Off Scammon's Lagoon on the northern border of Baja California Sur.*

Guerro Negro is not a tourist town, nor is this village of 11,000 a particularly attractive place. The town's main claim to fame is that it's the world's largest producer of salt. However, it earns a spot on our Ten Best List because it's the nearest town to Scammon's Lagoon, a major winter home of the California gray whales. Hundreds come here to bear their young, breed and play in the calm waters. Visitors can hire government-authorized boats to go out and observe—and even pet—these magnificent beasts. There also are places along the shore where you can watch them, including an old salt company pier; ask locals how to get there. December through March is the best time to see the whales; there's not much to see or do here the rest of the year.

The town's few motels often fill up during "whale season" so make advance reservations. Here are two AAA-recommended places: Hotel La Pinta, a 29-unit motel with TV movies and phones; around $65 to $75; c/o Mexican Condo Reservations, 5801 Soledad Mountain Rd., La Jolla, CA 92037; (800) 262-4500 or (619) 275-4500. Hotel El Morro, a modest 32-unit motel with TV; $30 to $40; Apdo Postal 144, Guerrero Negro, BCS, 23940 Mexico; phone 01152 (115) 7-04-14.

4 **LA PAZ** • *On the Gulf of California, in the lower half of Baja California Sur.*

This historic town exhibits a mixture of colonial charm and contemporary energy. La Paz is the capital of Baja California Sur and the peninsula's busiest port. With frequent ferry service across the Gulf of California, it has long ties with the mainland and it has never experienced the isolation of other peninsular towns. It's not a village; the population approaches 200,000. However, it still has a village charm with graceful old stone buildings splashed by bougainvillea, and quiet back streets. The setting is impressive; it's tucked into the southern rim of Bahía de La Paz. the largest natural harbor on the peninsula. While not sleekly modern like Cabo San Lucas, La Paz has an abundance of resorts, motels and restaurants. The bay of La Paz was discovered by a Spanish expedition in 1533 and it became an important source of pearl oysters two centuries later. A mission was established on the bay in 1749, a permanent settlement followed in 1811 and it became the territorial capital in 1829.

5 LORETO • *About midpoint in Baja California Sur, on the Gulf of California.*

The oldest settlement on the Baja Peninsula, Loreto is our second favorite community after Cabo San Lucas. It's a charmingly weathered colonial town of about 9,000 souls with a backdrop of palm groves and the rugged ramparts of Sierra de la Giganta. Loreto was founded as a mission settlement in 1697. It was from here that Father Junípero Serra began his epic journey to establish the first Alta California mission in San Diego in 1769. Loreto was the capital of Baja Sur until 1829, when it was practically destroyed by a hurricane and the seat of government was shifted to La Paz. It is today a pleasant coastal village built around a plaza and a monumental stone church. A stone *malecón* (seawall) protects the downtown area from the incoming surf. The seawall walkway recently was redone and it's is a grand place to relax and admire the view across the Gulf of California to offshore Isla Carmen. This is not a tourist town, although it soon may be. It has a few motels and resorts and more are being built. If you like the quiet life, come enjoy Loreto before it becomes the next Cabo San Lucas.

6 MULEGÉ • *Just inland from the Gulf of California in northern Baja California Sur.*

Despite its homely name, Mulegé enjoys one of the prettiest settings of any Baja community and it's a popular winter retreat for Americans. Located two miles upstream on Río Mulegé, it's surrounded by a tropical oasis of date and banana palms, olive groves and fig trees. Although popular with visitors, it remains a quiet, old fashion community with about 5,000 permanent residents. The nearby beach is popular for swimming, snorkeling, fishing and other water sports. Mulegé has several modest hotels, motels and restaurants.

7 ROSARITO • *Fifteen miles south of Tijuana on Baja California's Pacific Coast.*

If you want to get away from the bustle of the border and explore just a little of Baja's interior, this is a good destination. While hardly free of tourism, it enjoys a slower pace than Tijuana to the north and the booming port of Ensenada to the south. It also has a curious attraction—the Titanic Museum. A huge ninety percent scale model mock-up ship was built here for the film *Titanic*. While the Rosarito coast hardly resembles the North Atlantic, this was the scene of much of the shooting of that epic film. The mock-up was dismantled when filming ended, although a museum has been opened at the site, with props, photos and memorabilia from the movie. Rosarito isn't a sleepy Mexican village. It has a population of 100,000 and growing, and it has been a resort town since the 1920s. It has a few resorts, motels, condos, shops and restaurants, plus several miles of white, uncrowded beachfront.

8 SAN FELIPE • *In upper Baja California, about 120 miles south of Mexicali.*

San Felipe is a popular if somewhat barren looking town of about 20,000 year-around residents and thousands of winter snowbirds. Because of its nearness to California and Arizona, it's one of the most visited town on the Baja, and it can become rather chaotic and even unruly on holiday weekends. It's rather peaceful and a little bit charming the rest of the time, sitting on a bay rimmed by steep-walled mountains. Both commercial and sports fisherfolk come here to work the rich waters of the upper Gulf of California. San Felipe began as a fishing village in the 1920s. While it lacks the charm of the peninsula's older towns, it has abundant tourist facilities and it's close enough for a quick visit by folks who want to escape the tumult of border towns. Don't come in the summer, however; it's very hot. Otherwise, the climate is appealing if you don't like rain; annual precipitation is less than two inches.

9 TECATE • *On the California-Mexico border; about forty miles southeast of San Diego via State Route 94.*

If you'd like to see "typical" Mexican town without venturing deep into the Baja, Tecate is your place. Although it's a border city, it draws very few visitors and it's more authentically Mexican than some of the tourist spots far down the peninsula. Sitting in a high agricultural basin, this weathered town of 50,000 is built around an old fashioned plaza, with a relatively peaceful downtown area. Tecate's suburbs are rather industrial, since they have several American owned or American sponsored "offshore" factories, which provide most of the local employment.

One of these "industries" produces Tecate beer, which happens to be our favorite. Tours of the Cuauhtémoc Brewery at Avenida Hidalgo and Calle Carranza are conducted Monday-Saturday from 11 to 3, and you can sip suds in an attractive beer garden Tuesday-Saturday from 10 to 5:30; call 01152 (665) 4-20-11 for tour reservations. There are a few small motels and hotels in Tecate, although it's an easy day trip from San Diego.

10 TODOS SANTOS • *Lower part of Baja California Sur, just inland from the Pacific.*

"Welcome to the Hotel California." Local legend says that the Eagles' 1976 hit song was based on a Spanish colonial style hotel in Todos Santos. Whether true or not, this charming 1928 inn with graceful Spanish arches and sidewalk tables is a pleasant place to spend a lazy afternoon. Off Highway 1 and bypassed by crowds headed for nearby Cabo San Lucas, Todos Santos a quiet and properly rustic town built around a traditional plaza. It was founded as a mission settlement in 1733. Underground springs feed lush palm and cactus gardens, as well as farmers' fields on this coastal plain. Not entirely ignored by tourists, it has become something of an American art colony and it has a late January art festival. The town offers, in addition to grand old Hotel California, several motels, small resorts and restaurants. A fine beach is two miles away.

The public is the only critic whose opinion is worth anything at all.
— **Mark Twain**

Chapter sixteen

READERS' FORUM
AND NOW, IT'S YOUR TURN

Now that you've learned all about San Diego and its attractions, we'd like your input. We invite you to submit your own list of what's best in Sunshine City, using the form that follows. (You can photocopy these pages or write your selections on a piece of paper, if you don't want to dismember the book.) Of course, we don't expect you to come up with a nomination in each category. Any and all entries will be welcomed. You can choose some of the same selections that we have, or you can dare to disagree.

All who send us at least fifteen selections will receive a free copy of the next edition of *San Diego: The Best of Sunshine City*. They can be in any category you wish. Send your selections to:

Pine Cone Press, Inc.
631 N. Stephanie St., #138
Henderson, NV 89014
YOU CAN FAX YOUR LIST IF YOU WISH, TO (702) 558-4355.

READERS' SURVEY FORM

THE BEST ATTRACTION _____

THE BEST "HIDDEN" ATTRACTION _____

THE BEST SAN DIEGO ACTIVITY _____

THE VERY BEST RESTAURANT _____

THE BEST FAMILY RESTAURANT _____

THE BEST MEXICAN RESTAURANT _____

THE BEST OTHER ETHNIC RESTAURANT _____

THE BEST SEAFOOD RESTAURANT _____

THE BEST SPECIALTY OR THEME RESTAURANT ____

_____

THE BEST BREAKFAST CAFÉ _____

THE BEST OUTDOOR DINING AREA _____

THE BEST VIEW RESTAURANT _____

THE BEST FREE ATTRACTION _____

THE BEST CHEAP RESTAURANT _____

THE BEST CHEAP MOTEL/HOTEL _____

THE BEST HOTEL _____

THE BEST RESORT _____

THE BEST BED & BREAKFAST _____

THE BEST PERFORMING ARTS GROUP _____

THE BEST NIGHTCLUB _____

THE BEST COCKTAIL LOUNGE _____

THE BEST VIEW BAR _____

THE BEST SPORTS BAR _____

THE BEST SINGLES BAR _____

THE BEST PARTY BAR _____

THE MOST ROMANTIC BAR _____

THE BEST THEME BAR _____

THE BEST NOSTALGIA BAR _____

THE BEST BEER PUB _____

THE BEST PLACE TO SNUGGLE _____

THE BEST MOST ROMANTIC RESTAURANT _____

THE BEST SAN DIEGO VISTA _____

THE BEST PHOTO ANGLE OF THE CITY _____

_____

THE BEST SHOPPING MALL _____

THE BEST SPECIALTY STORE _____

THE BEST HIKING/WALKING PATH _____

THE BEST BIKE ROUTE _____

THE BEST PEOPLE-WATCHING PLACE _____

THE BEST ANNUAL FESTIVAL _____

THE DUMBEST THING YOU CAN DO IN SAN DIEGO _____

_____

THE BEST RADIO STATION _____

THE BEST COUNTY ATTRACTION _____

THE BEST COUNTY BEACH _____

THE BEST COUNTY CITY _____

THE BEST SCENIC DRIVE _____

THE BEST TIJUANA ATTRACTION _____

THE BEST BAJA ATTRACTION OUTSIDE TIJUANA _____

_____

YOUR FAVORITE BAJA TOWN OR CITY _____

NEW CATEGORIES YOU'D LIKE TO SEE IN THE NEXT EDITION?

_____

_____

_____

_____

- -

THANKS FOR CONTRIBUTING TO OUR SURVEY!

Please list your name and address if you want to receive a free copy of the next edition of *San Diego: The Best of Sunshine City*.

Name _____

Address _____

City/state/ZIP _____

Please send this form or a facsimile to:
Pine Cone Press, Inc.
631 N. Stephanie St., #138
Henderson, NV 89014
or FAX it to (702) 558-4355

INDEX: Primary listings indicated by *bold face italics*

REMARKABLY USEFUL GUIDEBOOKS
from Pine Cone Press

Critics have praised the "jaunty prose" and "beautiful editing" of Pine Cone Press guidebooks by Don and Betty Martin. Their remarkably useful guides are comprehensive, accurate, witty and opinionated. Ask your book store to order them if they're not in stock. Or you can order copies directly from the publisher and we'll charge you only a nickel shipping.

ADVENTURE CRUISING
This book focuses on small ship cruises, listing over a hundred cruise lines and hundreds of worldwide itineraries. *— 340 pages; $15.95*

ARIZONA DISCOVERY GUIDE
This detailed guide covers attractions, scenic drives, hikes and walks, dining, lodgings, RV parks and campgrounds. *— 408 pages; $15.95*

ARIZONA IN YOUR FUTURE
It's a comprehensive relocation guide for job-seekers, retirees, winter "Snowbirds" & others planning an Arizona move. *— 272 pages; $15.95*

THE BEST OF THE WINE COUNTRY
Nearly 300 California winery tasting rooms are featured, plus restaurants, lodging, attractions and wine tasting tips. *— 336 pages; $13.95*

CALIFORNIA-NEVADA ROADS LESS TRAVELED
This is a "Discovery Guide to places less crowded," a comprehensive driving guide to fascinating yet uncrowded attractions, interesting museums, hideaway resorts, great little cafes and more! *— 336 pages; $15.95*

LAS VEGAS: THE BEST OF GLITTER CITY
It's a delightfully impertinent insiders' guide to the world's greatest party town, with detailed descriptions of the Ten Best casinos, restaurants, shows, attractions, bargains, buffets and more! *— 256 pages; $14.95*

NEVADA DISCOVERY GUIDE
This guide covers all of Nevada, with a special focus on gaming centers of Las Vegas, Reno-Tahoe and Laughlin. A special section advises readers how to "Beat the odds," with gambling tips. *— 416 pages; $15.95*

NEW MEXICO DISCOVERY GUIDE
There's more to New Mexico than Carlsbad Caverns! This useful guide steers travelers from ancient native pueblos and Old West historic sites to the galleries and cafes of Taos and Santa Fe. *—386 pages; $16.95*

OREGON DISCOVERY GUIDE
This comprehensive book guides vacationers from wilderness coasts to snowy peaks to volcanic wonderlands. *— 448 pages; $17.95*

SAN DIEGO: THE BEST OF SUNSHINE CITY
This is a fun insiders' guide to California's second largest city, with detailed descriptions of the Ten Best beaches, resorts, restaurants, attractions, nightspots, walking/biking paths & more! *—288 pages; $15.95*

THE TOLL-FREE TRAVELER

This handy pocket or purse sized companion lists hundreds of toll-free phone numbers for airlines, hotel and motel chains, rental car agencies and more. It's also packed with useful travel tips. *—162 pages; $8.95*

THE ULTIMATE WINE BOOK

It's the complete wine user's guide, focusing on wine appreciation, wine and health and serving wine with food. *— 192 pages; $10.95*

UTAH DISCOVERY GUIDE

A busy guide to the Beehive State, it escorts travelers to Utah's canyon lands, modern Salt Lake City, Mormon historic sites, famous ski areas and the "Jurassic Parkway" of dinosaur country. *—360 pages; $13.95*

WASHINGTON DISCOVERY GUIDE

This driving guide steers motorists and RVers from one corner of the Evergreen State to the other, from Seattle to the Inland Empire, covering attractions, lodging and dining along the way. *— 372 pages; $13.95*

ORDERING FORM

Order from us and we'll charge only a nickel shipping! Add five cents to the list price ($3.20 fpr priority mail) and send a check or money order. Use this form or jot your selections on a slip of paper.

Name _____ Date _____

Address _____

City_____ State & ZIP _____

TITLE	Price incl. shipping
_____	_____
_____	_____
_____	_____

TOTAL (Nevada residents add 7% sales tax) _____

Send your order to: *Pine Cone Press, Inc.*
631 N. Stephanie St., #138
Henderson, NV 89014

A BIT ABOUT THE AUTHORS

The Martins have written nearly twenty guidebooks, mostly under their Pine Cone Press banner. When not tending to their publishing company near Las Vegas, Nevada, they explore America and the world beyond, seeking new places and new experiences for their readers. Both are members of the Society of American Travel Writers.

Don, who provides most of the adjectives, has been a journalist since he was sixteen, when classmates elected him editor of his high school newspaper. (No one else wanted the job.) After school, he left his small family farm in Idaho and hitch-hiked about the country a bit. He then joined the Marine Corps and served as a correspondent in the Orient and as a public information specialist at bases in California. Back in civvies, he worked as a reporter, sports writer and editor for several West Coast daily newspapers, then he spent several years as associate editor of a San Francisco-based travel magazine. He now devotes his time to writing, photography, sipping fine Zinfandel and—for some odd reason—collecting squirrel and chipmunk artifacts.

Betty, a Chinese-American whose varied credentials have included a doctorate in pharmacy and a real estate broker's license, does much of the research, editing and photography for their books. She also has sold articles and photos to assorted newspapers and magazines, and she has photos with a New York stock agency. When she isn't helping Don run Pine Cone Press, Inc., she wanders the globe—with or without him. Her travels have taken her from Cuba to Antarctica